Trim Carpentry Techniques

Trim Carpentry Techniques

Installing doors, windows, base and crown

CRAIG SAVAGE

The Taunton Press

Library of Congress Cataloging-in-Publication Data

Savage, Craig, 1947-
    Trim carpentry techniques : installing doors, windows, base and crown / Craig Savage.
        p.   cm.
    "A Fine homebuilding book"—T.p. verso.
    Includes bibliographical references.
    ISBN 0-942391-08-X : $17.95
    1. Trim carpentry.   I. Title.
TH5695.S29   1989
    694'.6—dc20   89-50517
                                                                              CIP

First printing: September 1989
Printed in the United States of America

A FINE HOMEBUILDING Book

Fine Homebuilding® is a trademark of The Taunton Press, Inc.,
registered in the U.S. Patent and Trademark Office.

The Taunton Press
63 South Main Street
Newtown, Conn. 06470

In a trade such as carpentry, there's really very little that's new. Now and again, new tools and materials come along to replace the old ones, but most of the techniques used by carpenters two centuries ago are still in use today in one form or another.

In the course of researching and writing this book, I spent a lot of enjoyable time in libraries, where I discovered that much of what's written about trim carpentry borrows liberally from the past. Interestingly, as my research progressed, I found that each new generation of books assumed that the carpenter knew less and less. Where an old text would simply say "lay off and cut a 45° angle," newer books suggest three ways to accomplish the task with a detailed analysis of each. The need for this detailed instruction is, I believe, a direct result of the decline of the apprentice system in the United States. Books like this one (and the video that accompanies it) are an attempt to fill the gap.

It takes a lot of hard work by many people to produce a book. While there's not enough space here to mention them all, special thanks go to Charles Miller, senior editor of *Fine Homebuilding* magazine, who suggested this book in 1986. Charles led me to many of the fine craftsmen who generously shared their methods with me, giving this book a breadth it would otherwise lack. Thanks too go to the owners of the houses shown in Chapter 1, who allowed me and my photographer, Dick O'Neill, unlimited access to their homes. I hope seeing their homes in print is a small compensation for the time they gave. Finally, if you find this book comprehensive and easy to read— and I hope you do—it's because of the work of Paul Bertorelli and the staff at The Taunton Press.

Craig Savage
Palm Desert, California
August, 1989

I dedicate this book to family and friends who had to cope while my mind was somewhere else, trying to dovetail one chapter into another.

Cover photo: Dick O'Neill.
Text photos by Craig Savage, Dick O'Neill
and The Taunton Press staff, except where noted.

Contents

Introduction

During the 25 years that I've worked in the construction business, I have tried to study and analyze the way that houses are built, from traditional timber-frame dwellings to state-of-the-art superinsulated boxes. Most of what I've learned has come from job-site experience, but I continue to read every book I can find on the building trades as a way of increasing my knowledge. In all my research, I never encountered a complete book about trim carpentry. No one, it seems, had ever bothered to write down in detail exactly what trim carpenters do and how they do it. This book is an attempt to do just that.

Anyone who has ever built a house starting with the foundation and finishing up with painting knows that trim carpentry is a small but important part of the total picture. In terms of board feet of lumber used, nails driven and labor expended, trimming a house usually ranks far behind the framing and the drywall work. But in many ways, the look of the trim—the doors, the windows, the baseboards and wall moldings—takes on an importance far out of proportion to the amount of time and money it takes to install it. Trim is the last thing done in a house, but the first thing you notice when you walk into a room. It's worth doing right.

Installing trim is a finicky, demanding job, closer to the cabinetmaker's work than to the rough-and-ready world of the frame carpenter. Although it requires patience, doing good trim work is well within the ability of anyone with moderate tool skills. All that you need is a basic toolkit, a broad understanding of trim theory and a repertoire of techniques that deal with the fact that the world isn't perfect: rough openings are often twisted, corners aren't square and floors are rarely level. In this book, I try to describe these techniques in ways that will appeal to amateurs wanting to trim their

own homes and to professional carpenters who have dabbled in trimwork but want a basic reference guide, along with some tricks of the trade.

What is trim?

Some tradesmen don't distinguish between trim carpentry and finish carpentry; they use the terms interchangeably. To my mind, however, there's a difference. Finish carpentry includes building staircases, fireplace surrounds, interior shelving and site-built cabinets, as well as installing doors, windows and moldings. Trim carpentry, on the other hand, is strictly confined to installing doors, windows and baseboard and ceiling moldings. These are the topics addressed in this book. If you want to expand your skills to include stairwork and cabinets, I refer you to some of the books mentioned in Further Reading on p. 181.

The purpose of trim is to cover up all the rough edges in a house and to lend a decorative, finished look to the windows, doors and walls. The trim carpenter's job is to take up where the frame carpenters and drywall mechanics left off, tying up the loose ends and making way for the last tradesman on the job, the painter. The trim carpenter has three main responsibilites: to select the molding (or at least advise on the selection) that's appropriate to the home's decor; to install the molding; and finally, to disguise the inevitable inaccuracies and mistakes that have occurred during the earlier stages of construction.

The most challenging task by far is deciding upon a trim style and selecting the moldings that will express it. This will usually be done by the client and the architect (if one is involved), by the trim carpenter and the client or by the trim carpenter alone. Were the house perfect in all regards, installing trim would be like building furniture: controlled and accurate from start to finish. Unfortunately, building a house is a study in calculated error. The surveyor's idea of accuracy is to the nearest inch, the foundation excavator's to the nearest ½ in. and the frame carpenter's to the nearest ⅛ in. Ultimately, the trim carpenter's work must gracefully compensate for all these approximations.

About this book

I've organized this book into roughly the same order that trim is done on site, beginning with design and ending with finishing. I'm assuming a range of circumstances, from readers who are thinking about trim even before ground breaking to those who will be remodeling or restoring an existing house. In any of these situations, a reading of Chapter 1 will give a good idea of just what's required to trim a house. I don't mean this chapter to be an all-inclusive essay on trim design, but it will provide enough information for you talk knowledgeably to your molding supplier or to a custom millwork house. The photos of finished work are meant to serve as design inspiration.

Chapter 2 deals with selecting and making moldings, a major part of any trim job. Certainly you can buy off-the-shelf moldings, but if you want a truly distinctive trim job, I strongly suggest you follow the advice in this chapter and have your moldings custom made or make them yourself. The results are usually worth the effort. Preceding the technical chapters on specific trim types is a chapter on preparation. In some ways this is the most important chapter in the book, for no amount of expensive molding and skill can overcome sloppy framing and drywall.

The chapters on windows, doors and base and crown describe proven techniques that I've used for many years. But as often as possible, I mention methods used by other carpenters that I encountered while researching this book. I have tried to be as thorough as possible but more important, the techniques are practical and can be realistically accomplished with relatively few tools. Although wainscoting and finishing are not specifically within the trim carpenter's realm, I have included chapters on them as well.

As does all trim, this robust crown molding gives a room a finished look and creates an appealing visual texture. It was designed by Peter Carlson for an Oakland, Calif., Victorian house.

1

Elements of trim

I did my first trim carpentry job, if you could call it that, when I was in high school. I'd been doing apartment maintenance on weekends, and my assignment was to repair a large crack between two pieces of moldy Marlite in a shower stall. Lacking a better solution, I decided to cover the crack with a piece of pine astragal molding purchased at the hardware store. There was no solid wood backing to which the molding could be nailed, so, following the owner's instructions, I glued it on with silicone caulk.

It's been 20 years since I "applied" that astragal, and even though my methods were embarrassingly crude, that molding did what trim carpentry has always done: it gave the interior a finished look by covering up the cracks and gaps that are an inevitable part of building a house. As applied to carpentry, the noun "trim" has two distinct meanings. In broad terms, it refers to any kind of interior finishwork in a house, including doors, windows, cabinets, built-in furniture and so on. But in specific terms, when carpenters talk about trim, they are referring to door and window casings, baseboards, ceiling moldings and, in some cases, wooden wall paneling and mantels. The meaning of the verb "to trim," to put in proper order, to make neat and tidy or to cut or lop off, is in some ways even more accurate, for this is just what trim carpenters do. They cap off the job, tidying up the minor (and sometimes major) imperfections left by the other tradesmen.

In a modern house, the chief purpose of trimwork is to decorate and embellish. Trim also has another function, to protect parts of the interior against the scuffs and dents of everyday living. For example, baseboard covers the base of the wall, shielding the plaster or drywall against damage from furniture and shoes; similarly, door jambs and casings protect the exposed edges of the wall coverings. In some cases, trim serves a structural function, too. For example, it reinforces window and door openings by physically connecting them to the house's framework.

If you extend your definition of trim to doors and windows, then trim also serves the important function of keeping the wet and cold out and the heat in. In fact, the crude moldings that constituted the earliest trim were probably more weather barriers than ornament. Used to seal the juncture of walls and ceilings against drafts, these moldings did then what caulks and building wraps do today.

Trimwork gives the interior of a house a distinctive visual texture, even though other decorative elements like floors, wall coverings, drapery and furniture are far more conspicuous. Trimwork, or in some cases, the lack of it, defines the style of a house. Imagine a Georgian mansion without its elaborate cornices or a Victorian without its gingerbread. Even in a house where movable furnishings set the tone, the trimwork creates the starting point from which a style or look emerges. From the outside, two houses might be identical, but once the trim is done, the interiors could encompass any style from formal paneled rooms to a reproduction of a turn-of-the-century Arts and Crafts parlor. The stylistic opportunities are vast.

Where trim comes from

In researching this book, I learned that historians can get quite fussy about cataloging the architectural styles of the past. One popular pictorial guide, *Identifying American Architecture*, lists some 39 American architectural styles, beginning with the Spanish Colonial period of the early 1600s and ending with Art Moderne, circa 1930 to 1945, each with its own interior and exterior treatment. Studying such sources leaves

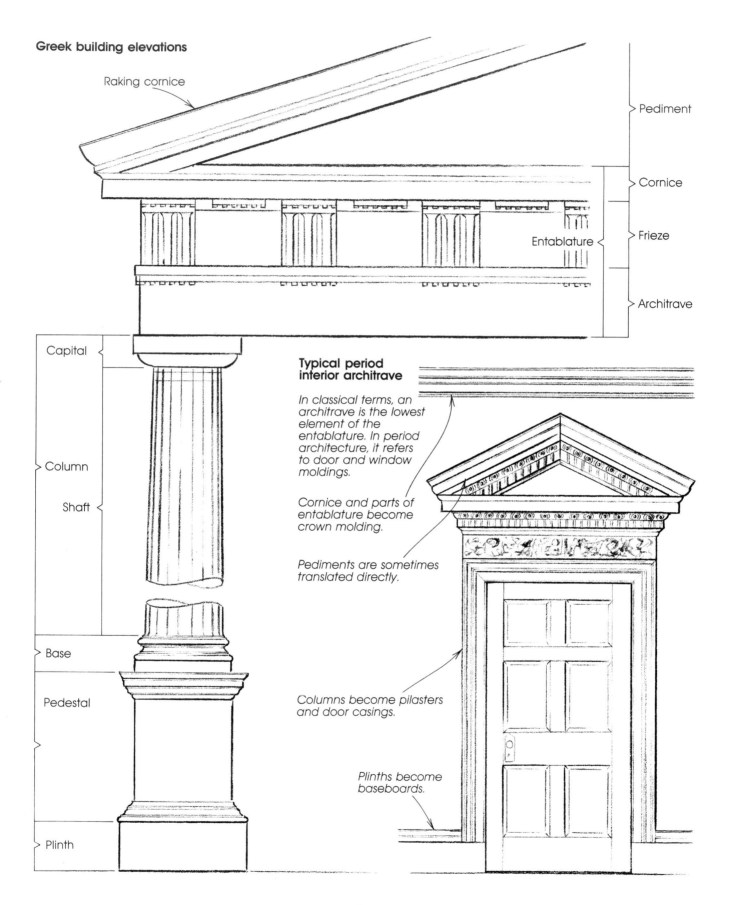

Greek building elevations

Raking cornice

Pediment

Cornice

Entablature

Frieze

Architrave

Capital

Column

Shaft

Base

Pedestal

Plinth

Typical period interior architrave

In classical terms, an architrave is the lowest element of the entablature. In period architecture, it refers to door and window moldings.

Cornice and parts of entablature become crown molding.

Pediments are sometimes translated directly.

Columns become pilasters and door casings.

Plinths become baseboards.

me with the distinct impression that even though they are separated by several centuries, the earliest styles share more similarities than differences with what I call modern trimwork. It's easy to see how the relatively crude moldings used in some of America's earliest dwellings evolved into more elaborate treatments, only to be simplified again as tastes changed.

There are, of course, large differences among architectural styles, in the size and profiles of moldings and in the way they are positioned in the room. But the major elements of what we call modern trim—the baseboard and wall moldings, door casings and crown moldings—were all inspired in some way by elements of Greek and Roman architecture. In some cases, the individual molding profiles are drawn directly from Greek and Roman examples.

Greek (and later Roman) builders discovered that in order for a building to look correctly proportioned and pleasing to the eye, it has to have a certain logical progression of elements. These major elements are the plinth, the column, the capital, the entablature and the pediment. In one form or another, some or all of these elements are still found in modern architecture but especially in interior trim.

The drawing on the facing page shows how the major elements of classical architecture and the basic molding profiles evolved into modern interior trim. In some period architecture (high-style Georgian, for example), elements like columns, entablatures and pediments were translated quite literally into interior features. In classical architecture, the architrave was the lowest element of the entablature, but in period architecture, an architrave is an elaborate door or window trim system. As such, an architrave is really a scaled-down version of a temple entrance, complete with pilasters and a gabled pediment. Elsewhere in the house, robust baseboards might suggest plinths, and cornices (or crown moldings) were made to look like entablatures.

Hampton National Historic Site in Towson, Md., was built between 1783 and 1790, and its elaborate trim is considered high-style Georgian. The pedimented architrave shown above is more than 10 ft. high. It is a good example of how 18th-century architects and housewrights translated classical architectural details into interior trimwork. Baseboard, shown at left, is a stylized interpretation of Greek temple details.

Eight basic molding shapes

Scotia: concave profile, greater than a quarter-round

Cavetto: large concave quarter-round

Ogee (cyma reversa): alternate convex, concave profile with listels

Listel

Reverse ogee (cyma recta): alternate concave, convex profile with listels

← Listel

Astragal: small convex half-round

Torus: large convex half-round

Ovolo: convex quarter-round between listels

Fillet: small, flat section used to separate other profiles

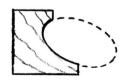
Greek moldings are based on the ellipse.

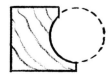
Roman moldings are based on the circle.

Above, a pediment detail from Hampton National Historic Site. The drawing at right shows the eight basic molding shapes, which are derived from Greek and Roman architecture.

Period architects and housewrights were far from slavish in their devotion to classical design, but they did follow some broad guidelines concerning the placement and selection of moldings. When viewing a typical interior wall from eye level (about 5 ft. or 6 ft., on average) we expect to see a certain graduated progression of visual elements. We know that a building's foundation has to be strong enough to support the structure above, so we expect it to look strong and solid. It follows then that the heaviest moldings—the baseboards—are usually at the bottom of the wall and that each higher horizontal band of molding—the chair rail, plate rail and crown molding, for example—are or appear to be slightly narrower. "Appear" is a key word because the plane from which a molding is viewed has a lot to do with its apparent width and depth.

As Greek builders discovered, moldings are best viewed straight on, from right angles. That's fine for temples but inside a room, this just isn't possible: from eye level, we look down on the baseboard and up at the crown molding. To compensate for this, moldings are often mounted or constructed in such a way that they appear to be at nearly right angles to the viewer. Thus moldings above the eye lean forward and those below the eye lean backward, as shown in the drawing at right. This canting, called the facial angle, can be be achieved in two ways. Below-the-eye moldings like baseboards are constructed so that the lowest part of the molding—in this case, the shoe—stands proud of the trim's primary plane. This gives the appearance of a rearward lean. Above-the-eye crown moldings, on the other hand, are simply fastened at an angle—typically 30° or 45°—to both wall and ceiling.

In classical architecture, plinths, columns and so on were made up of combinations of eight simple profiles, shown in the drawing on the facing page. Their shapes form the basis of the molding we use today. The profile of a molding has a lot to do with how and where it's used. Baseboards and other horizontal trim well below eye level are mainly ogees or coves along the top edges and sections of rounds or coves along the bottom edges. Other profiles will work too, but some look awkward. For instance, ogees or reverse ogees placed right on the floor project too deeply into the room and appear to float off the floor, thereby defeating the baseboard's job of appearing to anchor the wall.

Moldings that are placed high on the wall, chiefly crowns, are made up of deep coves, cyma rectas, and wide flats with narrow soffits. Rounds such as the ovolo and torus don't work well. Light striking these shapes from below tends to wash them out, making them appear as uneven flat surfaces. On the other hand, horizontal moldings at or slightly below eye level —chair rails, plate rails and dado caps for paneling— will look right if they are composed chiefly of a flat surface supported from below by a sharply receding structure made up of rounds or coves and cyma rectas.

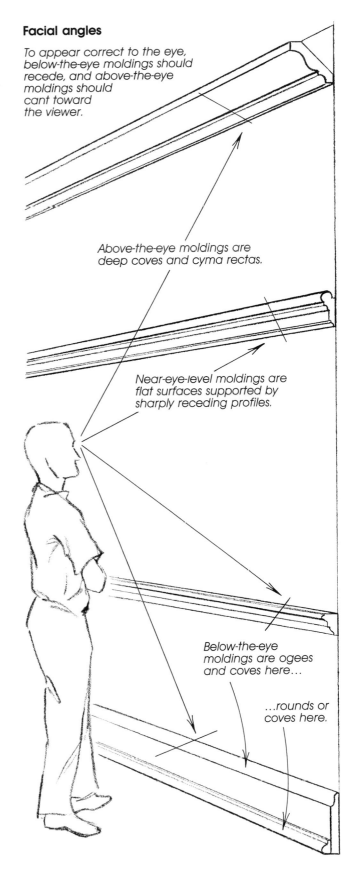

Facial angles

To appear correct to the eye, below-the-eye moldings should recede, and above-the-eye moldings should cant toward the viewer.

Above-the-eye moldings are deep coves and cyma rectas.

Near-eye-level moldings are flat surfaces supported by sharply receding profiles.

Below-the-eye moldings are ogees and coves here...

...rounds or coves here.

In this Laguna Beach, Calif., house, architect Jeffrey Sumich manipulated the style and placement of moldings to give the trimwork a traditional feel without resorting to slavish reproduction of period styles. Sumich's casings, installed by Gary Gordon, are shown in the photo above. They consist of wide, fluted pilasters butted to plinth blocks, right. Built-up moldings, above right, suggest a formal cornice.

Vertical moldings for door and window casings should generally be rounds—the astragal and torus—separated by wide flats or by broad, shallow rounds that read as flats. The outer edges of casings are often treated with beads or coves. These shapes produce a sharp vertical shadow line that crisply defines the molding's edges.

These guidelines are not cut-and-dried rules. If you look at enough trim, you'll discover that builders and architects often violate or at least bend the classical rules, sometimes successfully, sometimes not. However, if you're designing your own trim by combining off-the-shelf moldings or by making your own moldings, they will serve as a sensible starting place.

Modern trim

All modern trimwork consists of molding of some kind. Doors, windows and paneling are exceptions, of course, but even these elements are aesthetically set off by some sort of molding. Simply defined, a molding is a decorative plane or curved strip used for ornamentation or finishing. I sometimes think of a molding as any board that isn't performing a structural function, but even that is a fuzzy definition since structural members—timber beams and posts—were (and still are) occasionally embellished with carved profiles.

What we call modern trim (or at least the moldings we use to make it) has evolved largely since the advent of the Machine Age. Before moldings were turned out by the lineal mile on machines, carpenters "stuck" moldings on boards with hand planes whose cutters faithfully reproduced the classic profiles, or very nearly so. To a large extent, design variation years ago was as much a function of what molding planes the carpenter happened to have as it was of the architect's plans.

In the late 19th century, the introduction of the molding machine, or "sticker," changed the way designers and carpenters viewed moldings. Now they could simply pick profiles out of a catalog and stack them this way and that until a pleasing combination was achieved. By the turn of the century, this revolutionary technology was widespread enough to make elaborate trim affordable even to home owners of modest means. As a result, a multitude of individual trimwork styles developed and flourished. Some were patterned off classical examples, while others were inspired by the architectural movements of the day, including the Arts and Crafts style of Charles and Henry Greene in California, Frank Lloyd Wright's Prairie School and the the Craftsman style of Gustav Stickley, to name a few 20th-century examples.

Not all of these styles were consistently successful. Victorian houses, for example, are appreciated for their colorful gingerbread exteriors. But when carried to excess, Victorian trimwork, with its wide, multi-part crowns and bulky window and door casings, can be op-pressive, especially if finished in dark-stained oak, as some Victorian trim was. At the opposite extreme are the stripped-down boxes inspired by the International Style of the 1920s and 1930s. These houses come as close as possible to being trimless, and most of us would find them somewhat sterile.

Today, it's possible to reproduce any interior style from a period reproduction to a Craftsman bungalow. These styles are well documented; entire books have been written on the subject and a few are listed in the Resource Guide on pp. 179-181. More important, a surging interest in accurate restoration has made it profitable for molding suppliers to make reproductions of classically inspired moldings. If these high-quality moldings aren't available locally, you can order them by mail, have them made or make them yourself, as described in Chapter 2. You don't have to let the local discount lumberyard's dismal selection of molding determine what your trim will look like.

A trim sampler

A succesful trim job has to start out with an aesthetic purpose and a point of view that goes beyond just nailing up a few feet of Ranch casing. Although my own tastes tend toward minimal use of simple moldings, a client will sometimes want a room with the feel of a particular period, but not a strict reproduction. This usually calls for more elaborate moldings, which I have made by a custom millwork shop or make myself. I mix and match profiles until I develop a combination my client likes.

The photos on pp. 10-21 show some examples of what I consider sucessful trimwork. I've selected work—both my own and the work of other finish carpenters—that shows how trim can visually tie together a room or an entire house. I consider all of the examples shown here to be contemporary, even though some of them have a traditional feel, like the home of Penny Hassman of Laguna Beach, Calif., shown in the photos on the facing page. This trim was designed by architect Jeffrey Sumich and installed by Gary Gordon, a Laguna Beach trim carpenter.

If you compare these photos to the drawing on p. 6, you can see that it has most of the major elements of the period architrave, including a pair of fluted pilasters and a carved frieze. However, the architect didn't intend the trim to be a period reproduction, so the cornice is more elaborate than one you'd expect to find in a period house, and both the scale and relief of the molding are more robust. This trim was composed of a combination of off-the-shelf and custom-made moldings. To create the cornice, Gordon simply stacked the moldings, beginning at the bottom and working his way toward the ceiling.

Other examples of how a period feel can be achieved without slavish reproduction are shown on the follow-

ing pages. In the first example (see the photos here and on the facing page), a restored Italianate Victorian house in Oakland, Calif., carpenter Peter Carlson installed the wide multi-part casings, baseboard and crown molding that are the hallmark of Victorian interiors. Most Victorians, however, have elaborate painted trim, which was often made of plaster instead of wood. For this restoration, Carlson had the molding made of redwood. All the trim was finished with a clear Varathane varnish.

Victorian houses are noted for elaborate painted trim, often made of plaster. Carpenter Peter Carlson's restoration of this Oakland, Calif., Victorian is a departure from the norm. The wide baseboards, left, and crown moldings, above left, are made of redwood, finished clear with Varathane. Carlson installed wide, multi-part casing around the doors and windows, as shown above. The paneling is tied to the window by an elaborate stool and apron, as shown on the facing page. (Photos by Charles Miller.)

The second example is the house of California contractor Rodger Whipple, whose trim details are shown below and on the facing page. He had in mind the Arts and Crafts aesthetic of Charles and Henry Greene, California architects noted for their rich wood interiors. Whipple had done restoration work on the Greenes' well-known Gamble House in Pasadena and wanted to incorporate similar trim in his own residence.

Whipple employed the key feature of Greene and Greene trim, namely, the lavish use of wood detailed by angular, layered elements whose edges have been softly rounded. The junctures of various trim elements—side casing to head casing, for example or baseboard to casing—are emphasized by a difference in thickness or by decorative shaping. In his family room, kitchen and

Some of the trim details California contractor Rodger Whipple used in his own house are shown here. The top and bottom rails of the doors have trademark 'cloud-lift' rails, below. A similar shape is used to detail the end of the head casing, which extends past the side casing, above. Where horizontal and vertical members join, one element is made thicker, or a bevel or roundover is used to accent the joint. The photo at left shows a stein sitting on a narrow plate rail installed near the top of the wainscoting.

Contractor Rodger Whipple styled his trim after the work of Charles and Henry Greene, two turn-of-the century California architects whose Arts and Crafts interiors still inspire contemporary craftsmen.

The trim shown here was installed in a Spokane, Wash., home by carpenter Shawn Gabel. Gabel used high wainscoting, right, to tie the room's trim together and, as an accent, finished the doors and newel-post caps with varnish. Although you'd expect to find a chair rail atop wainscot, Gabel installed a crown-type profile instead, a pleasing variation shown below left. The photo below right shows how baseboards were tied into door casings. Newel posts repeat the detailing used in the wainscoting and are capped with clear-finished walnut, as shown on the facing page.

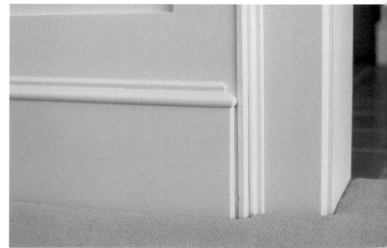

dining room, Whipple constructed redwood wainscoting that looks like frame-and-panel work but is in fact nailed directly to backing on the wall. Alternating panels are ¾ in. and ⅝ in. thick, creating a board-and-batten look that's a Greene and Greene trademark.

Another approach to tying a room together with wainscoting is shown here and on the facing page. This trim was built and installed by Shawn Gabel in Spokane, Wash. It's unusual on several counts. First, the wainscoting is nearly 5 ft. high, a departure from the usual 3-ft. height. It is capped off—succesfully, I think—by a crown molding, rather than the chair rail you'd expect to see. Gabel also nicely combined stain-grade and paint-grade work by finishing the doors, the stair rail and the newel-post caps with varnish.

For this house he built in Sandpoint, Idaho, author Craig Savage integrated the trim with built-in furniture. The moldings were made on site of jatoba, a very hard tropical wood. Head casings are a mock cabinet-head design. They were screwed to the wall, after which the screw holes were plugged.

Occasionally, I have been asked to design an entire trim system around a decorative motif. Such was the case for the house I built for Mark Story in Sandpoint, Idaho. My wife Lena, who is an artist, designed the house and worked out the trim details with the client through drawings and mockups. Interestingly, Lena's starting point for the trim design was a Greene and Greene motif. However, as we refined the design, we decided to limit the use of wood paneling to one small area in the bedroom and we greatly simplified the door and window trim, eventually settling on the mock cabinet-head design shown in the photos above left and on the facing page.

The trim itself is made of jatoba, a Brazilian wood that's about as hard as concrete and just as punishing to sawblades and router bits. Because no moldings were available in jatoba, I made my own on site, using the methods explained on pp. 30-41.

It's possible to achieve pleasing, even stunning, results with ordinary methods and materials. The photos on pp. 20-21 show one example. Tom Sain, a carpenter in Sandpoint, Idaho, made and installed this trim in his own house, which my wife Lena designed in 1986. It's hard to imagine a simpler approach. Sain made the baseboards and casings out of plain vertical-grain fir whose edges were lightly rounded with the router.

Trim needn't be elaborate to be elegant. Idaho carpenter Tom Sain made the trim for this house out of vertical-grain fir, whose edges were lightly rounded with a router. The baseboards join the casings at chamfered plinth blocks. The wood is finished clear, and the nail holes were left unfilled.

As shown in the photos at left and on the facing page, Sain dressed up the door casings with plinth blocks. The head casings have a mock cabinet-head treatment similar to what I did in the Story house. To create a bold reveal at the plinth blocks, Sain planed the casings and baseboard to $\frac{9}{16}$ in. thick. The plinth blocks are $\frac{3}{4}$ in. thick, and their edges were chamfered with a router bit. All of the molding was made on site with a router table, using the basic method discussed on pp. 30-39.

The photos on the preceding pages show only a few ways in which a house can be trimmed. If you don't have a specific idea of the trim you want, I'd suggest referring to some of books listed in Further Reading on p. 181. These will provide a starting place. Probably the hardest part of designing trim is latching on to a few basics from which you can build. For example, a photo in a book might give you some ideas for baseboard details, which you can then carry over to the casings. As Lena discovered in designing trim for Mark Story's house, it's sometimes easier to start with an existing design or style and then modify it to suit your own tastes and needs.

A Saturday morning spent looking at custom molding in local millwork shops will generate ideas, too. As discussed on pp. 28-30, a millwork shop usually keeps samples on hand. If you see a molding you like, the shop will already have on hand the knives to make it, so the cost won't be much more than for an off-the-shelf molding.

Trimming a house starts with selecting the molding. Whether you buy it, have it custom made or design and make your own, quantity, quality and cost are the main considerations.

2

Selecting, buying and making molding

The success of any trim job depends as much on the quality of the molding as it does on how the trim itself is designed. There are three ways to obtain molding: you can buy what's available off the shelf, have molding custom made to your specifications or make your own. Which you choose depends on how big the job is, what kind of quality you're after and, as usual, how much money you wish to spend.

From time to time, I have used all three sources, sometimes in the same job. Fortunately, molding manufacture has undergone somewhat of a renaissance in recent years. Thanks to a resurgent interest in restoring period homes and the popularity of Post-Modern architecture, high-quality molding is easier to find than it used to be. If you can't find what you want locally, you can even order it through the mail (see the Resource Guide on pp. 179-181 for mail-order sources).

Off-the-shelf molding

Buying molding off the lumberyard shelf is clearly the quickest solution, but you need to cultivate your sources carefully. Local lumberyards and hardware stores buy molding from specialty mills that do nothing but churn out lineal miles of the stuff. These yards offer low prices but not much variety, which explains why lumberyards usually have three or fewer crown profiles and only a couple of casing and baseboard designs. There's nothing really wrong with these moldings. At best, I've found them to be bland, bastardized versions of classical shapes that don't cast distinctive shadow lines (see the photo below). Inexpensive moldings are sometimes made of low-grade lumber that's sanded with shaped abrasive wheels, which produce a pasty profile that lacks crispness. The really cheap stuff isn't even wood at all but extruded plastic with a simulated wood-grain finish.

The top sample at left is lumberyard-grade crown; the bottom sample is custom-made crown. The cheaper molding's profile has been rounded over. The custom molding has crisp, well-defined edges.

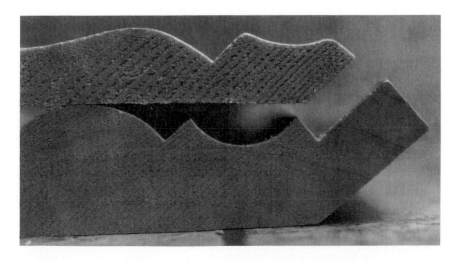

Some typical stock moldings

Base caps

Base caps attach to top of baseboards.

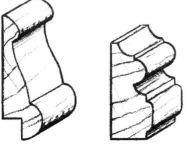   

Baseboards

Widths range from 5¼ in. to 7⅝ in.

Backs are relieved to bridge irregularities.

Base shoes

Base shoes attach to front of baseboards, at floor.

 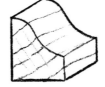 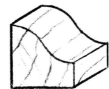

Crown moldings

Widths range from 2½ in. to 8 in.

Door stops

Window and door casings

Widths range from 2¼ in. to 5¾ in.

Backbands

Widths range from 1⅜ in. to 2½ in.

Backbands extend the casings' width and create a higher-relief molding.

Casing

Picture rails

Hook for paintings

Chair rails

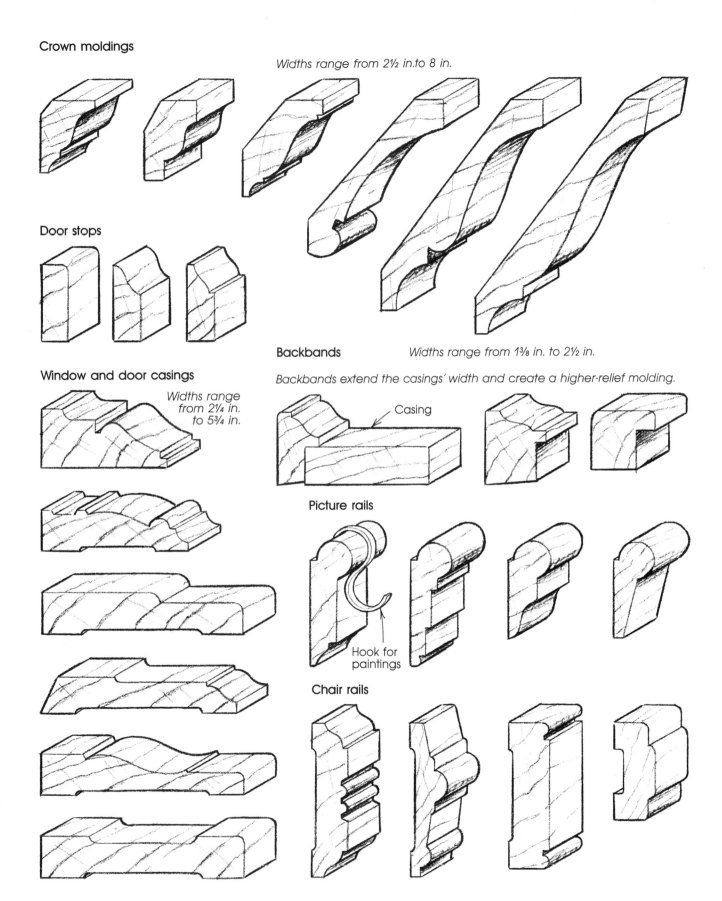

Variety and quality in lumberyards will vary widely. Local discount outlets are likely to have the poorest selection; in most cases, these places won't be worth bothering with. Yards that supply the building trade with factory-made doors and windows are usually a better bet. These suppliers will probably have bins stocked with various lengths in the common profiles shown in the drawing on pp. 24-25. If they don't have the moldings in stock, ask for a catalog and see if they can order what you want.

Molding grades and species

Trim carpenters divide the quality of their work into paint grade and stain grade, two terms that also loosely describe the grades of molding sold by most suppliers. These grades really translate into joints that can be caulked and joints that can't, and they dictate the tolerances kept by the carpenter. Paint-grade work assumes that the painter, with judicious application of caulk and primer, will cover up minor blemishes and less-than-perfect joints. Stain-grade work, on the other hand, is finished clear, so the carpenter has to do near-perfect joinery.

Paint-grade moldings are usually made of softwoods, while stain-grade moldings are of more expensive hardwoods. There are exceptions to this. Poplar, a hardwood, is often sold as paint-grade molding because it's relatively cheap and wears better than pine. In the West, it's not uncommon to see vertical-grain fir, a softwood, used for both stain-grade and paint-grade molding. In most cases, millwork shops will stock paint-grade moldings in white pine or in locally inexpensive species like yellow pine or fir. They may have on hand small quantities of stain-grade moldings in hardwoods like oak, birch or walnut but usually, if you want these species, you'll have to have the molding made.

Obviously, whether to stain or paint is a primarily an aesthetic consideration. But there are other things to think about when buying (and making) molding, as the chart at right shows. Of primary importance to the carpenter is the wood's workability. How well does it cut, sand and shape, and how does it hold a nail? A soft wood is easier to install because it bends and compresses readily to conform to irregularities, and it nails well. Very hard woods like oak or cherry must be pre-drilled for nails, so they are time-consuming to apply. Woods with tight grain, like pine, basswood and cedar, cut cleanly, leaving a surface that's ready for stain or paint. Conversely, woods with alternating sections of soft earlywood and hard latewood—Douglas fir, for example—can be difficult to bring to a presentable surface. Also, an open-grained wood will have to have its grain filled if you plan to paint it or expect a transparent finish to be a smooth film.

As surfaces in a house go, trim is subject to moderate wear and tear. Trim survivability depends on sev-

Woods suitable for trim

Species	Color
Ash, white	Creamy white to light brown
Beech	White to reddish brown
Birch, yellow	White to dark red
Birch, yellow: Select Red (heartwood)	Dark red
Birch, yellow: Select White (sapwood)	Creamy white
Butternut	Pale brown
Cherry	Reddish brown
Fir, Douglas: flat grain	Reddish tan
Fir, Douglas: vertical grain	Reddish tan
Lauan: Light Philippine Mahogany	Light to reddish brown
Maple, hard	White to reddish brown
Maple, soft	White to reddish brown
Oak, red: plainsawn	Reddish tan to brown
Oak, red: riftsawn	Reddish tan to brown
Oak, white: plainsawn	Greyish tan
Oak, white: riftsawn	Greyish tan
Pine, Idaho	Creamy white
Pine, Northern	Creamy white to pink
Pine, Ponderosa	Light to medium pink
Pine, sugar	Creamy white
Pine, yellow: shortleaf	Pale yellow
Poplar	Pale yellow to brown with green cast
Red cedar, Western	Light to dark red
Redwood: flat grain (heartwood)	Deep red
Redwood: vertical grain (heartwood)	Deep red
Spruce, Sitka	Light yellowish tan
Walnut	Sapwood: creamy white Heartwood: medium to dark purplish brown

This chart has been adapted from *Guide to Wood Species Selection: including sawing methods, treatment and finishing.* Courtesy Architectural Woodwork Institute, Arlington, Va.

Figure	Grain	Hardness	Dimensional stability	Paint-grade finish	Stain-grade finish	Remarks
High	Open	Very hard	10/64 in.	Rarely used	Excellent	Bold grain, springy and strong
Low	Closed	Very hard	14/64 in.	Excellent	Good	Low cost, low stability
Medium	Closed	Hard	12/64 in.	Excellent	Good	Widely used
Medium	Closed	Hard	12/64 in.	Rarely used	Excellent	Rich color
Medium	Closed	Hard	12/64 in.	Rarely used	Excellent	Uniform appearance
High	Open	Medium	8/64 in.	Rarely used	Excellent	Rich appearance, limited supply
High	Closed	Hard	9/64 in.	Rarely used	Excellent	Rich appearance
High	Closed	Soft	10/64 in.	Fair	Fair	Low cost, tendency to splinter, grain raises easily
Low	Closed	Soft	6/64 in.	Good	Good	Good stability
Low	Open	Soft	10/64 in.	Fair	Good	Limited application for architectural woodwork
Medium	Closed	Very hard	12/64 in.	Excellent	Good	Extremely hard
Low	Closed	Medium	9/64 in.	Excellent	Rarely used	Not widely used
High	Open	Hard	11/64 in.	Rarely used	Excellent	Excellent architectural wood, low cost, widely used
Low	Open	Hard	5/64 in.	Rarely used	Excellent	Excellent architectural wood, limited supply
High	Open	Hard	11/64 in.	Rarely used	Excellent	Wide range of grain patterns and colors
Low	Open	Hard	7/64 in.	Rarely used	Excellent	Limited availability
Low	Closed	Soft	8/64 in.	Excellent	Good	True white pine, wide range of applications
Medium	Closed	Soft	8/64 in.	Excellent	Good	True white pine, wide range of applications
Medium	Closed	Soft	8/64 in.	Excellent	Good	Most widely used pine, wide range of applications
Low	Closed	Soft	7/64 in.	Excellent	Good	True white pine, wide range of applications
High	Closed	Medium	10/64 in.	Good	Good	An economical hard pine
Medium	Closed	Medium	9/64 in.	Excellent	Good	Ideal interior hardwood, excellent paintability
Medium	Closed	Soft	6/64 in.	Good	Good	High natural decay resistance, limited availability
High	Closed	Soft	6/64 in.	Good	Good	Superior exterior wood, high natural decay resistance
Low	Closed	Soft	3/64 in.	Excellent	Excellent	Superior exterior wood, high natural decay resistance
Low	Closed	Soft	10/64 in.	Good	Good	Limited availability
High	Open	Hard	10/64 in.	Rarely used	Excellent	Fine domestic hardwood, extremely limited widths and lengths, high cost

Note: The column headed "Dimensional stability" refers to the amount of movement possible in a 12-in. wide board if its moisture content were to change from 10% to 5% or vice versa. These dimensions represent extreme conditions.

eral factors, including wood hardness, rot resistance and dimensional stability. The carpenter's best indication of how well a trim wood will stand up to the appliance mover or the cat's claw is hardness. The harder the wood, the more durable the trim. Rot resistance is a consideration in damp locations or where the trim will touch masonry, which will cause it to wick moisture. For these applications, choose a rot-resistant wood like redwood, cedar or cypress.

As the relative humidity in the house changes with the seasons and with routine household activities such as cooking and bathing, trim woods absorb and release moisture. Changes in moisture content cause the wood to swell and shrink across the grain so, in effect, the width of the molding changes constantly. A coat of finish slows moisture exchange, but trim still moves enough to open up joints, especially if the moldings are very wide. As the chart shows, some woods are more dimensionally stable than others. If the moldings are to be very wide and you have a choice of woods, pick a species that's dimensionally stable, like sugar pine or riftsawn oak. In any case, before you install the trim, stack it in the house for a few weeks with ½-in. stickers between layers, preferably after the drywall and

paint are well cured. This will allow the wood to reach equilibrium moisture content with the interior of the home and perhaps reduce grief from moisture-induced wood movement. The sidebar on pp. 32-33 gives advice on ordering molding from a supplier.

Custom-made moldings

In northern Idaho, where I've done most of my trim carpentry, the selection of moldings is limited, to say the least. Local lumberyards carry two styles, (if you can call them styles), Ranch and Streamline. If you want something different, you either make it yourself or have it made by a custom millwork shop.

Almost every town has a specialized millwork shop of some kind. These shops ply the general woodworking trade, making custom cabinets, staircases and interior fixtures and lots of moldings. Depending on its size, the custom shop will have on hand a wide selection of decent stock moldings and will be able to make just about any molding a customer can dream up. I've found that the best way to locate a custom millwork shop is not through the Yellow Pages but by picking the brains of other contractors and carpenters.

On a typical molding or sticker machine (facing page), knives (below) are custom-ground to the customer's specifications and bolted into a cutterhead (left). Stock is fed into one end of the machine, and finished molding emerges from the other.

A well-equipped millwork shop has specialized molding machines, sometimes called sticker machines. These machines have one or more cutterheads that can be fitted with knives to make molding in various profiles, as shown in the photos above and at right. Flat stock is inserted into one end of the machine and fed past the knives by automatic rollers. The finished molding emerges from the opposite end. It's not uncommon for high-volume millwork shops to have on hand hundreds of molding knives in various profiles. If they don't stock the molding you want, they may be able to make it from knives left over from another job. A resourceful molding operator can sometimes duplicate a profile by using portions of existing knives. If this isn't possible, you can have knives custom made by the shop machinist.

To order knives, the millwork shop will need a full-scale drawing of the molding profile you want or a sample of the molding to be reproduced. This profile will be scribed to steel blanks and ground to shape. The cost of this service is liable to vary widely. Some shops use optical layout systems that duplicate profiles in a matter of minutes; others do the job entirely by hand. Expect to pay anywhere from $60 to $150 for

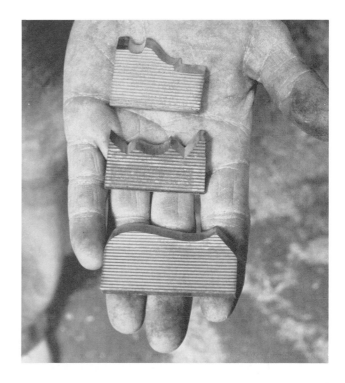

You can make your own molding using a combination of routers and molding heads (right). Half-inch shank bits are best for making molding; smaller bits are suitable for fine detail work. The bit at bottom right is a combination bit specially made to cut moldings. Below are some of Savage's shopmade moldings.

knives, depending on the size and complexity of the molding. One company I use charges $12.50 per inch of knife width plus a $25 setup charge. So for a 2-in. wide molding, I'd pay $50 for a single-knife cutterhead. Some molding machines have two or three cutterheads, however, and you'll be charged accordingly. The multi-knife machines produce a smoother surface that needs less sanding, so the additional knife cost may be worth it. If you subtract wood and knife-grinding costs, you can expect to pay about 8 cents per lineal foot for a typical custom-molding job.

The mill operator will want to know whether the molding is to be stain grade or paint grade and will ask what wood you want your molding to be. The chart on pp. 26-27 gives some advice on selecting species. Regardless of the species, however, make sure the wood used has a moisture content not much above 7%. Wood that's too moist machines poorly. You're at the mercy of your mill operator when it comes to the finished product. But it's a good idea to hang around the

mill and inspect the first few pieces that come off the sticker machine. Dull or imbalanced knives or too high a feed rate may leave a rippled surface that won't show up until paint or stain is applied, when it's too late to sand the ripples out. A feed rate that's too slow will burnish the wood, causing it to take stain unevenly. A tiny nick in just one knife will leave a conspicuous line or scratch in the molding. In hardwood, this will take lots of sanding to remove.

If you wet the surface of a sample piece with lacquer or paint thinner and hold it obliquely to a light source, you'll be able to spot ripples, burnishing and nicked knives. Draw these flaws to the operator's attention, and ask that they be corrected.

Making your own moldings

Except on large jobs requiring more than 500 lineal feet of trim, I prefer to make my own moldings, either in the shop or on site. Unless you're set up to make

Shopmade router table

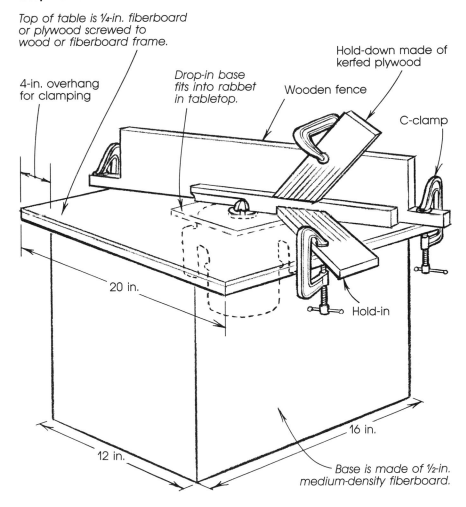

Top of table is ¼-in. fiberboard or plywood screwed to wood or fiberboard frame.

4-in. overhang for clamping

Drop-in base fits into rabbet in tabletop.

Hold-down made of kerfed plywood

Wooden fence

C-clamp

Hold-in

20 in.

16 in.

12 in.

Base is made of ½-in. medium-density fiberboard.

moldings for a living, however, don't count on saving money by making your own. For one thing, you'll pay more for molding-grade lumber than a millwork shop will, since these shops are often given volume discounts on lumber. And even if you're willing to work for nothing, the labor involved in making molding is substantial. The best argument for making your own lies in the satisfaction of producing a distinctive, one-of-a-kind decoration for the house you're trimming.

There are three ways to make moldings on site: with a router; with a molding head on a table saw or radial-arm saw; and with a molder/planer, a specialized machine that's really a combination thickness planer and shaper. I don't own a molder/planer but I have plenty of routers and bits, so I'll concentrate on the router and molding-head methods. Also, routers are relatively inexpensive, and in recent years, manufacturers have introduced a wide range of bits that make it practical to produce moldings in many profiles. Some typical bits and profiles are shown in the photos on the facing page.

As discussed on pp. 56-57, for making moldings, you'll need a powerful router (at least 1 hp) that's equipped to accept ½-in. shank bits. A smaller router and ¼-in. shank bits just won't be up to the job. The small bits tend to chatter and sometimes break under the heavy cutting load of molding work. A router can be used freehand by passing it over work that's been clamped to a bench or sawhorse. Conversely, the machine can be mounted upside-down in a table and the work fed past the stationary bit. The latter method works best for making molding, chiefly because moldings are usually cut into the edges of boards and it's easier, safer and more accurate to feed the stock past a fixed bit.

The router table that I use is shown in the drawing above. For making molding, a router table should have a large enough surface to support the longest stock to be molded, and it should have an adjustable fence to vary the stock's distance from the cutterhead. Some router tables have a slot for a miter gauge to support stock for molding. My router table has 4 in. of overhang to provide plenty of surface for clamping fences and hold-downs. Some carpenters (myself included) buy an extra router base and bolt it beneath the extension wing of the table saw. A hole bored through the extension wing allows a bit to poke through, converting the saw into a router table, complete with fence and miter gauge.

The fence need be only as tall as the molding is thick or wide. However it is safer to have a fence larger than the piece being molded. A fence 4 in. high provides plenty of clamping space for hold-downs and acts as a partial safety guard by covering the bit. I use a straight piece of scrap for a fence. It has small horns on the ends so I can clamp it without the clamps interfering with the feed.

How much molding do you need?
Compiling materials take-offs

SHEET 2 OF 6									
JOB _Garett Addition_			BID DATE _9/27/88_						
LOCATION _3739 SMOKE TREE_			ADD'S _____						
ARCHITECT _Simmonds_			ALT'S _____						
PLANS DATED _8/8/88_ ADDENDUM DATE _____ BIDS MAILED _____									
RM	DET	AMT	DESCRIPTION	MATERIAL	LNGT	FOOT COST	UNIT COST	TOTAL COST	
#1	BDR Base	50'	RANCH STYLE BASE	PINE	RND	.35	.35	17.50	
#1	BDR Case	70'	" " Case	"	14'	.32	.32	22.40	
#1	BDR STL.	16'	1"x6"x4' STOOL	"	16'	1.12	.56	8.96	
#2	BDR Base	70'	RANCH STYLE BASE	"	RND	.35	.35	24.50	
#2	BDR Case	65'	" " Case	"	14'	.32	.32	20.80	
#2	BDR STL.	16'	1"x6"x4' STOOL	"	16'	1.12	.56	8.96	
	HALL Base	40'	RANCH STYLE BASE	"	RND.	.35	.35	14.00	
	Hall Case	90'	" " Case	"	14'	.32	.32	31.36	

Form B

SUB TOTAL $ 148.48
OVERHEAD 10 % $ 14.85
PROFIT 10 % $ 14.85
TOTAL THIS SHEET $ 178.18

Whether you buy molding or make your own, you need to have some method of calculating how much you'll need. Contractors call this calculation a materials take-off, because it's usually "taken off" the plans. With a logical take-off method, you'll avoid wasting money by buying too much molding and wasting time by having to place a second order to finish the job.

When I'm doing a take-off I try to work only with an approved set of plans, if one is available. If I'm lucky, the architect has provided a door and window schedule and perhaps a listing of the lineal footages of trim required. Still, I use the schedule only as a check for my own calculations. If you provide the plans, some millwork companies will do the take-offs for you and then supply "trim kits," bundles of trim for each door or window. You still need to double-check the accuracy of the plans, but you save having to calculate the totals yourself. Whether plans exist or not, I visit the site anyway, tape measure in hand. I use a tally form like the one at left to keep track of my needs.

Standing trim—Estimators divide trim into two categories: running trim and standing trim. Running trim is trim that can be ordered and installed in random lengths. This includes baseboards, chair rails, picture rails and crown

Hold-downs and hold-ins are a must for making molding on the router table. These fixtures ensure a consistent cut and a crisp, even profile. I make featherboard-type hold-downs out of Baltic birch plywood. These fixtures, also known as fingerboards, are simply pieces of plywood with multiple kerfs sawn into one end. They act as springs, holding the molding stock firmly against both fence and table. If the bit should happen to catch in the wood, a featherboard will prevent a kickback. To set a featherboard, I first cut a few inches of molding. Then, with the stock held against the fence and the router stopped, I clamp the featherboard in place with a slight compression against the molding. If the hold-downs are too snug, the stock won't feed smoothly; if they are too loose, the molding will chatter as it's fed.

---

moldings. Standing trim is trim whose length must be specified for a particular purpose, usually door and window casings and perhaps wainscoting frames, or trim that must be made up for a specific application, such as an entryway.

I start my take-offs with the interior doors. This guarantees that I'll look at every room in the house. Since doors are standing trim, I try to keep my calculations as accurate as possible so I can use standard molding lengths. A typical 6-ft. 8-in. high interior door needs four 7-ft. pieces of side casing (two for each side of the door). This length allows for the 4 in. of waste consumed by the miters. Because molding is sold in multiples of 2 ft. with the minimum length usually 6 ft., I have two choices: I can buy five 8-ft. lengths for the side and head casings or two 14-ft. lengths, which, sawn in half, will yield all four 7-ft. side casings. Trimming the 8-footers would leave four pieces of waste about 1 ft. long; the two 14-footers cut in half will leave only short scraps. The head casing for a typical door, say 2 ft. 10 in. wide, needs to be 38 in. to 42 in. long (again, allowing for miters) so two of these will come out of a single 7-ft. piece. Thus, three 14-footers will case a door up to 2 ft. 10 in. wide, with one 7-ft. piece left over for the next door.

If the moldings aren't available in 14-ft. lengths, I'll call out two 10-ft. lengths and two 8-ft. lengths per door. Each 10-footer will give me a 7-ft. side casing and (just barely) a 3-ft. head casing. The 8-footers will yield the other two side casings, with 1 ft. of waste. If

you're not mitering the trim, you can figure your molding totals closer to the bone. I add at least one extra set of standing door and window trim to my final count. I always have to replace at least one chumped piece during a job, so I've learned to allow for it. I stash any extra pieces in the attic, figuring that another carpenter might someday need the trim for a repair or for a sample for the mill.

Windows are treated exactly like doors, but only one set of casings is required since the outside trim is entirely different. Each piece of window trim is counted separately, and like the doors, actual cut lengths are figured and called out on the order. Also, some doors will need stool and apron stock, as described in Chapter 6.

Running trim—Figuring running trim is fairly simple. As I'll explain in Chapter 7, running molding can be scarf-joined, so it's not nearly so critical to calculate exact lengths. This is just as well, given the way that mills price molding. Baseboards, chair rails, picture rails and crown moldings are typically made to order, so the mill will probably bill you by the lineal foot. Since the mill is using random-length lumber to make the molding, it will deliver and bill you for random lengths.

To estimate running trim, I total the running lengths of the walls on a per-room basis and add 10% for waste and chumped cuts. Working with random lengths, I try to install the longest pieces on the longest walls first. On walls interrupted by doors and windows, I don't add the waste factor

because the openings usually allow for plenty of extra molding. On very long walls where you don't want to splice shorter lengths together, call out 18-ft. lengths, but expect to pay the mill extra for them.

If you're going to make your own trim, doing an accurate take-off is a lot easier than calculating how much lumber you'll need to make the molding. There's a law written on a scrap 2x4 somewhere that says no matter how much molding you make for a custom job, you'll inevitably need just a foot more. To avoid this frustration, I do my take-off in the usual way, then, after determining what widths of boards are available, I figure how many pieces of molding blanks I will be able to rip out of each board. I allow for saw-kerf waste and then add between 25% and 55% for culling low-grade, twisted or warped boards. The large waste range is a function of the wood used. A clear, soft, vertical-grain wood like redwood wastes 25%; a grainy hardwood like walnut wastes closer to 55%. The high waste figures also allow for testing setups and the inevitable sniping of the beginning and end of each piece. Making molding uses lots of wood, and it's better to recognize it sooner than later.

Typical stock bits

Straight bit for rabbets and grooves

Corebox bit for fluting and coving

Cove bit with pilot

Chamfer bit

V-groove for fluting and veining

Roman ogee

Roundover with fillet or quirk

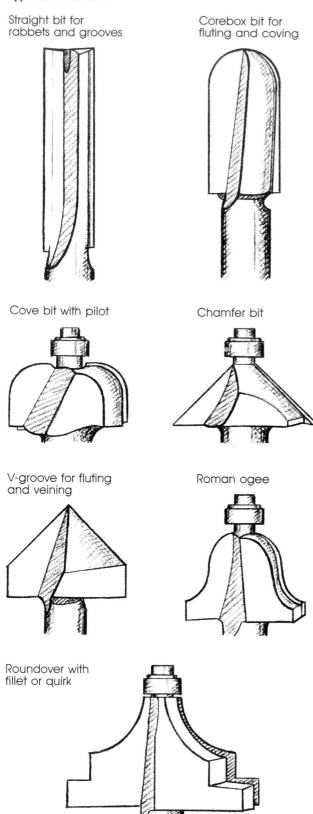

Router bits—Until just a few years ago, there wasn't much choice when it came to router bits; Sears probably had as good a selection as anybody. These days, however, bits come in such a wide range of materials, sizes and profiles that you can practically turn a powerful router into a small shaper. Bits are sold in three shank sizes: ¼ in., ⅜ in. and ½ in. Stick with the ½-in. shank bits. Besides being better able to deliver the router's power to the cutting face without chattering or snapping, ½-in. shank bits are available in greater variety than smaller bits. You may, however, want to keep some smaller shank bits around for joinery or for delicate moldings.

Router shanks are generally made of tool steel, and the cutting part of the bit is made of high-speed steel or tungsten carbide. There are good arguments for each material. High-speed steel, although cheaper than carbide, doesn't stay sharp as long. But because it is readily shaped by grinding, you can change a bit's profile to suit the job at hand. Carbide, on the other hand, costs three or four times as much as steel but because it stays sharper much longer, it's worth the extra money. Half-inch shank bits are usually available only in carbide, although it is possible to find ½-in. steel bits. I use only carbide bits unless I need a few feet of a custom profile, in which case I grind a steel bit myself.

Some router bits have a pilot or guide bearing attached to the shank, above or below the cutter. This bearing acts as a fence by keeping the bit's cutting edge at a constant distance from the stock and in effect controls the cutting width. The drawing at left shows four piloted bits. The bearing keeps the cutting edge exactly at the tangent of the bit's maximum cutting width. Bits with pilot bearings (at least the small ones) are meant to be used with the router held freehand. If you're using a piloted bit in the table with a fence, you can either remove the bearing or let it into a notch chiseled into the fence. To make curved moldings or to carry a straight molded profile around the corner of a board, remove the table's fence and feed the work directly against the pilot bearing. In any case, the edge the bit bears against must be perfectly smooth, or irregularities will telegraph to the finished profile.

Router bits are available (individually or in combination) in profiles that come close to matching the eight classical shapes discussed on p. 9 and shown in the drawing on p. 8. The drawing on the facing page shows a typical but far from comprehensive selection. A number of companies, the Furnima Co. of Canada, for example, make bit sets specifically designed for molding. Some of them are actually reproductions of English wooden hand-plane profiles. If you want profiles that these bits can't make, you can have a carbide bit made (see the Resource Guide on pp. 179-181) or you can modify a high-speed steel bit yourself by grinding the profile you want. Usually I buy a cutter for a specific purpose, adding to my cutters as each client requests a particular detail or molding. My collection has expanded to the point where I can create or copy almost any shape or pattern from my cutter box.

I store my bits in a block of wood drilled with holes 1/64 in. larger than the shank diameter. This arrangement keeps them from banging into each other and chipping the carbide which, for all its hardness, is really quite brittle. Occasionally, to remove pitch buildup and dirt, I wipe the cutting edges with a strong detergent like Formula 409. If the bearings are clogged with contact cement from plastic-laminate work, remove the buildup with lacquer thinner, then lubricate the bearing with a drop of light machine oil. Keep the shanks free of dirt, too, or they might freeze in the collet. If this happens, tap the bit with a brass hammer on some point other than the cutting edge. Turn the shank between taps to free it from the collet. Clean the collet with steel wool, and add a dab of nose grease (body oil from your face) to keep the shank from freezing up again.

Setting up for molding—Making moldings with a router is basically a subtractive process—you keep routing away wood until the only thing that's left is the desired profile. This is accomplished by using one or more router bits and by varying both the cutting depth and the cutting width. Cutting depth is set by reaching beneath the table and raising and lowering the router itself so more or less of the bit extends above the surface of the table. Cutting width is controlled by moving the fence toward or away from the bit. For minimum cutting widths, a notch cut into the fence allows it to move right on top of the bit so that only a small portion of the cutting edge is exposed.

Although very versatile, a router is not a shaper. It has limitations. With its relatively low horsepower and small bit diameter, a router isn't capable of cutting in a single pass the kinds of large moldings a shaper can make with ease. Most routed moldings must be made in several passes, sometimes with combinations of bits set at different cutting depths and widths. Often, a single bit can cut more than one profile, as shown in the drawing below. This bit, a Roman ogee, will cut a

Combination bit for cutting multiple profiles

Vary the the cutting depth and width to obtain different profiles.

radius or quarter-round when adjusted flush to the tabletop but will produce a quarter-round with a fillet when adjusted to cut 1/16 in. deeper. Using this sort of adjustment, it's possible to make hundreds of different profiles with a small assortment of bits.

The width of the moldings will determine what type of bit you can use. Since router bits rarely have a cutting depth greater than 2 in., a 6-in. wide fluted casing, for example, will have to be made with a straight flute bit and with the stock lying flat on the table. A narrower molding could be fluted with the board held

Multiple profiles from one bit

It's possible to make several profiles by varying cutting depths.

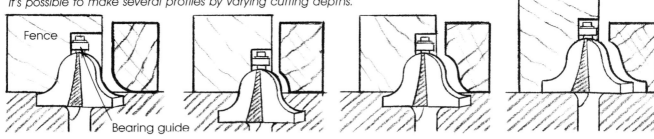

Fence

Bearing guide

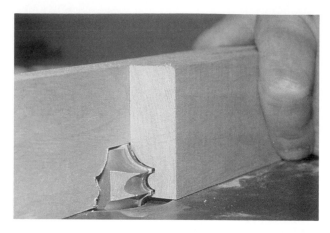

The photos above show the series of cuts necessary to make a chair rail with a combination bit. The first two cuts establish the profile, and the last is a cleanup cut with a straight bit. Whenever possible, feed the wood into a bit shielded by the fence rather than between the bit and fence. A piece that's already molded, however, will have to be fed with its flat back against the fence, as shown in the photo above. (Photos by Stephanie Johnson.)

in the vertical position, using a different cutter, of course. If I have a choice of feeding horizontally into a small-diameter bit or vertically into a larger one to produce the equivalent profile, I prefer to feed the stock vertically. This is because a larger bit has a higher speed at the cutting edges, which produces a cleaner cut with less burning.

Regardless of the type of bit you use, try to set it up so the bit can be partially shielded by the fence, as shown in the photos at left. One way of doing this is to anchor the fence loosely at one end with a clamp, then pivot it slowly into the spinning bit until only half the cutting diameter is exposed. If the bit has cutting surfaces on its top edge, you can position the fence over the bit and then slowly feed it up into the fence. With piloted bits, you'll have to cut a clearance notch into the fence with a chisel or handsaw.

Cutting molding—I make most molding from standard dimension lumber, usually from 1X stock that's ¾ in. thick. If you want thicker molding or a hardwood species not sold in nominal thicknesses, buy rough stock and have it planed to the desired thickness. A molding that will have a simple edge treatment, say a baseboard, should be ripped to its final width and then molded. So the wood will cut consistently as it feeds past the bit, straighten the edge of each board to be molded on the jointer and make sure both edges are parallel. If you are making narrow moldings and starting with wide boards, begin by jointing both edges and molding both edges. Then rip the moldings off the wide board, rejoint the edges and mold again, as shown in the drawing on p. 39. It's far easier and safer to feed a wide board than a narrow strip. You can continue the mold/rip sequence until the board is too small to feed safely.

I always set up the router table and run a few test pieces before committing my good lumber. I go over a mental checklist of safety items before turning on the router. I make sure the fence is properly set and securely clamped. The bit must be tight in the collet and the cord out of harm's way, where it won't be tripped over. Sometimes, under heavy cutting loads, the bit will tend to creep out of the collet, deepening the cut and ruining the piece. To prevent this, insert the bit into the collet until it bottoms, then back it out ⅛ in. before tightening the collet. The small space between the bit and the bottom of the collet will reduce vibrations, keeping the bit from creeping. I use a scrap to test my setup, and I adjust both fence and cutting width until the profile looks right. The test piece should be of the same species as the molding so you'll get a good idea of feed rate and cutting quality.

As shown in the drawings on pp. 38-39 and the photos on the facing page, the wood can be fed from the bit side only or, if there's no other way, between the bit and the fence. It's possible for the wood to get trapped between the bit and fence, causing splintering or a kickback. The drawings show a typical cutting sequence for the Furnima bit, and these apply to other cutters, too. In general, try to make the deepest (but narrowest) cuts first, so as to leave as much material as possible bearing on the table. The lightest, widest cuts are saved for last, when there's less material to steady the wood during feeding.

Feed the wood into the router bit firmly but slowly. Feeding too fast will cause a poor surface, but feeding too slowly will cause burning. The router's sound will give a good clue about feed rate. If the motor maintains its speed without bogging down and the bit produces large, clean chips, the router is cutting optimally. A bogged-down motor or smoking indicates too fast a feed rate, a cut that's too deep or wide or a dull bit. The rules that apply to feed rate are obvious. When the cut is very deep or wide, make it in several passes or feed the work more slowly. Similarly, to achieve a smooth cut in very dense, hard wood, make multiple passes. As a general rule, feed the wood against the rotation of the bit, which forces the work into rather than away from the fence.

Molding heads—Another popular way of making molding is with a molding head mounted on a table saw or radial-arm saw. Molding heads are made by several manufacturers, including Sears and Delta. Basically, a molding head is a fat metal disc with slots cut into it for one, two or three molding knives. The head bolts to the saw arbor, and it's usually fitted with some sort of guard. By changing the knives or using them in combination, dozens of molding profiles are possible, including some pretty ugly ones, which is one reason I use molding heads so rarely. The photo at right shows a typical molding head.

Molding heads are very dangerous. Three or four knives spinning at 2,700 rpm make a terrible din, and they can do horrible damage to a misplaced hand. The knives have been known to fly out of the head. Without fail, use guards and hold-downs and wear eye and ear protection when you use molding heads. When the furnished guard won't fit—as is sometimes the case on the radial-arm saw—try to fashion one out of wood or, as shown in the photos on p. 40, operate the cutterhead through a wooden fence.

Molding-head knives come in a wide selection, especially from Delta, which has been selling a molding-head system for many years. I have never seen carbide-tipped molding knives, but you can buy steel blanks for grinding your own profiles. The molding head's chief advantage over the router table is its ability to reach farther in toward the center of a piece of molding to cut overhanging or undercut profiles in a single pass. Also, the molding head can be tilted to alter the angle of cut, something that is very difficult to do on a router table.

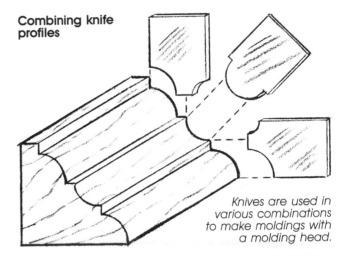

Combining knife profiles

Knives are used in various combinations to make moldings with a molding head.

Several manufacturers make molding heads in single-knife, double-knife or three-knife models. This single-knife head has 18 knives whose profiles can be combined to make hundreds of moldings.

Molding cutting sequence

These drawings show the steps in making a baseboard and base-cap molding.

Baseboard

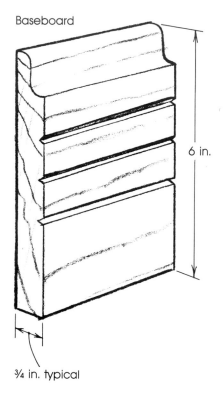

6 in.

¾ in. typical

Step 1

Select clear, straight-grained wood.

Joint edges straight.

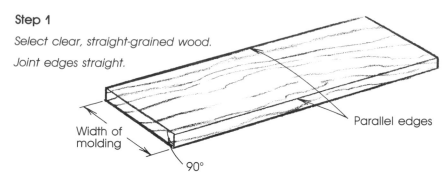

Parallel edges

Width of molding

90°

Step 2

In several passes at progressively greater depths, make deepest cuts first.

Router fence

Molding stock

Corebox bit

Hold-in

Step 3

Next, round over top edge of molding.

Roundover bit with pilot removed

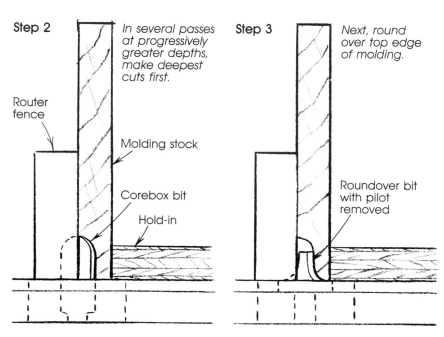

Step 4

Make one cut, move fence, make second cut, etc.

Hold-down clamped to fence

Sand molding to fair profile.

Feed flat edge against fence.

Veining bit

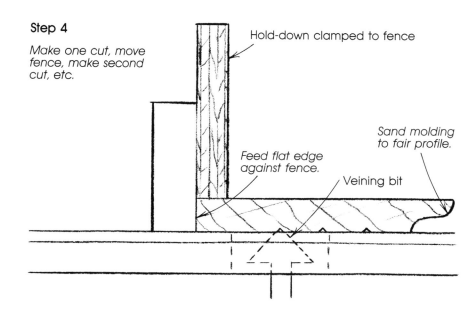

Step 1

To make base cap using similar profile, mold both edges.

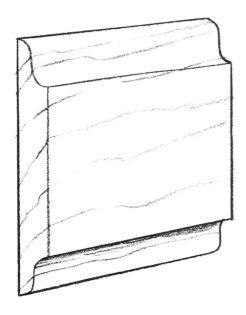

Base cap

Finished cap fits over baseboard.

¾ in.

2¼ in.

Baseboard

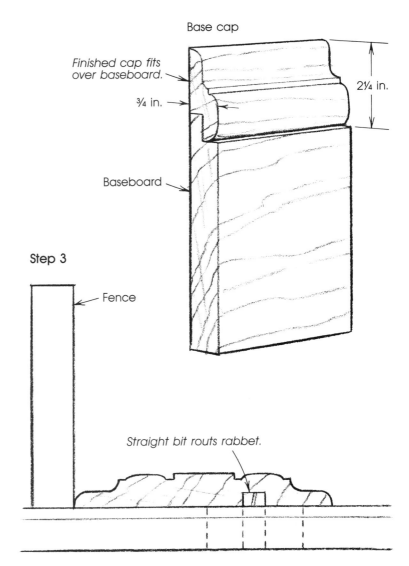

Step 3

Fence

Straight bit routs rabbet.

Step 2

High fence provides better support.

Use portion of combination bit for desired profile.

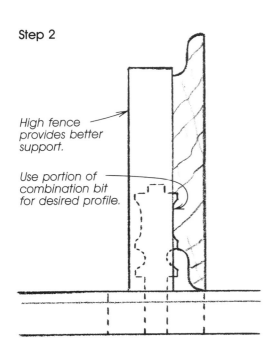

Step 4

On table saw, rip molding off large piece and sand edges smooth.

To rip second piece, flip stock edge for edge and reset fence. Never trap molding between fence and blade.

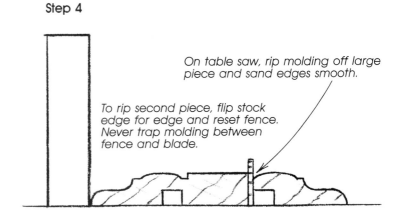

Although it isn't practical to use the table saw's guard with a molding head, always hold the stock firmly against the fence with a featherboard. When possible, feed the stock against the fence, rather than between the fence and cutter, as shown at right.

To set up a radial-arm saw for molding work, carefully plunge the head through a wooden fence, as shown below. Then feed the wood into the cutter between a featherboard and the fence. A semicircular plywood disc screwed to the fence immediately above the knives offers further protection. It has been omitted here for clarity.

The photos above show typical molding-head setups for the both the table saw and the radial-arm saw. Before turning on the saw, make sure that the knives are seated securely at the bottom of their slots. Check that the setscrews are tight. Tighten them in sequence around the cutterhead, a little at a time, to equalize stress in the slots. On the radial-arm saw, the cutterhead can be raised, lowered, moved in and out and tilted, but normally, the head is operated with the motor's axis at 90° to the table. This makes best use of fences and hold-downs. I screw an auxiliary fence to the table, then carefully pull the spinning cutterhead into the fence until it projects far enough through the other side enough to cut the desired profile.

On a table saw, there's really no choice but to feed the wood into the vertically mounted cutterhead. This means that if you're molding the edge of a board, you'll also have to hold the wood against the fence. This is not a problem if you use good hold-downs and straight, clear stock that won't hang up during the feed. As with the router table, try to arrange cuts so the bulk of the stock is outside the cutter, not between the cutter and the fence. If it's practical to do so, attach a wooden auxiliary fence to the saw's regular fence, then carefully raise the cutter into the wooden fence, exposing only that part of the knives necessary for the cut. Keep the cuts as shallow as possible, and make multiple cuts if you need to. Not as evident in the photos is one more

Making cove molding on the table saw

By taking very shallow cuts and feeding stock diagonally across the blade, large cove cuts can be made.

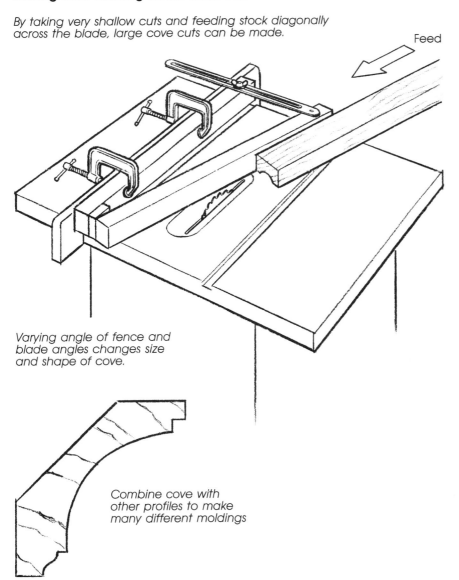

Feed

Varying angle of fence and blade angles changes size and shape of cove.

Combine cove with other profiles to make many different moldings

safety rule: always feed the stock against the rotation of the cutterhead.

If you need a molding of very small profile, begin by thicknessing your stock to the desired dimension. Then, with a jointer or hand plane, joint one edge perfectly straight and square to the face. Run the molding through the machine in one or more passes, then rip it off the larger piece. Never attempt to mold a piece narrower than about 3 in.

If the knives are sharp, a molding head will produce a crisp profile in most woods. Problems occur when the wood has irregular grain or knots, both of which tend to chip out if the wood is fed too fast. Feeding too slowly in some wood, especially cherry, may burn the wood. The fix is the same in both cases: sand to remove the blemish.

One neat trick that you can do on the table saw is to combine molding-head cuts with large cove cuts, which can be made with an ordinary sawblade. As shown in the drawing above, a wooden auxiliary fence is clamped diagonally to the blade. With the blade initially set for a $\frac{3}{16}$-in. cutting depth, feed the stock slowly across the blade, making a shallow concave cut. Raise the blade $\frac{3}{16}$ in. after each pass, and continue in this manner until the desired cove size is achieved. Using the concave profiles in conjunction with rabbets, grooves and molding-head profiles can create some very distinctive moldings.

The trim carpenter's toolkit has to balance speed, accuracy and portability. Carrying tools in sliding bins like these protects them from damage and theft.

3

The trim carpenter's toolkit

My first serious construction job, during the summer of my senior year in college, was the perfect introduction to light construction. We were building duplexes on steep hillsides, and my duty was to watch Matt, my boss, do a task, so that I could then do the same thing for the rest of the job. After each lesson Matt would get into his truck, sneak a shot of bourbon, and drive around until I needed the next lesson. From this arrangement, I learned each step of the construction process and never forgot it. I also learned not to drink on the job.

Once the duplexes were drywalled and ready for trim, Matt delivered a 20-oz. Vaughan hammer to the job site along with two yellow-handled Stanley butt chisels. He presented the tools and bundles of molding with little fanfare, then launched into a demonstration of door hanging. Following Matt's instruction, I trimmed all the duplexes with my two chisels and a hammer. I had to borrow a nail set and Yankee screwdriver, and I used a beat-up old miter box and a sharp crosscut saw to cut miters and butt joints. With this minimal equipment, I got the job done. Eventually I learned enough resourcefulness from Matt to leave his tutelage and become a contractor on my own.

My collection of finish-carpentry tools has grown enormously since I worked for Matt. And even though my toolkit fills an entire truck and then some, I've learned that it's possible to trim a house with just a half-dozen tools. Piece-rate workers (professional carpenters paid not by the hour but by the amount of trim they install) work fast and have little time for small talk. Consequently, they seldom carry more tools than will fit into a tool belt. The minimal kit includes a finish hammer, a block plane, a four-in-hand rasp, a nail set, a combination square, a pencil and a utility knife. All molding is cut with the trim carpenter's business license: the power miter box, or chopsaw.

At the other extreme is the patient craftsman who knows no time limits. He has boxes overflowing with tools, brings a table saw to the job and wishes he could bring his jointer. Inquire about how a particular gauge block works or why he uses a Lion miter trimmer instead of a chopsaw and you'd better glance at your watch: each tool has its own story and you're apt to hear it if you ask. But for most of us, tool choice reflects a balance between practicality, speed and accuracy, and it should be based on personal work habits. In this chapter, I'll describe both the trim carpenter's basic toolkit and a list of "nice-to-have" tools that might speed the work along a little. For the addresses of tool manufacturers mentioned, see the Resource Guide on pp. 179-181.

Marking and measuring tools

To make a flawlessly fitting miter, a trim carpenter needs to work to tolerances of a few thousandths of an inch from measurements taken with a tape graduated to sixteenths of an inch. So how does the carpenter overcome the limitations of the measuring tools? The answer requires an explanation of the difference between accuracy and fit. Accuracy is an absolute: if a stop molding needs to be 78½ in. long to fit snugly between the threshold and the head jamb, no greater or smaller dimension will do, since neither the jamb nor the threshold can be altered. Fit, on the other hand, has to do with how various parts relate to each other, without regard to their absolute dimensions. Thus, a mitered casing that looks perfect might really be 43° on one leg and 47° on the other to compensate for an out-of-square window.

Cabinetmakers work to finer tolerances than trim carpenters. Because cabinetmakers have control of the

To fit accurately, trim must be measured, marked and sawn accurately. Shown above are the trim carpenter's basic measuring and marking tools. Beginning at top left, proceeding clockwise: standard office pencils and a carpenter's pencil, a shopmade marking knife, tram-mel points for marking large radii and two marking gauges. At center are a pair of dividers, a commercially made marking knife and awls (one of which is a household ice pick). Immediately above the awls is a butt marking gauge for marking door hinges.

Carpenter's pencil

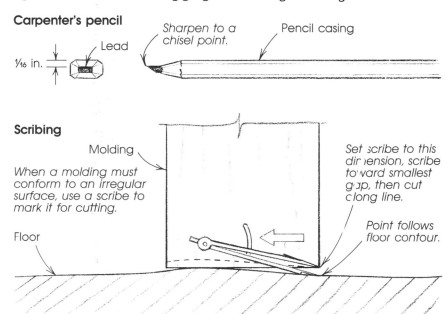

1/16 in.

Lead

Sharpen to a chisel point.

Pencil casing

Scribing

Molding

When a molding must conform to an irregular surface, use a scribe to mark it for cutting.

Floor

Set scribe to this dimension, scribe toward smallest gap, then cut along line.

Point follows floor contour.

product's final dimensions, they can afford to worry about absolute measurements. Things aren't nearly so cut-and-dried for trim carpenters. Even in the very best construction, drywall varies in thickness and framing studs taper in width and thickness, so constant dodges and fixes are required. Moreover, when the painters and drywallers begin work, the humidity swings wildy, playing havoc with the dimensional stability of wood trim. To compensate, the trim carpenter needs accurate tapes and marking devices, plus some simple but indispensable jigs for sizing parts relative to each other rather than to some ideal dimension.

Tapes and measuring aids—The Stanley 1-in. wide retractable tape measure (or the equivalent from another manufacturer) seems to be the standard among both finish and frame carpenters. No other measuring tool is as accurate or fast. I know carpenters who use a wooden folding rule and swear by it, but the retractable steel tape is my choice. Mine is 25 ft. long and rigid enough to cantilever 6 ft. to 8 ft., so I can get measurements where I couldn't otherwise reach. Another version made by Stanley is called a dual-reading tape. It's graduated on both edges. This is helpful in two ways. It reads right-side-up whether you are pulling from the left or right, and since you're never reading the thing upside-down, you won't transpose 45 to 54 or misread 66 as 99.

Here are some tips to improve measuring accuracy. Hook the tape over the end of a board and knife-mark a crow's foot at some convenient measurement, say 2 ft. Then tack a scrap piece to the end of the board to serve as a bumper, push the tape to the bumper and look at the 2-ft mark. It should be right on the crow's foot. If it isn't, adjust the sliding tip to compensate. Do this by carefully bending the tip of the tape until it reads the same hooking or pushing. Sometimes you'll hear carpenters say they're burning an inch or just plain "burning one." They aren't talking about a cigarette break. "Burning an inch" means measuring from the 1-in. graduation rather than from the end of the tape and then subtracting the extra inch from the readout. Burning an inch results in a more accurate measurement because it automatically eliminates any play in the tape's hook. Unless you want to make two cuts, remember to subtract the inch before you transfer the total dimension.

I have a couple of folding wooden rules but for the most part, they collect dust in my toolbox. One of them has a sliding depth gauge on one end, making it handy for getting accurate inside measurements, say between two window jambs. By opening the ruler to nearly the width of the opening, I'm able to get precise inside measurements by extending the depth gauge. The truth is, though, I've learned how to bend my Stanley tape into a corner, estimate the curvature and come up with measurements that are close enough.

Marking tools—Although not everyone realizes it, the common carpenter's pencil is a cleverly designed tool. It has a rectangular section with a wide flat that keeps it from rolling off the workpiece and also provides a handy place for the lumberyard's name. Best of all, the lead is exactly $\frac{1}{16}$ in. from the edge of the pencil, making it an ideal scribing tool. The flat sides will follow a perpendicular surface, drawing a line $\frac{1}{16}$ in. away from the actual scribe line.

Carpenter's pencils come with leads of varying hardness. I've seen hard, medium and soft used to describe hardness, as well as 2H and 4H. Harder lead is best for trim work. It keeps a sharp point longer and makes a finer line. The drawing on the facing page shows the proper way to sharpen a carpenter's pencil. If you prefer, an ordinary (No. 4 lead) pencil similarly sharpened puts a line $\frac{3}{32}$ in. off the side of the pencil, which is the perfect amount to remove from a door to scribe it into a jamb. By the way, don't pay for carpenter's pencils—expect to be given them. It's an old tradition.

Some carpenters eschew pencils altogether. An old-timer once told me, "If you're going to use a fat pencil line, then you might as well use a crayon." He used only a knife, and he showed me how a knife point can be set into an etched mark on a steel ruler for pinpoint accuracy. There are many kinds of knives to choose from but any of them, if kept sharp, will produce a crisper (though harder-to-see) line than will a pencil.

I carry a utility knife for most of the work I do. It's an appropriately named tool, good for cutting sheet plastic, felt, Tyvek, insulation and, if you don't watch it, thumbs. It'll also score a door bottom for cutting and remove slivers from fingers. Mine is a Stanley #10-099, available at any hardware store. It has built-in blade storage and a retractable blade, so I always have blades and I don't slice up my belt every time I put it away.

You can also buy specialized marking knives from some of the companies listed in the Resource Guide on pp. 179-181. These knives are beveled on one side and flat on the other. The flat side rides perpendicular to the straight edge, giving the most accurate results possible. The knifed line is really a shallow cut so a sharp chisel or the point of a carbide saw tooth indexes accurately in the center of the cut. Also, a knifed line lessens the probability of chip-out from the exiting teeth of a circular saw. However, for really accurate work, you'll have to decide whether to cut down the center or to either side of the line. It doesn't really matter which, as long as you're consistent.

Scratch awls are used to mark along the grain and to mark centers for drilling or nailing. Unlike a knife, the awl doesn't tend to wander off when marking along the grain. Still, on woods with wild grain or where soft earlywood alternates with hard latewood, the awl may follow the grain instead of the straightedge. If so, reverse the direction you're pulling the awl so the grain pulls the awl into the straightedge.

Plumb, level and square, the trim carpenter's holy grail, are measured with the tools shown here. Beginning at bottom right, proceeding clockwise: 12-in. and 8-in. squares, a bevel gauge, a folding rule and a combination square. At left are a Stanley bevel gauge and a plumb bob; in the middle is a Japanese *tomegata* metal miter square. Above the miter square are a machinist's square, a 9-in. torpedo level and a 2-ft. level.

A scribe is a tool used to draw or cut a line to the outline of a template or an uneven surface. The surface may be a crooked wall or floor or anything you're trying to match a straight piece of trim to. In addition to the carpenter's pencil, some carpenters use a dime-store compass as a scribe. Regardless of the type of scribe you have, it's used the same way. With the trim held as close as possible to its final position, the scribe is held perpendicular to the irregular part (wall, floor, jamb or what have you) and an outline of the irregularity is transferred to the trim, which is then sawn to match the uneven surface (see the drawing on p. 44).

Squares and bevel gauges—You do need to have at least one accurate square but there's no point in getting obsessive about perfection. Square is a relative thing. Sometimes the framers will have gotten things so badly out of whack that the best you can hope for is trim that matches the opening and hides the errors as inconspicuously as possible. For setting up machines,

my chopsaw for instance, I use a small 6-in. machinist's square that I'm certain is square beyond question. Using this square, I have a confident starting place so I know my chopsaw or table saw is square. When I know my tools are adjusted accurately, I can look to other causes for trim misalignments.

Combination squares, a right angle and 45° miter square attached to a sliding metal ruler, are useful for layout and measuring and are also small enough to carry in a tool belt. For quick checks of rough openings, I use a standard framing square. Despite claims to the contrary, framing squares aren't always accurate fresh from the factory. If you want a really accurate tool, you'll have to do some tune-up. The top drawing on the facing page tells how to check and true up a square. I also have a smaller steel square, which I use for narrow jambs where the regular size won't fit.

Since mitering is a major part of trim carpentry, you'll need at least one miter square, either one dedicated to the purpose or a combination square. I have a Japa-

Testing squares and levels

Checking a square

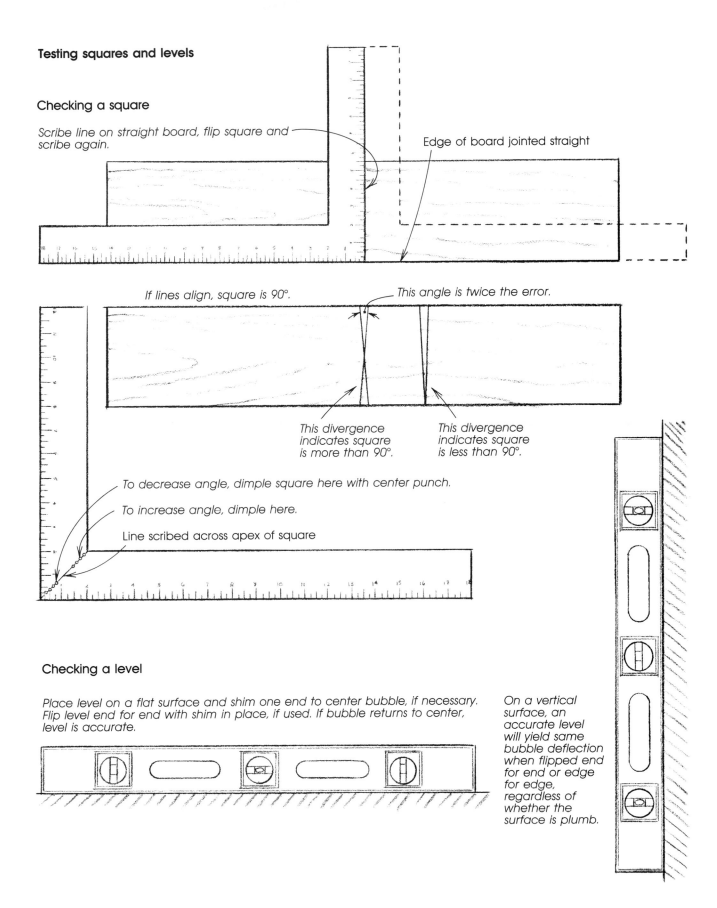

Scribe line on straight board, flip square and scribe again.

Edge of board jointed straight

If lines align, square is 90°.

This angle is twice the error.

This divergence indicates square is more than 90°.

This divergence indicates square is less than 90°.

To decrease angle, dimple square here with center punch.

To increase angle, dimple here.

Line scribed across apex of square

Checking a level

Place level on a flat surface and shim one end to center bubble, if necessary. Flip level end for end with shim in place, if used. If bubble returns to center, level is accurate.

On a vertical surface, an accurate level will yield same bubble deflection when flipped end for end or edge for edge, regardless of whether the surface is plumb.

nese *tomegata* miter square that I bought from Woodline—The Japan Woodworker. With it, I set my table saw to 45° and check to see that my miter box is making accurate cuts. Quite often, miters aren't 45°, or some other odd angle needs to be measured or marked. For odd angles I have two sliding bevel gauges, one with an 8-in. blade and the other with a 10-in. blade.

Levels and plumb bobs—Taken to the trim carpenter's cynical extreme, a level is good only for telling how inaccurate the framing is. Whether it's the framer's fault or not, badly out-of-plumb walls and out-of-level floors have to be corrected or compensated for. An accurate level will tell how much the walls and floors are off so you'll know when a fix is necessary and when not. I rely on two levels, a 2-ft. magnesium level and a 6-ft. aluminum model. The short level is useful for quick checks of headers and small window openings; the long one is best for setting doors plumb or as the occasional straightedge. I also carry a small 9-in. torpedo level in my bag. It's good for leveling window stools and head casings. In a pinch I use the torpedo with a long, straight board to increase its virtual length.

As an alternative to levels, plumb bobs are easier to carry and reliable beyond question. They're no good for testing level, of course, but a bob will indicate whether a rough opening is plumb or twisted. My toolbox contains two plumb bobs, a heavy one that's less affected by the wind for outdoor work and a lighter one for stair and door work. You can improvise a plumb bob by tying a piece of cotton twine to a heavy eyebolt or to any other heavy, pointed object. Hung from a nail, the bob's string describes plumb from the nail to the point of the bob. The bob should be suspended so its point is just above the floor.

Shopmade tools

Earlier, I explained that much of the measuring a trim carpenter does has more to do with conforming to existing conditions than with some fixed ideal size. Several shopmade tools, shown in the drawing on the facing page, help in this regard. One is the story pole. A story pole is simply a stick of scrap wood on which certain important dimensions have been marked, such as window and door casing heights, window-stool heights, cabinet locations and so on. It provides physical storage of layout information. By simply placing a story pole where the measurement must be made, you save using your tape over and over. Horizontal dimensions, such as window-apron offsets, can also be marked on the story pole.

Another tool that relies on physical rather than arithmetic measurement is the preacher, also called a base gauge or casing gauge. When fitting baseboard to casing, the preacher projects the casing edge to the front face of the baseboard, where the length can be accurately marked, then cut. The preacher is a notched piece of wood that slips over the baseboard while resting against the casing. A line drawn along the face of the preacher transfers the length and angle of the cut that will fit the baseboard into position against the casing.

To set the ³⁄₁₆-in. reveals on doors and windows, I usually use my combination square, but some carpenters make up a gauge for this purpose. A jamb gauge, or reveal gauge, is simply a piece of scrap with a ³⁄₁₆-in. rabbet sawn along one or several edges, as shown in the drawing. You set the gauge on the edge of a jamb and mark a line on the jamb edge. The casing is then butted to the line, creating a consistent ³⁄₁₆-in. reveal. Reveals of other sizes can be cut into the gauge's other edges.

Even with an accurate square or measuring diagonally from inside corner to inside corner, it's very difficult to test a rough opening for square. Some carpenters make up a pair of pinch rods or sticks. The sticks are made to a length just a little less than the dimension to be tested, and they're roughly pointed at one end. To test an opening, hold the pair edge to edge in one hand, then insert them diagonally into the opening. With the other hand, extend the sticks until their points fit into the corners, as shown in the drawing. Without changing the sticks' position relative to each other, test the opposite corners. As with the story pole, the pinch rods measure the physical distance rather than the arithmetic dimension across the opening. If the diagonal measurements are identical, the opening is square.

Also handy to have are shopmade sawhorses and benches. Years ago, an employer who wanted to test a job applicant's skill would order the carpenter to make a couple of sawhorses. Today most carpenters would walk out to their trucks and unfold a couple of metal ones or, better yet, a Black & Decker Workmate. A chopsaw can be clamped at a convenient height on the Workmate's top. Its vise will hold work as large as a door or as small as ¼-in. cove molding. Two Workmates spanned by a plank or two make scaffolding for high work.

Many trim carpenters build a 12-in. high step bench as a work support and mini-scaffold. This bench is just the height to stand on when trimming head casing on doors and windows, and you can span a pair of them with a plank for doing ceiling trim. A tray beneath the work surface has a space for tool storage. Although I rely mostly on my chopsaw, I occasionally use a wooden miter box, whose chief advantage is portability. Sometimes, electricity isn't available on the job site, or setting up the chopsaw isn't worth the bother. The drawing on p. 87 shows how to make a wooden miter box.

Handsaws

Although a few carpenters prefer them as a primary sawing tool, handsaws have been largely supplanted in trim carpentry by the power miter box, or chopsaw. A

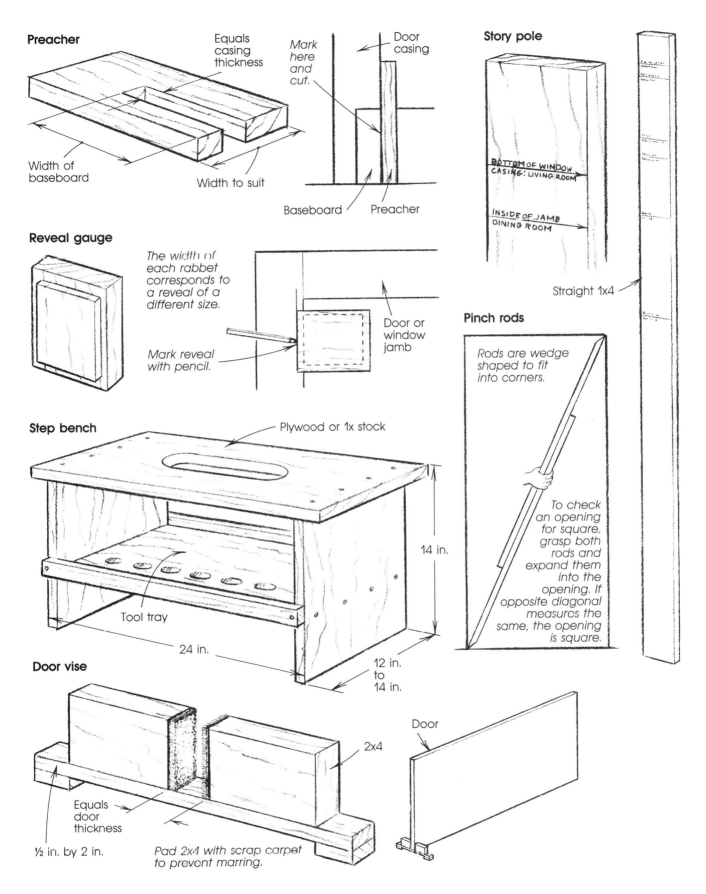

Preacher

Equals casing thickness

Width of baseboard

Width to suit

Mark here and cut.

Door casing

Baseboard   Preacher

Story pole

BOTTOM OF WINDOW CASING: LIVING ROOM

INSIDE OF JAMB DINING ROOM

Straight 1x4

Reveal gauge

The width of each rabbet corresponds to a reveal of a different size.

Mark reveal with pencil.

Door or window jamb

Pinch rods

Rods are wedge shaped to fit into corners.

To check an opening for square, grasp both rods and expand them into the opening. If opposite diagonal measures the same, the opening is square.

Step bench

Plywood or 1x stock

Tool tray

24 in.

14 in.

12 in. to 14 in.

Door vise

Equals door thickness

½ in. by 2 in.

Pad 2x4 with scrap carpet to prevent marring.

2x4

Door

49

The power miter box, or chopsaw, has largely replaced the handsaw for most trimwork, but rip and or cross-cut handsaws, shown at left, still have a place in the toolkit. At top right is a coping saw, used for cutting copes at inside corners.

chopsaw is accurate, fast and, given its versatility, a real bargain, even for a one-off job. Still, I've found that I can't get along without at least two handsaws. For getting into tight spots or for quick cuts, I carry a 20-in. Sandvik crosscut saw with 12 teeth per inch. It fits nicely into my toolbox and can be used with the wooden miter box shown in the drawing on p. 87.

I consider my second handsaw indispensable. It's a 6-in. coping saw with a fine-tooth blade, usually 16 to 22 teeth per inch. As its name implies, a coping saw is used to shape or cope one piece to conform to another. It's also handy for scroll and pierce work and light-duty cut-off. A coping saw's thin blade is kept in tension by a stiff C-shaped metal frame—the stouter the frame, the greater the tension and the smoother the cut. Hardware-store coping saws are usually pretty flimsy. I

recommend one of the sturdy European coping saws with pivoting blade clamps that eliminate blade fatigue and breakage. These are sold by Lee Valley, Garrett Wade and other suppliers—see the Resource Guide on pp. 179-181 for the addresses.

Years ago, a number of companies, including Stanley, sold elaborate metal miter boxes equipped with the fine-toothed backsaws that were then the trim carpenter's standard sawing tool. If you look diligently, you can probably find one of these fine miter boxes at a used-tool sale. You can also buy a new one made by a Swedish company called Nobex and available in this country through Sandvik. The Nobex is light and accurate. It has a tensioned blade much like a hacksaw that rides in guides that hold it rigid for absolutely straight cuts.

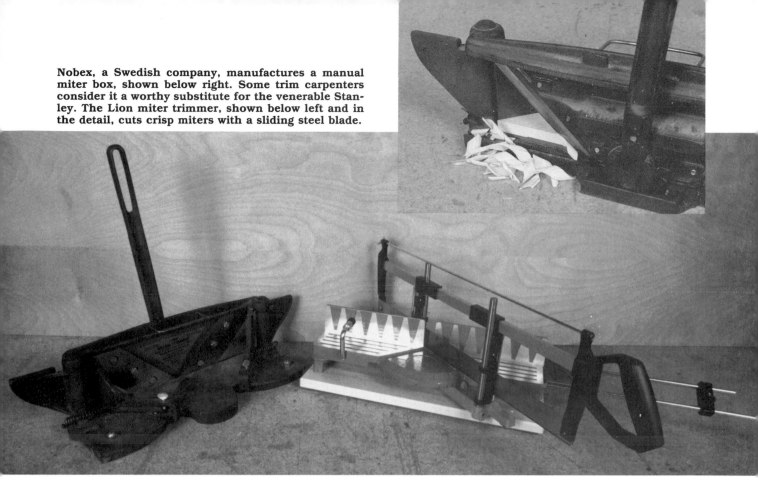

Nobex, a Swedish company, manufactures a manual miter box, shown below right. Some trim carpenters consider it a worthy substitute for the venerable Stanley. The Lion miter trimmer, shown below left and in the detail, cuts crisp miters with a sliding steel blade.

Worth a mention here is the miter trimmer, a stout, razor-sharp steel knife attached to a heavy lever. The knife slides back and forth in a rigid guide mechanism, and the wood can be positioned by a fence that's continuously adjustable for angles of cut between 45° and 90°. With a mechanical slicing action, this tool pares off shavings just thousandths of an inch thick, trimming miter and butt joints to perfection. The best-known trimmer, the Lion Miter Trimmer, is made by the Pootatuck Corporation, but an inexpensive trimmer of this type is sold by Grizzly Imports.

Planes and chisels

No matter how sharp the saw, trimwork always seems to need a shaving removed here and there and for that, planes are indispensable. A finish carpenter needs planes for two tasks: a long one for straight trimming work (as in fitting doors) and a shorter one for trimming joinery. Despite the demise of planemaking in the United States, there are still a lot of metal bench planes from which to pick. Record, the English manufacturer, makes four bench planes 14 in. or longer. Which plane you pick for door work is a matter of personal preference. Some carpenters swear by their 22-in. fore planes; others get by with a cheap, hardware-store 9-in. smooth-er. I prefer Record's No. 5 jack plane, which, at 14 in., is long enough to produce a flat, smooth cut but is short enough to work as a smoother; it also fits into my toolbox. I also have a venerable Stanley jack plane.

For trimming joints or planing in a tight space, a sharp block plane is a must. It's small enough to fit into a tool pouch, and it's compact enough for single-hand operation while you secure the workpiece with the other hand. The block plane is used for back-beveling edges, trimming miters and flushing up surfaces. There are several styles of block planes. The most popular are Stanley's No. 09½ block plane and the No. 60½ low-angle block plane (Record makes identical planes, with the same identification numbers). Either or both are suitable for trim carpentry. The low-angle plane cuts end grain better, making it ideal for trimming miters and butts, but the real advantage of this plane is in its feel. With its low center of gravity, the low-angle plane fits sweetly into the palm of your hand.

Fresh from the factory, all planes need tuning. It's a time-consuming process but worth the effort. A warped sole or balky depth adjustor makes for frustrating planing. But when the blade is sharp and true, shavings peel effortlessly and it's fun to use the tool. To start out, the blade must lie perfectly flat against the frog, the angular bracket inside the plane body to

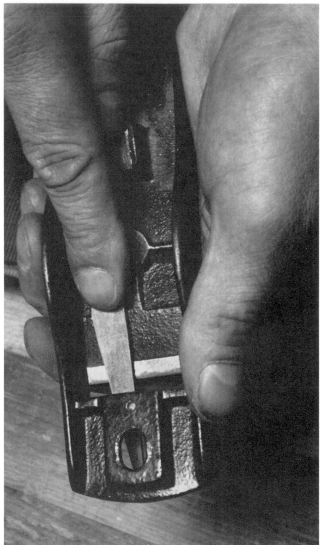

Essential edge tools, above, include a set of steel-handled chisels, a 1-in. socket chisel and a set of Stanley butt chisels. The large plane is a jack, the smaller a Stanley block plane. Also shown are a Stanley Surform rasp and a pair of steel cabinet scrapers, which are handy for removing saw marks.

True a plane's sole by lapping with automotive valve-grinding compound on ¼-in. plate glass, right. So the back of the iron will seat firmly, true the frog and mouth with a mill file, above right.

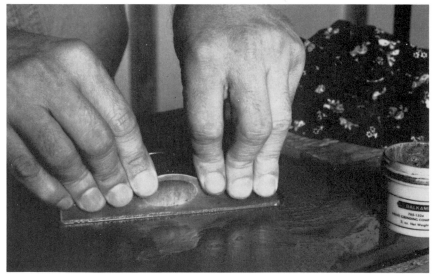

which the blade is clamped by the lever cap. Some frogs are removable, while others are cast right into the plane. In either case, insert a piece of carbon paper between the iron and the frog and rub back and forth. The paper will mark high spots on the frog, and these should be dressed down with a file until the iron makes as even contact with the frog as possible. Pay special attention to the plane's mouth, where the blade passes through the sole. As shown in the top right photo on the facing page, file the mouth opening so the back of the blade is fully supported by the mouth.

If there's a cap iron, make sure it lies flat and tight against the front of the blade. File or lap to flatten and square it. To ease chip removal, you can fair out the curve of the cap iron and smooth it with a file. With the frog adjusted and tightened, check the plane's sole for flatness, using a steel straightedge. Most soles are warped, either in length or width. You can flatten the sole yourself by lapping it with water-based automotive valve-grinding compound on a piece of ¼-in. plate glass, as shown in the bottom photo on the facing page. Smear some compound on the glass, and then, without rocking it, lap the sole in a figure-eight motion. When the entire sole appears evenly flat grey with no surface untouched by compound, you're done.

Finally, the blade itself must be sharp. I don't wish to launch into a treatise on sharpening here but I've been through enough sharpening fixtures, jigs, stones, wheels, strops and diamond gewgaws to have strong opinions. I began with oilstones but I was never really satisfied. Finally, I bought a Makita 9820-2 motorized grinder and a set of Japanese waterstones. The Makita has a water-cooled wheel of medium-fine (1000) grit that polishes edges to near mirror smoothness without any risk of burning. It will sharpen plane irons, jointer and planer knives, chisels, gouges, scrapers, drill bits and router bits. An accessory wheel will sharpen carbide tools.

The nice thing about sharpening with waterstones is that they produce a very sharp edge that is also mirror smooth. And since water is the lubricant, not oil, there is no chance of leaving a hard-to-remove stain on the wood.

Chisels—While searching my cluttered bench for a hammer not too long ago, all I could find was a pipe wrench. It reminded me of an old mechanic's saying: "All tools are hammers except chisels, and they're screwdrivers." There's more truth to this than most of us will admit, but over the years, I've come to appreciate good chisels. In fact, I've gotten a little crazy about them. I have a complete set of the Stanley tang-butt chisels, in widths from ¼ in. to 1½ in.

For mortising door hinges and lock sets and for general paring, a ¼-in. wide chisel and 1-in. wide chisel are useful. If I could have only two chisels, I'd pick this pair. I carry mine in my belt in separate leather pouches. The narrow chisels are suitable for joinery or for paring

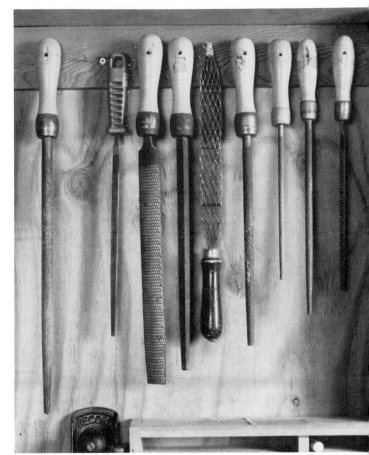

Files are indispensable for fine-fitting cope joints. Rasps, like the one shown fifth from the right, are useful for trimming overhanging drywall.

small pieces of molding. I also own a set of Sears Craftsman all-steel chisels: no plastic or wooden handles. These are utility tools, good for shearing off nails and for heavy prying.

Rasps and files—Paring with a chisel and planing are the most accurate ways of removing wood, but there are situations when it's quicker to cut an unseen back bevel or chamfer with a rasp or file. Rasps and files are both sold by cutting grade. Rasps are graded as wood, cabinet and patternmaker's, with wood being the coarsest. Cabinet rasps are further divided into bastard, second cut and smooth. Files are graded in ascending order of smoothness of cut: coarse, bastard cut, second cut and smooth. For shaping moldings I like to use second-cut cabinet rasps and bastard-cut files. A few rat-tail files and round rasps are good to keep on hand for back-cutting acute curves, as when contouring intricate coped joints.

I also carry a four-in-hand rasp, also known as a shoe rasp. Viewed in section, one face is curved and

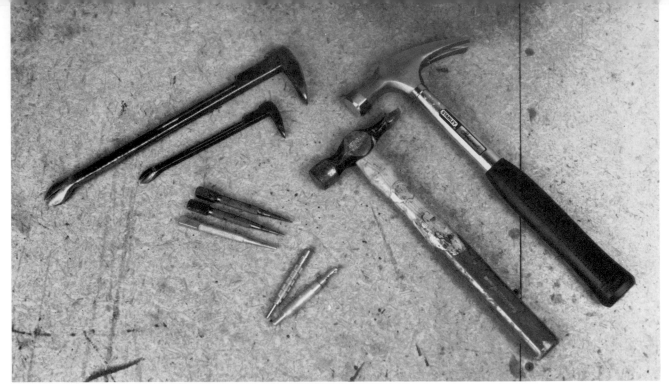

A trim carpenter's toolkit should include a 16-oz. or 20-oz. hammer, such as the steel-handled Stanley shown at right, and the smaller Warrington hammer for driving brads. At upper left are two Japanese nail pullers and three nail sets. In the foreground are two tools that are used for marking on-center holes for hinges and hardware: a spring-loaded center punch and a Vix bit.

the other is flat. It fits easily in the tool pouch. The four-in-hand's name seems to arise from the fact that it has four patterns: a fine and medium wood rasp and fine and medium wood file. Although I'm a little embarrassed to admit it, I own a Stanley Surform plane. I consider it a worthless woodworking tool, but it's perfect for one very important application: trimming back drywall that stands proud of a jamb.

Hammer, nail set and pullers

The hammer is the finish carpenter's most used tool, so it pays to buy a good one. Pick a hammer with good balance and feel and one with a broad, smooth head, not the milled head framing hammers have. Weight is subjective. I like a 20-oz. hammer, but some carpenters prefer lighter or heavier heads. I'd consider 16 oz. the minimum. Straight, sharp, rip-style claws are preferable to the standard claw style. Some carpenters swear by wood handles, others prefer steel or fiberglass. I've used all three, but I finally settled on a steel-handled Stanley after the head on my 20-oz. Vaughan flew off its umpteenth wood handle and plopped into the water off a dock I was working on. The Stanley hammer has a tubular shank, which gives good feel when nailing yet still damps the shock of each blow.

Smaller hammers, namely the Warrrington hammer, are nice to have for fine work in tight spaces. The Warrington is really a cabinetmaker's tool. It has a unique crosspeen head that allows you to start small nails without hitting your fingers.

Nail sets are punches designed to drive or "set" nails below the surface of the wood. The working end of the set is ground with a small cup that keeps it from slipping off the nail. Because sets are made from hardened steel, the cups occasionally chip, especially if they are used to set hardened nails. Throw away a damaged nail set. It's cheap enough to replace, and there's no reason to destroy a piece of molding with a nail set that slips off the mark. Nail sets come in four sizes, ranging from $\frac{1}{32}$ in. to $\frac{4}{32}$ in. I suggest buying all four and using the size that corresponds to the nail size you're using. For setting nails in tight corners, an offset nail set is available from Lee Valley Tool. It has two cupped ends, one $\frac{1}{32}$ in. and the other $\frac{2}{32}$ in., mounted on a 6-in. bent rod.

If you do things right the first time, you aren't supposed to need a nail puller, but there are times when "twice but right" is the rule. In these cases, you need to remove nails and try again. The most common nail puller is called a cat's paw, and it's widely available in hardware stores. Although the cat's paw does the job (usually) there's a better tool made by a Japanese company, Yamaguchi, and sold by Woodline–The Japan Woodworker (see the Resource Guide on pp. 179-181). This puller is L-shaped with sharp forks that grasp the most stubborn nails. It comes in several sizes; the smallest is about 6 in. long and is perfect for trimwork.

Power miter boxes, or chopsaws, are the trim carpenter's tool of choice for sawing miter and butt joints. Chopsaws should be equipped with extensions to support long stock during cutting.

Portable power tools

Power tools have changed the way trim carpenters work and for the better, in my opinion. Even though much of a trim carpenter's day involves patient hand-work, power tools make it possible to do more work faster and with greater accuracy. The power miter box, or chopsaw, has done more to revolutionize the trade than any other single tool. The chopsaw is essentially a circular saw attached to a spring-loaded pivot. The blade arcs down across the wood, making quick, accurate crosscuts between 0° and (depending on the model)

47°. Chopsaws are available with 10-in., 12-in. and 14-in. blades. Which size you buy depends on several factors. The larger blades have more teeth, which means a smoother cut on larger moldings. When set up with extension tables, a 14-in. saw will cut framing lumber as well. On the other hand, a 14-in. saw is awkward to drag around, and blades for it are more expensive than for a 10-in. saw.

I've owned three brands of chopsaws and I can't honestly recommend one over the other, but here are some features to consider when you buy one. Some saws

For accurate repeat cuts, a movable stop can be clamped to the chopsaw fence. The fence shown here is also equipped with a built-in measuring tape, an added refinement.

have power brakes that stop the blade instantly when the switch is released; others have a thumb-operated manual brake. I prefer the power brake because it automatically stops the blade and lets me get on to the next cut sooner. Most chopsaws have positive stops at 22½°, 45° and 0°. These might seem useful, but when you need to fudge a miter at 45½° the stops are a pain because they want to slip the half-degree back to the even angle.

Older chopsaws had wooden tables that had to be replaced from time to time, but most now have metal tables with a slot that allows the blade to pass through. Clamping accessories to hold the work are nice to have, but a couple of 4-in. C-clamps or small handscrews are more versatile and you can use them elsewhere. To keep it reasonably portable, a chopsaw's table is usually no longer than about 16 in. Consequently, molding longer than 4 ft. will need extra support. Several manufacturers make chopsaw extension tables that support the work at a convenient work height and have adjustable stops for repeated cuts to length. I use an elaborate extension table made by Saw Helper. The Saw Helper has an adjustable stop on its fence that can be set for accurate repeat cuts.

Of equal importance to the saw is the blade. I've been told that a really sharp steel blade gives the smoothest cut but I've never come across one, and it wouldn't be sharp very long anyway. I've found it pays to buy a good carbide-tipped sawblade. For general trimwork, a blade that represents a good trade-off between smoothness of cut and durability is a 60-tooth alternate top bevel for soft woods and a 60-tooth triple-chip for hard woods.

If you plan to make your own molding or door and window jambs, a router is essential equipment. I own several routers of different size and horsepower. For making moldings, you'll need a machine with at least 1 hp. A smaller router just won't be up to the job. A

Even on a small job, a pneumatic nail gun can pay for itself in short order. With a single squeeze of the trigger, nail guns can shoot and set nails of various sizes. Always wear eye and ear protection when using a nail gun.

router can be used freehand by passing it over work that's been clamped to a bench or sawhorse or, conversely, the machine can be mounted upside-down in a table and the work fed past the bit, as described on pp. 35-37. The latter method works best for making molding, chiefly because moldings are usually cut on small boards and it's easier, safer and more accurate to feed small pieces past a fixed bit. If you don't already have a router and plan to buy one, I'd suggest getting a plunge router made by one of several manufacturers, including Makita, Hitachi, Elu and Porter-Cable. Used freehand, plunge routers are quite versatile, and with the base locked, they can be mounted in a router table.

Two other portable power saws are handy to have but not essential. For coping molding and for utility sawing, I have a jigsaw fitted with a hollow-ground 10-tooth-per-inch blade. I also have an electric power plane. Before the drywall is installed, a power plane can straighten studs and flush up uneven framing around headers. Once you're into the actual trimwork, a power plane will smooth and straighten boards and trim the edges of doors to a final fit. Several manufacturers sell these planes, and I suggest you buy the type with a removable fence. Power planes with fixed fences won't plane flat surfaces, so their utility is limited.

Out West, more carpenters are using pneumatic nail guns, an idea that rankles some seasoned vets. However, the advantages of driving and setting nails with the single pull of a trigger are obvious. Besides saving time, a nail gun reduces the shock that trim and backing must absorb when you hammer and set nails. And with one hand free of holding the nail, you can position your work precisely before firing. Of course, the gun itself and its attendant compressor and hoses aren't cheap and will have to be hauled to the job site, but a nail gun can quickly pay for itself.

A table saw is more luxury than necessity for the trim carpenter, but it's useful for cutting miters and for making molding. This saw has been mounted on a stand with rollers so it's easy to move around the job site.

Stationary power tools

On big jobs or those requiring lots of complex work, it's nice to have stationary power tools like a table saw, a radial-arm saw and a jointer. I have two table saws, a Delta 10-in. contractor's saw and a 9-in. Makita portable table saw. These two tools are excellent for ripping jamb extensions or making molding, as described on pp. 40-41. And, if set up carefully, a table saw can replace the chopsaw for mitering. I've also mounted a router underneath one of the extension wings of my Delta table saw so the saw doubles as a router table.

Although not as accurate as a table saw, a radial-arm saw is more versatile. Like the table saw, a radial-arm works well with a dado or molding head and it's generally a better crosscutting tool, which makes it nice to have for framing. However, radial-arm saws are bulky and heavy and tend to drift out of adjustment when they are moved. All things considered, it's a happier tool when left in the shop. Worth a mention here is Delta's Sawbuck, a bushing-guided, sliding circular saw that's really a clever combination of chopsaw and

radial-arm saw. The Sawbuck is mounted on its own lightweight stand that folds up for easy transportation. The Sawbuck makes accurate crosscuts, miters and compound bevels in lumber as large as 2x12. It will not rip, however.

Notes on safety

At the turn of the century, when trim carpenters worked almost entirely with hand tools, the biggest danger they faced was falling off a ladder or nasty cuts from planes and chisels. Power tools have changed all that. The chopsaw is the trim carpenter's principal tool and even when used correctly, it is dangerous. Always, always use the saw's guard and make sure the blade brake works. In some of the photos in this book, the guard has been removed or lifted out of the way for clarity, but I recommend that it always be in place.

Keep the chopsaw in good repair. The spring that holds the saw in the retracted position has been known to break, causing the saw to descend into the cut position without warning. Whenever the saw is running, keep your hands well clear of the blade. Also, don't show off with a chopsaw or any power tool by using it for purposes for which is was never intended. In other words, don't try to cut freehand when fences with hold-downs and stops are clearly needed. Never try to rip with a chopsaw.

Make sure you've got the right blade and that it's sharp and correctly installed. When changing blades—and this goes for all power tools—unplug the saw and drape the cord over the bench so you can see it. Kickbacks can be a problem with chopsaws, but they can be prevented by securing the work firmly against the fence with your hand or clamps. A sharp blade and a slow, deliberate feed will minimize the chances of a kickback. One trick to extend a chopsaw's width of cut is to lift the outside edge of the molding off the table. This is asking for a violent kickback. Don't try it.

Table saws and radial-arm saws are very prone to kickbacks when ripping, especially if the wood is warped or twisted. On a table saw, minimize kickbacks by feeding slowly and by avoiding cuts in which the blade is angled toward the fence, trapping the wood. If too much feed pressure is required to complete the cut, stop the saw and correct the problem. You'll improve your chances of surviving a kickback if you habitually use push sticks and stand well to one side of the blade when ripping. The same general advice applies to radial-arm saws. Some carpenters won't rip on them at all, however, reasoning that they're just too cumbersome to do the job safely.

When operating any power tool, use some kind of eye protection, either a full face shield or goggles. Hearing protectors are also a good idea, as are a nuisance-dust mask in a dusty environment and a respirator approved for organic solvents when using paint or lacquer thinners. Eye protection is particularly important when using pneumatic nailers, which tend to shatter molding from time to time.

Finish carpenters are lucky because they usually work in dry, warm houses. But sometimes, you'll find yourself having to work in a moist basement or a damp room. When you do, make certain that power tools are properly grounded, either with three-prong grounded plugs or double-insulated construction. Don't defeat grounding by snipping off the third prong or bypassing a grounded outlet with a two-conductor extension cord. Some carpenters make up extension cords tied into a junction box with a ground-fault circuit interrupter, a sensitive, fast-acting circuit breaker that cuts off current flow in situations that might otherwise lead to serious shocks. Ground-fault interrupters should be in the 15-amp to 20-amp range.

Hand tools can cause serious injuries, too. Ironically, it's usually the dull ones that do the most damage. Blunted edges tend to slip off the work, but they're plenty sharp enough to cause horrible cuts and even

permanent injury. Keep hand tools sharp. Protect them in the toolbox with leather or plastic scabbards. Position the work and the tool so that any slips will be directed away from your hands and body.

Finally, use common sense around the job site. Keep the work area picked up and swept clean. Get rid of shavings and cut-offs before you start to trip over them. Stow any tools and cords that aren't in use. If you can, schedule the most hazardous work in the morning, when you're alert and fresh. Save the long afternoons for handwork, where a mashed thumb or minor cut will be the highest price you'll pay for a moment of inattention.

By the time the trim carpenter begins work, the framers have moved on to the next job. Before a stick of molding is nailed, the trim carpenter must check—and correct—shortcomings in the framing and drywall.

4

Preliminary work

I know a few carpenters who pride themselves on being able to trim out a 1,200-sq. ft. house in a single day. For dashing back and forth to a chopsaw for 10 hours and with no other concern than to cover the cracks with molding, they can earn $300 a day. On the other hand, some carpenters will spend two days hanging and trimming one door, earning $75 for the job.

Either way, the carpenters are confronted with a starting point not of their own making. The quality of the finished trim will depend to a large extent on how well the framers did their jobs and how carefully the drywall was hung, taped and finished. It's sad but true that the finish carpenter—whose work is the most visible—is often expected to find and correct the sins of others, or at least hide them.

The $300-a-day pieceworkers won't have time to ponder a fix for out-of-plumb walls and bulging drywall. They will have accumulated a fat bag of tricks to camouflage substandard work so the trim will at least look right. But even in inexpensive houses and modest remodels, there's no excuse for trim carpenters having to correct problems that could have been avoided early in construction. Whether you're building your own house or having it done by a contractor, there are steps that can be taken almost at ground breaking that will make for smooth trimwork.

Getting the framing right

No matter how skillfully it's hung and taped, drywall won't disguise a twisted or out-of-plumb wall; openings framed out of square at the start are likely to stay that way. Even if you've kept the framers on a short leash or done the framing yourself, there will be some problems to correct before the drywall goes in. Ignoring them will simply make the trim that much harder to do.

One way of achieving straight walls and openings that are plumb, level and square is to use good lumber in the first place. Most veteran carpenters say framing lumber gets worse every year. The big trees are gone. Those that are harvested are often full of defects and internal stresses that wreak havoc when nailed into a frame. First of all, framing lumber should be dry. It doesn't matter if it got that way by kiln or air; it just has to be dry before you build with it.

Exposed to direct sunlight, sopping-wet studs will warp horribly, twisting or crowning the wall before the drywall goes up or popping the nails later on. I buy kiln-dried lumber exclusively, even though it costs about 3% to 5% more. When it's delivered, I test it with a moisture meter, but you can also lift a few pieces and tell pretty easily if they are dry. Or you can whack a board with a hammer—if it splashes you in the face or if moisture rises in the "camel track," it's not dry. In the West, the lumber comes from the mill with an "S-dry" stamp. I used to think that this meant "sponge dry," but it really means that the mill has surfaced the lumber in a dry state, with an average moisture content of 19%.

The better mills wrap their lumber for shipping so it won't get wet during transport. At the job site I cover my lumber with black sheet plastic to keep it dry. Your lumber supplier has the most control over the quality of the boards you're going to receive. I tell my suppliers flat out not to send junk because I'll ship it right back at their cost. If you have to use wet lumber, use it fast. Lock the frame with plenty of nails as soon as possible, and protect the building against the elements with builder's felt or a commercial building wrap like Tyvek. Shielding the framing against rapid drying by direct sunlight and wind will slow moisture loss in the lumber, thereby limiting degrade.

Crowns, crooks and cups

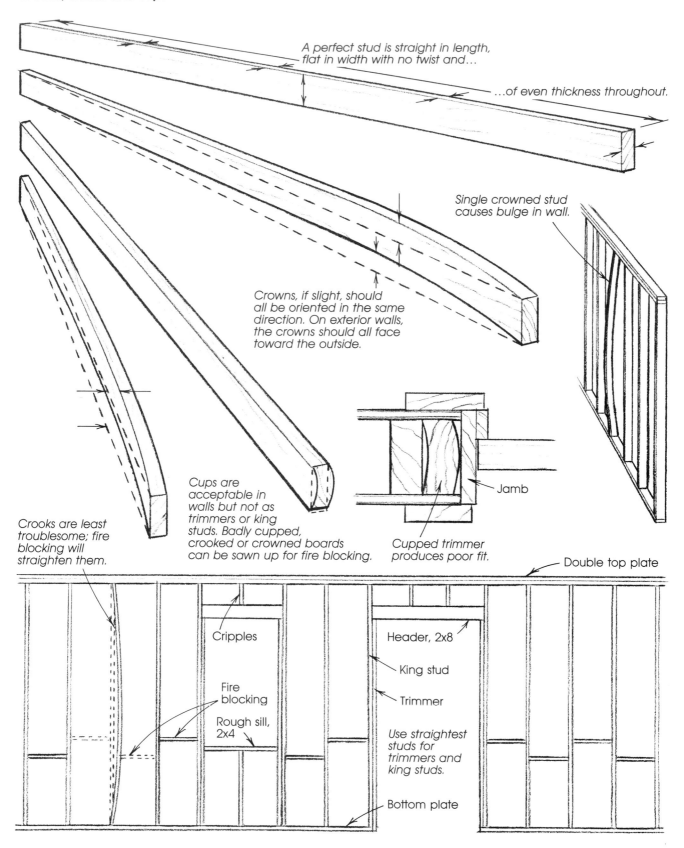

A perfect stud is straight in length, flat in width with no twist and...

...of even thickness throughout.

Single crowned stud causes bulge in wall.

Crowns, if slight, should all be oriented in the same direction. On exterior walls, the crowns should all face toward the outside.

Cups are acceptable in walls but not as trimmers or king studs. Badly cupped, crooked or crowned boards can be sawn up for fire blocking.

Jamb

Cupped trimmer produces poor fit.

Crooks are least troublesome; fire blocking will straighten them.

Double top plate

Cripples

Header, 2x8

King stud

Trimmer

Fire blocking

Rough sill, 2x4

Use straightest studs for trimmers and king studs.

Bottom plate

62

Sometimes lumber comes to the job site "thick and thin." This means that the boards vary substantially along their length in thickness or in width. Lumber like this obviously makes it difficult to do accurate framing. Frame walls are usually built flat on the floor deck, then erected. Laid edgewise on the deck, the studs are aligned by the flat floor deck into a single plane. If the studs happen to be thick and thin, the edges touching the deck will be flush, but the "up" side will have irregularities. On exterior walls, this usually isn't a problem because the wall is normally erected with the "up" side facing out. Exterior sheathing, siding and stucco easily bridge the irregularities. But interior walls get drywalled on both sides, so I try to even out dimensional variations by centering the stud in the plate before driving the first nail. Splitting the difference this way, I can reduce a troublesome ⅛-in. error to 1/16 in., a gap that the drywall will bridge smoothly.

Even if you've paid extra for kiln-dried, high-grade lumber, you should expect to find a few warped, cupped or crowned pieces. Sort through your lumber pile and set aside the worst pieces, as well as the exceptionally straight ones. The bad ones can be sawn up for fire blocking, the short horizontal members nailed across the stud bays. Save the best stuff for king studs and trimmers, the two major framing elements that form door and window openings. Studs with crooks—that is, with bends parallel to their edges—aren't usually much of a problem since the wall's fire blocking will tend to straighten them.

Crowns, also called bows, are bends along the studs' edges. The odd minor crown framed into a wall won't cause too much grief for the trim carpenter. If you build with a lot of crowned studs, though, walls may have noticeable undulations that make it difficult to run baseboard and crown molding. Crowned king studs or trimmer studs complicate door hanging, too, because it's next to impossible to build an opening that's plumb and square. It's good carpentry practice to orient crowned studs in the same direction, either all up or all down. The result is a wall with an unnoticeable gentle curve rather than a flagrant zigzag. I prefer to orient all of the crowns up for two reasons: the wall will be less likely to rock on the deck as I'm nailing; and the bowed studs will face outward, to be covered up with siding or sheathing.

Nailing it down—Nailing the framing properly will keep studs and plates from popping loose and shifting, ruining the trim and the drywall. In most cases, proper nailing means enough nails of the right size. Some carpenters use sinkers, thick-shanked 12d framing nails coated with cement. The thick shank and cement coating resist pullout, but these nails tend to split boards, especially near the ends. Most framers I know still use 16d common nails for framing because they're less likely to split the wood.

Clinched nails keep the trimmer from twisting off the king stud. First, drive a 16d nail into the trimmer, then bend it over. A pair of clinched 8d nails locks the larger nail in place.

Built-up header

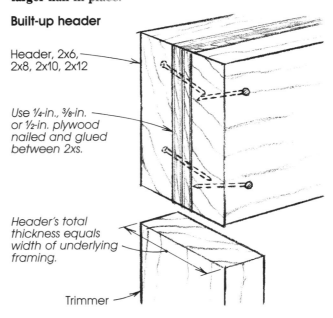

Header, 2x6, 2x8, 2x10, 2x12

Use ¼-in., ⅜-in. or ½-in. plywood nailed and glued between 2xs.

Header's total thickness equals width of underlying framing.

Trimmer

One nailing trick I've seen used on trimmers—the stud that supports the header and to which the door and window jambs are nailed—is to clinch the trimmer to the king stud with bent-over nails, as shown in the photo above. Clinching it on both sides keeps a trimmer—especially one made of 2x6 stock—from cupping or being twisted off the king stud by a heavy door, either of which will spoil the door's closing action. If the trimmers aren't clinched, at least make sure they're nailed or screwed solidly. Otherwise there's a chance they'll bounce when a casing nail is driven into them. The bounce can pop drywall nails or screws or open up taped joints. Headers over doors and windows are often made of nailed-up pieces of wide 2x stock. Even if the lumber is well seasoned, these may warp or cup. One way to avoid this is to sandwich plywood between the 2x stock and nail it well, as shown in the drawing above.

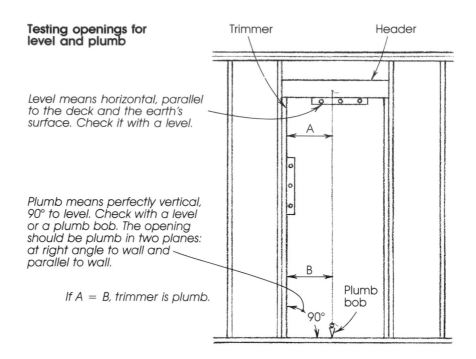

Plumb, square and level—Even near-perfect framing will need minor remedial work before drywall installation. Some of the fixes can also be done after the drywall is installed, but it's best to correct faults sooner rather than later.

First, some nomenclature. Most trouble with door and window trim is caused by openings that aren't plumb, level, square and straight (see the drawings above and on the facing page). A straight frame has all its parts in the same plane, with no projecting studs and no misaligned plates. Plumb means straight up and down, perpendicular to the earth's surface or at least to the house's deck. A plumb bob suspended from a string causes the string to be perfectly vertical, with the point of the bob exactly beneath the point of suspension. The two points define plumb, and the string connects them. For a true opening, both the face and the edge of the trimmer stud must be plumb. If they are out of plumb, a door may creep open, or it will be difficult to get a consistent reveal between the door and its jamb.

Level means parallel to the earth's surface and at 90° to plumb. The header and the rough sill of a window, for example, should be level. In fact, they should be level in two directions, across the opening and through the opening. Level is generally less critical than plumb since the window or door is usually secured with wedges slipped between the jambs and the trimmer, effectively suspending it between the rough sill and header. Nonetheless, it's a good idea to get rough sills and headers as level as possible because there will be times when doors and windows will fit flat against them.

Square means a 90° angle between two members, like the header and trimmer or the rough sill and trimmer. If both trimmers are plumb and the header is level, they will automatically be at 90° to each other and thus square. The trimmers will also be perfectly parallel, greatly simplifying door and window hanging.

Finding and fixing framing problems—How you go about checking framing for trueness is a matter of personal preference, but I usually begin by checking for straightness. I look for minor irregularities in the frame with a straightedge made of a 6-ft. long, 4-in. wide piece of ¼-in. tempered Masonite or a 6-ft. aluminum level. Holding the straightedge against the walls will reveal bowed or crooked studs. In a long wall, a few mildly bowed studs won't matter, but on walls meant to have cabinets or wainscoting, fix them. Also, just one badly bowed stud, situated one or two away from a window opening, will put the opening in wind, making it a pain to trim.

The worst studs should be replaced, but when they can't be, here's a simple trick for straightening a stud in place. With a handsaw or reciprocating saw, cut a diagonal kerf three-quarters of the way through the long edge of the stud in the center of the bow, as shown in the drawing at right on the facing page. Drive a screw or nail through the kerf, pulling it together and straightening the stud. If this trick fails, try straightening the bow with a hand plane or power plane after setting the nails well below the wood's surface to avoid nicking the blade. Kerfing the stud, by the way, will work even after the drywall is installed. Simply saw

Testing openings for square

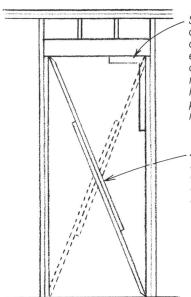

Square means a 90°
angle between vertical
and horizontal
elements; check with
a square or with pinch
rods. If the header is
level and the trimmer
plumb, the opening
must be square.

Adjust pinch rods to
measure diagonal
dimensions; if they
are equal, the
opening is square.

Straightening a stud

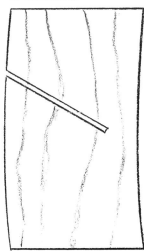

First, saw a diagonal
kerf with a circular
saw, reciprocating saw
or handsaw.

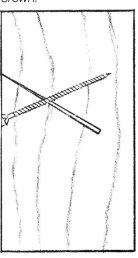

A 2½-in. drywall screw
pulls the kerf closed,
straightening the
crown.

Correct framing errors before the drywall is hung. To flush a header sprung off its trimmer, above, pare with a chisel. The stud at left was misaligned with its plate, creating a hump in the drywall. To fix it, remove the nails, align and renail.

It's best to correct a twisted opening at the framing stage rather than cobbling a fix after the fact, as is being done here. If strings stretched across the opening just touch, the opening is true.

With a framing square, Savage checks a door opening for square. Checking both trimmers for plumb and the header for level is another way to test for square.

the stud right through the drywall, pull it in straight with a screw and patch the drywall with compound.

On long walls where bottom or top plates are butt-joined or where headers meet trimmers and king studs, misalignments at the joints will create a curve or hump in the drywall. Planing or chiseling off the projecting wood before drywalling will save trouble later.

I know of two ways to check a door or window opening for straightness, or more accurately, flatness. One is to pass the straightedge across the opening diagonally and vertically, marking any high spots with a pencil. After setting all the nail heads below the surface, plane the high spots flat with a portable power plane. The second method, called cross-sighting, won't reveal local irregularities, but it will detect a grossly twisted opening. As shown in the photo at left on the facing page, tack 8d nails at each corner of the opening and then stretch strings diagonally between the nails. If the strings don't touch, or if they touch and bend slightly, the opening is probably twisted (in winding) because one or both of the trimmers is out of plumb.

Correct this condition by checking the trimmers for plumb. But first, see that the bottom plates have been nailed tightly to layout lines struck on the deck. Misaligned plates might be the source of the twist. If the plate is off the line, I adjust it by toenailing a galvanized spike (20d) or 3-in. drywall screw through the plate and into the floor joist. The angle of force pulls the plate back to the line and the wall into plumb. If this doesn't work, I saw off the nails with a reciprocating saw fitted with a metal-cutting blade, reposition the plate and nail or screw it down.

A level is the quickest way to test for plumb, but a plumb bob will also work. You'll need to check trimmers for plumb in two planes, as shown in the drawing on p. 64. Minor variations of ³/₁₆ in. or less aren't critical, but anything greater should be corrected. A badly out-of-plumb trimmer can sometimes be trued by moving the bottom end out, either by changing the width of the opening or by moving the plate in relation to its layout line. Sometimes, a good whack with a hammer is all it takes. But if the trimmer is grossly mispositioned, saw the nails, tap the plate into position and then fasten with nails or drywall screws. In really bad framing I use a couple of ³/₄-in. blocks taped to the ends of my level. The blocks hold the level off the trimmer, but indicate if the two points at the top and bottom of the trimmer, upon which they rest, are plumb. You can buy door-hanging levels with blocks that flip out of the way when you need a straight edge (see the Resource Guide on pp. 179-181 for a source).

Adjusting the width of the opening is more complicated and depends on the style of framing used, as shown in the drawing above right. In California, most carpenters frame with both the king stud and trimmer sitting on top of the bottom plate. The plate, which spans the door opening as the wall is framed, is sawn

Adjusting rough door openings

California style

To change the width of the opening, remove nails, reposition trimmer and king stud, and renail.

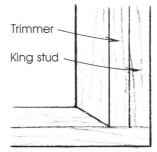

Trimmer

King stud

Conventional style

To widen the opening, remove nails and reposition king stud. To make opening smaller, wedge trimmer, then clinch nail.

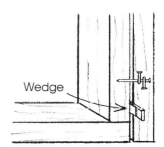

Wedge

out later. To move the trimmer in or out, remove the nails from both studs, reposition and renail. If, as a result, the plate projects into the opening, saw it off flush. In other parts of the country, the king stud sits on the plate, but the trimmer is nailed on after the wall is erected so it extends right to the floor. A wedge or twisting the claw of your framing hammer between the trimmer and king stud will move the trimmer out. Lock it down with the clinched-nail trick described on p. 63. To move it in—that is, to widen the opening—remove nails and trim the plate.

You can test the header and trimmer for gross errors in square with a framing square, as shown in the photo at right on the facing page. But because a framing square is only 24 in. long, it won't detect minor run-out. The best test for overall square is to place a 6-ft. level on the trimmer and a 2-ft. level on the header, checking for plumb and level at the same time. If the trimmer is plumb and the header is level, the opening has to be square. If the trimmer is out of plumb or the header out of level, you'll have to adjust one or the other —usually the trimmer, as described above.

One last thing to check before the windows are installed and drywall hung is the placement of building wrap. The wrap is important for the structure's water-tight integrity, and how it's installed makes a difference to the trim carpenter. In Idaho, we wrap a house with Tyvek before the siding goes on. The Tyvek is applied over the window and door openings, then cut carefully so it folds into and around the header, trimmer and rough sill of window and door openings. The paper should stop just short of the rough opening's inside edge. Be careful not to bunch wrap in the corners of the openings, or the windows and doors might not seat flat into the opening. This could cause the jambs to bow in, making it difficult to install casing.

Grounds and backing

In the days before drywall replaced plaster as the favored wall-covering material, carpenters needed a way to nail molding to the wall. Since plaster alone won't hold nails, strips of wood called grounds were laid into the walls ahead of plastering to provide a secure surface to which moldings could be nailed or screwed. Even before plaster became popular, grounds were in common use in brick or stone houses whose interiors were covered by paneling. In these, grounds consisted of wooden plugs called noggins, which were let into the wall in place of a brick or stone. As plaster became more common, grounds evolved into strips embedded flush with the plaster so that moldings, skirtings and paneling could be securely nailed. These grounds also acted to stop or "screed" the plaster around door and window openings, and they gave the plasterer both a straight edge and a thickness gauge by which to measure the work.

We still use grounds today, even with drywall, but most carpenters refer to them as backing. For some trimwork, all the backing that's needed is the standard 2x framing. Most trimwork, casing and baseboard mainly, is narrower than the underlying framing, so studs, plates, trimmers and headers offer a secure enough nailing surface to work as backing. But where wide casings and crown molding or chair rails will be installed, backing will have to be nailed to the frame before the drywall is hung.

Plan on installing backing wherever molding will be nailed at points where there's no framing to nail into. Rough headers on doors and windows and rough sills on windows are normally wide enough to serve as grounds for horizontal moldings. If you're planning to install an elaborate cabinet head whose width will extend well above the header, however, you'll have to add 2x4 or some other kind of backing. Similarly, casings 4 in. or wider will extend beyond the rough framing so they'll need extra backing too, usually in the form of vertical 2x4 blocks nailed to the king stud or horizontal blocking on 16-in. centers, as shown in the top drawing on the facing page.

Backing for a long, continuous molding like chair rail or plate rail or a complex crown molding can be made of 2x4 blocks nailed between the studs. An even better solution is to let a 1x4 strip into notches cut in the studs, as shown in the drawing. If I'm framing a wall that will get a chair rail, I lay the backing right on the wall where I want it and then scribe its width on the edges of the studs. I set my circular saw to the thickness of the backing, then make two cuts to the lines, followed by several more cuts to waste the groove. I knock out the waste with my hammer, then clean out and smooth the notch with a chisel. I nail the backing into the end studs only and fasten it securely at every stud only after the wall has been erected and plumbed.

Backing for wide crown molding and baseboards can be done the same way, but look out for nails when sawing the notches. There are a couple of other ways to add blocking for baseboard and crown molding. Some carpenters double or triple bottom plates and top plates as the wall is being framed. If the wall is already framed, you can add blocking after the fact. Extremely large crowns will need special backing along the walls that run parallel to the ceiling joists. In this case you must nail blocking between the bottoms of the joists on 16-in. centers. Be sure to extend blocking tight in the corners so the ends of the molding can be secured. Regardless of its complexity, blocking must be fixed in true vertical and horizontal planes. If it isn't, the molding may not align with the backing, and you'll miss a few nails.

Trimming concrete and metal stud walls—Trimming concrete walls presents special problems for which there are basically two solutions, as shown in the bottom right drawing on the facing page. One is to have the backing in place when you pour the wall, which means that you'll have to use pressure-treated lumber to guard against rot as the backing absorbs moisture from the concrete. The treated backing is set in place, firmly nailed or screwed to the forms, and the pour is made. When the forms are stripped, the backing is carefully separated and stays put in the wall, as shown in the drawing.

The second method, and the one that most carpenters use, is to install the backing after the concrete has cured. The backing then serves as a means of attaching both drywall and trim, and it creates a space for insulation between the concrete and the drywall. Backing on concrete can be 1x2s or 2x4s or anything in between, fastened with expansion bolts or with powder-actuated fasteners. Use the same strategy as with a frame wall—install backing wherever molding will be nailed.

Although it's not common in residential framing, light-gauge steel framing is gaining popularity, chiefly because it's more fireproof and, in some parts of the country, less expensive than wood. For the trim carpenter, trimming a wall framed with steel studs requires more thought and quite a bit more time since most of the trim will have to be screwed instead of nailed. Backing can be installed just as in a wood wall, using either steel framing material or plywood ripped to the width of the steel studs. Molding can be nailed directly to the wood backing, but you'll have to use trim-head drywall screws where metal is the backing material. As their name suggests, trim-head screws have a very small head, leaving a hole that can be filled with putty, sanded and finished. Stain-grade trim fastened to a steel-framed wall will need to have the screw holes countersunk and plugged. This process is described in Chapter 9.

Installing backing

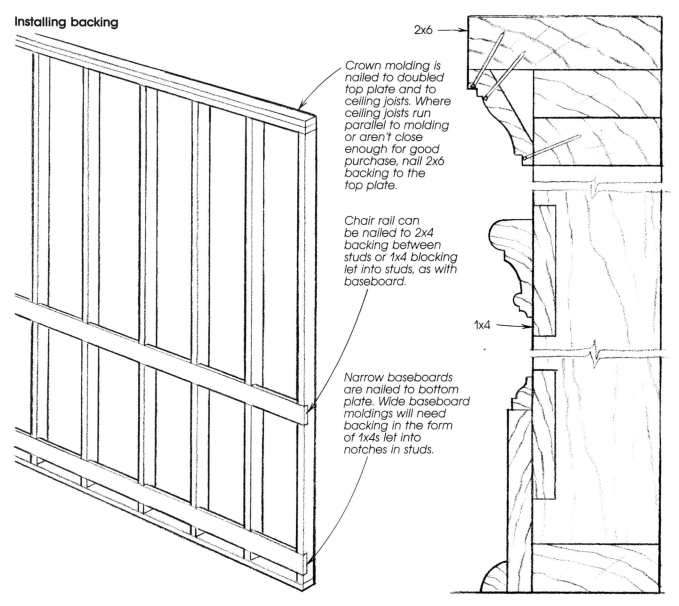

2x6

Crown molding is nailed to doubled top plate and to ceiling joists. Where ceiling joists run parallel to molding or aren't close enough for good purchase, nail 2x6 backing to the top plate.

Chair rail can be nailed to 2x4 backing between studs or 1x4 blocking let into studs, as with baseboard.

1x4

Narrow baseboards are nailed to bottom plate. Wide baseboard moldings will need backing in the form of 1x4s let into notches in studs.

Backing for metal studs and concrete walls

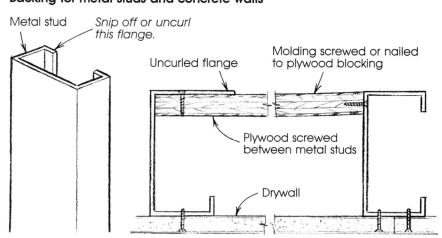

Metal stud

Snip off or uncurl this flange.

Uncurled flange

Molding screwed or nailed to plywood blocking

Plywood screwed between metal studs

Drywall

Concrete backing

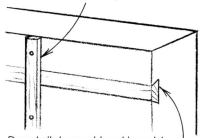

Furring strips fastened to concrete wall with powder-actuated fasteners or masonry nails

Dovetail-shaped backing strip nailed to inside of form remains embedded in wall when forms are stripped.

Drywall that projects above the jamb can be made flush with a Surform plane. A penciled line on the drywall shows the outward limit of the taper.

After the drywall goes up

Once the drywall is up, trimwork can begin in earnest, but there are a few more things to check. First, using your straightedge and a square, check around the drywall surfaces that will get trimmed. Often, drywall compound will have been built up near the inside and outside corners. If molding is applied over this mess, it won't sit flat. I use a Stanley Surform plane to flatten out the high spots. Inside corners can be pared with a chisel.

Window and door jambs are generally ¾ in. to 1 in. thick, and when installed, their edges should be flush with the surface of the drywall. Of course they never are. Differences in stud thickness, several layers of building paper and other minor discrepancies add up and prevent the jambs from projecting in their full amount, or they may project too much. If the difference is ⅛ in. or less in either direction and you are using a casing with a relieved back, you can go ahead and begin trim work.

If the drywall is proud—meaning that it protrudes beyond the jamb more than ⅛ in., something must be done in order to bring the two flush. Sometimes a few more drywall nails or screws can "suck in" the offending protrusion.

When that doesn't work, lots of carpenters simply pulverize the edge of the drywall, hammering the offending edge every ½ in. or so. This is an inelegant solution at best. To see a craftsman banging away at the drywall in order to place a delicate molding over the resulting mess smacks a little of desperation.

A better way is to shave down the offending drywall protrusions with the Surform, as shown in the photo at left. Flush up the surfaces of the drywall and the jamb by shaving away both the paper and drywall. Work a flat tapered surface out as far as you can, but be careful not to plane beyond the finished casing line. It's messy work that requires a drop cloth to protect a finished floor.

When there's a major discrepancy (¼ in. or more) and the jamb fails to come even close to the surface of the drywall, you will have to add more wood to the jamb by nailing or gluing on jamb extensions, as described on pp. 78-81. The opposite problem occurs if the jamb protrudes into the room beyond the wall plane. In this instance the jamb should be planed flush with the surface of the drywall, as shown in the photo on the facing page.

A small block plane is the easiest tool to handle and does the least amount of damage to the neighboring drywall. If the projection is large and a lot of material has to be removed, I use a jack plane or a power plane. Plane the jamb flush to the drywall, stopping just before you dig into the paper. With a block plane it's possible to bevel the jamb so that it's slightly proud along its inside edge, that is, the edge away from the drywall. This makes installing casing easier.

When to trim: before or after paint?

Trim is one of the last things to go into the house, but there are a couple of schools of thought on exactly when it should be installed. Most modern houses have drywall walls, and the trim is normally applied after the drywall is taped and/or textured. The question is whether to install trim before or after the walls are painted and the floors varnished, carpeted or tiled. Ideally, every vertical surface should have a coat of paint, including the walls behind the trim and the backside of the trim itself, which will be less likely to warp if a film of paint or varnish inhibits the wood's absorption of moisture. This would argue for an order of events like this:

1. Tape and/or texture drywall;
2. Install a wood or tile floor (but not carpet);
3. Prime the wood trim (before installing) and prime the walls;
4. Sand and finish the floors;
5. Install the trim and cabinets;
6. Complete the electrical, plumbing and air-conditioning installation;
7. Complete painting the walls and trim.

This work flow is ideal, as long as the painters are willing and able to cut in the trim neatly by hand with a brush. However, many painters these days (especially in areas where building is booming) work strictly with an airless sprayer. They'll park the sprayer in the middle of the house and snake its hoses into each room, painting the entire house in little more time than takes to write about it. Production painters want the trim installed before they begin work. They mask off the walls, spray the trim, then mask the trim and spray the walls. It's a fast method and a cheap one, although not always neat. Some airless painters will agree to spray walls that haven't been trimmed out, in which case the walls are painted, the electrical and plumbing are finished and the trim is prepainted before it is installed. This method requires touchup painting by hand once the trim is hung, but it has the advantage of not requiring much masking.

In most cases, the trim carpenter won't have much to say about the sequence, but will be called onto the job somewhere between foundation construction and the move-in date. But a contractor or owner-builder will have a choice, and if the ideal order of events described above (or a modified version of it) fits the schedule, follow it. If you're trimming an addition or a remodel yourself and want to move in before the job is done, sand and finish the floors and paint the walls, then trim at your leisure.

Jambs that stand proud of the drywall surface should be planed flush. Be careful not to plane too deeply, or you risk tearing the drywall's surface paper.

After the house is closed in and the drywall is hung and taped, the windows can be trimmed. Here Savage has constructed a jamb extension in one piece and is installing it on the window jamb.

5

Windows

Windows play a curious, sometimes contradictory role in a modern house. They're supposed to "let the outside in" by providing a nice view yet still keep cold drafts at bay. Windows are supposed to shut tightly but open effortlessly and be easy to clean but hard to break. With the advent of high-tech glass coatings, a window is now expected to let light in while excluding heat, or let heat and light in, depending on the climate. And, of course, windows are always supposed to blend into the home's decor.

Fortunately, window technology has come a long way even since the turn of the century, when the double-hung sash window was state of the art. In those days, machine-made sash had come into wide use but trimming a window was still a major operation, involving hours of assembly and tedious fitting. Modern windows, some with precut molding kits, make the job go much more quickly, but the trim carpenter's task remains the same: to finish off the rough opening and to install sills, stools, aprons and casings that match the trim in the rest of the house. In this chapter, I'll describe how these tasks are done. Much of what I'll cover here, especially the sections on joinery and casing work, also applies to door trim, so I won't repeat it in Chapter 6.

Parts of a window

These days, virtually all windows are factory-made and arrive on site ready to nail into the rough opening. Complete window units arc sold in five major styles with dozens of minor variations, as shown in the drawing at right. Some windows are sold with trim kits; others require that the finish carpenter supply and fit the trim. All windows consists of two major parts: the window frame and the sash. The window

Window types

Double-hung
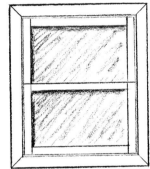

Casement

Sliding

Awning
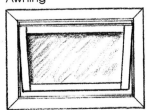

Hopper

73

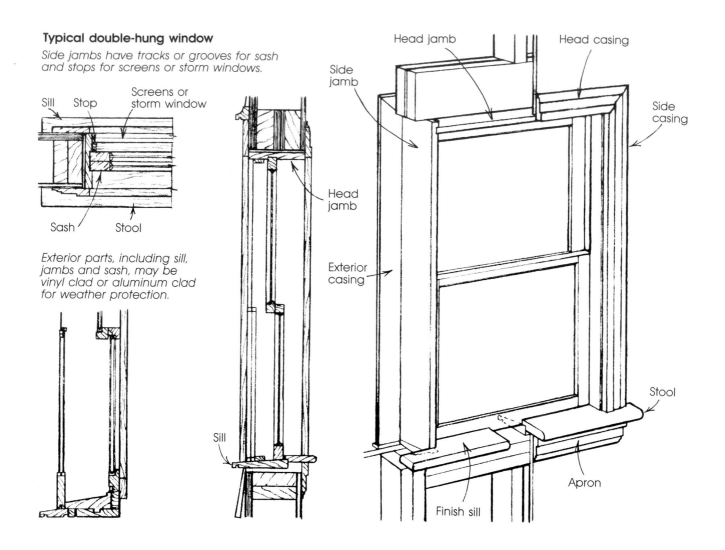

Typical double-hung window

Side jambs have tracks or grooves for sash and stops for screens or storm windows.

Sill   Stop   Screens or storm window

Sash   Stool

Exterior parts, including sill, jambs and sash, may be vinyl clad or aluminum clad for weather protection.

Side jamb

Head jamb

Exterior casing

Sill

Head jamb

Head casing

Side casing

Stool

Apron

Finish sill

frame is analogous to the door jamb and in some parts of the country, it's even called a window jamb. The sash is the frame that holds the glass; it's the part that moves when the window is opened and closed. Normally, frame and sash are separate parts with the frame set into the rough opening and the sash set into the frame. Windows that open and close are said to be "operable," and the sash is mounted in tracks or hung on hinges.

As shown in the drawing above, the frame consists of two vertical members called side jambs and two horizontal members, a head or yoke at the top and a sill at the bottom. As mentioned above, the sash is a separate piece that fits into the frame. Unlike doors, windows don't follow a universal standard for overall size, a fact that has gotten a lot of carpenters into trouble. If a window's size is given as 48 in., this number could refer to the overall sash size, the jamb's exterior dimensions or the rough-opening size. If you can, it's best to buy your windows first and then measure them to determine the rough opening. If this isn't possible, make

sure that you're certain of the required rough opening before the framing is complete.

As with a door jamb, a window frame's head jamb is normally let into dadoes in the side jambs. The sill is also let into the side jambs but at a 12° angle toward the outside of the house, so it can shed water and direct it beyond the siding. In some newer windows, particularly casements, the sill is not angled. Instead, a beveled piece is glued to the outside edge of the sill, as shown in the drawing above left. Flat sills simplify trim installation because it's easier to fit a stool cap to a flat sill than to one that's angled.

Trim carpenters use two basic methods to trim a window: the picture-frame method and traditional or stool-and-apron method. Picture-frame trim consists of four pieces of molding: two side casings, a head and a sill casing. As the name suggests, these moldings frame the window like a picture. The casing's function is to cover the gap between the window jamb and the framing and to act as a gusset between the two, making the jamb more rigid.

Traditional window trim also has a head and two side casings, but instead of a sill casing, a stool and apron are installed at the bottom of the window, as shown in the drawing at right. As described above, the stool is really an extension of the sill into the room, but it is a separate part. When you say that you are placing something on the window sill, you are really referring to the stool. The apron is attached beneath the stool and is meant to cover the gap between the rough sill and the bottom edge of of the stool. It's usually made from a piece of casing molding, but well-stocked molding suppliers sometimes carry special apron moldings.

Deciding on window-trim style

During the 20th century, tastes in trim have come full circle, from the gaudy excesses of turn-of-the century Victorian parlors to the practically trimless interiors of Modernist boxes. Because these styles are relatively recent and well documented, it's possible to reproduce them or to use them as starting places for new designs, as discussed in Chapter 1 and Chapter 2. Regardless of the window itself, the trim around it lends style and texture to the home's interior. In most cases, the trim you use on the windows will be duplicated on the doors.

Even within a given decorative style, many variations are possible. Using the same molding, for example, a window can be trimmed picture-frame style, with full stool-and-apron, with a cabinet head, with butt joints and plinth blocks or in some combination of these styles. One of the simplest trim styles is the trim carpenter's holiday: the drywaller simply nails up a metal corner or radius molding where the casing would otherwise be, then runs the drywall right into the opening so it butts against the window jamb. A wooden stool is often installed over the rough sill, however.

Besides personal taste, several other factors should influence the window-trim style you select, not the least of which are time and money. The picture-frame method is faster by far, although not necessarily easier, given that it requires miters at all four corners. One advantage of picture-frame molding is that you use the same molding around the entire window, and it's usually the same stuff used on the doors. This simplifies ordering somewhat. The picture-frame style blends into the wall, especially if it's painted the same color. Simple casings not overly wide or adorned with deep, complicated profiles look best with picture-frame work. Curtains can be hung over the picture-frame style with little interference, and horizontal or vertical blinds fit nicely into the frame. Curtains and blinds don't always fit so well with stool-and-apron trim.

Traditional stool-and-apron trim is more complex, but it is also more distinctive because it lends itself to more variation. Stool-and-apron trim is often used with double-hung windows, but it can be adapted to other

Window-trim styles

Picture frame

Stool-and-apron
with mitered head casing

Stool-and-apron
with corner blocks

Typical casing profiles

← 2¼ in. →

Stool-and-apron
with butted head casing

Stool-and-apron
with cabinet head

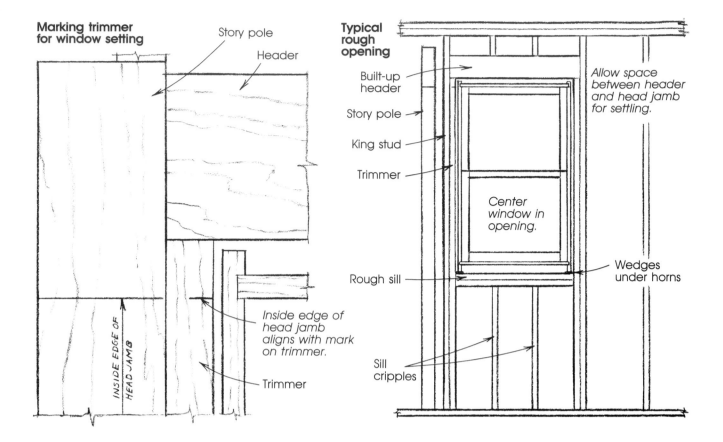

Marking trimmer for window setting

Story pole

Header

INSIDE EDGE OF HEAD JAMB

Inside edge of head jamb aligns with mark on trimmer.

Trimmer

Typical rough opening

Built-up header

Story pole

King stud

Trimmer

Rough sill

Sill cripples

Allow space between header and head jamb for settling.

Center window in opening.

Wedges under horns

To level the window, wedges are placed under the jamb horns. The space between the rough sill and finished sill will be filled with blocking to provide backing for the sill casing or apron.

designs. Stool-and-apron trim can be mitered or butt joined. Stool-and-apron are often wider and thicker than picture-frame casings. But because each stool and apron must be cut and fit separately, this style is very time-consuming. Still, the stool is a nice touch. It gives visual weight to the bottom of the window, and besides, stools are a good place to put plants.

Two stool-and-apron variations I like are the corner block and cabinet head, shown in the bottom drawings on p. 75. Corner blocks give the window a nice architectural feel that can be carried over to the doors, too. In more elaborate work, a cabinet head—really a nonstructural lintel that caps the window—is a nice touch. Cabinet heads can be bought or made up on site from several different kinds of moldings. For more on cabinet heads, see p. 92.

Installing a window

The framers usually install the windows including the outside trim and the siding, leaving the finish carpenter to deal with the interior. Sometimes, though, the trim carpenter performs the entire job, so I'll touch here on the major points of setting a window, beginning with the rough opening (see the drawing above).

Traditionally, wooden window frames were nailed into the rough opening suspended between wooden

Once the rough opening has been prepared, the window is set from the outside of the house. The window is temporarily tacked through its nailing flange or through the exterior casing. It's then plumbed and leveled with wedges before being permanently nailed.

wedges, just as with a door jamb. But more and more, they're fitted with prenailed casing or a metal or plastic flange that overlaps the outside of the rough opening. In this case, the window is plumbed and leveled, then nailed through the casing or flange, through the sheathing and into the trimmers. Wedges are inserted between the bottom of the sill and the top of the rough sill to position the window temporarily for nailing. It's best to put these wedges beneath the horns, that portion of the side jamb that extends past the window sill, as shown in the photo on the facing page.

As described on pp. 64-67, the rough opening must be plumb, level and square and large enough to accommodate the window jamb. Leave at least ¼ in. and preferably ½ in. between the rough header and window head jamb for any settling the house might do. Also, there must be space between the side jambs and the trimmer for insulation. Before the window is set, the building wrap should be carefully cut, folded into the opening and stapled, as explained on p. 67 and shown in the drawing on p. 98. In cold climates, a plastic vapor barrier is sometimes stapled to the interior walls before the drywall goes up. This plastic should be folded into the door and window openings toward the outside of the building and over the top of the building wrap. The interior vapor barrier should cover the trimmers but stop just short of the exterior sheathing. However,

be careful about using plastic. If the house is otherwise very tight, it may become too stuffy or damp.

Setting and shimming the window starts with marking the rough opening, as shown in the drawing on the facing page. With a tape or story pole, mark the trimmers at the height the inside (bottom) edge of the head jamb should be, taking into account the space between the rough header and window head jamb. This measurement should also account for any alignments with other trim, windows, doors, plate rails and so on. Usually, all the window trim in the same room will align at the top edge, so one story-pole mark will suffice for an entire room.

Once the trimmer is marked, you can set the window. But before you do, apply a bead of caulk behind the nailing flange or a pre-attached wooden casing if there is one. I use urethane caulk because it's cheap, flexible and cleans up with water. With the caulk applied, have a helper push the window in from the outside and hold it in place. Center the window so that the space between side jambs and trimmers is approximately equal. Place wedges under each bottom corner (or under the horns, if the window has them) and raise the window until the inside edge of the head jamb aligns with your marks on the trimmers, as shown in the photo on the facing page. Temporarily tack or screw through the exterior casing or nailing flange, but only on one side and near the bottom corner so the window can still be moved a bit. Check to see that the head jamb is aligned with your marks, then check the sill for level. If the sill isn't level, adjust the shim opposite the secured jamb leg until it is level.

Next, check the side jambs for plumb and straight. It's usually safe to assume that factory windows are square, so if the sill is level, the jambs should be plumb. If this turns out to be the case, nail or screw the pre-attached exterior casing or nailing flange diagonally opposite the first tack. If for some reason the jambs aren't plumb but the sill is level, you'll need to adjust the wedges to split the difference. With the window locked squarely in the opening, I check the head jamb for level one more time, check the marks on the trimmer, then nail permanently. I drive nails on 12-in. centers, whether fastening through a flange or through an outside casing. Sixteen-penny galvanized casing nails or 3-in. drywall screws are the fastener of choice here. Screws can be driven through a flange, but unless you want to counterbore and plug the screw holes, stick with nails when fastening through a pre-attached wooden casing.

Some carpenters stop right here and assume that the fastened exterior casing and later the interior casing will lock the window in place. But this isn't really so. Without further nailing, the window jamb is really rather flexible, especially on the inside edge, where the casing will be installed. To fasten the window more securely, I install shims between the trimmer and jamb and nail about every 16 in. with 16d finishing nails. Then I fill the gaps between the trimmer and jamb with foam insulation. Don't overdo the insulation: this stuff expands with considerable force, and if you use too much, you can bow the jambs inward.

The last step is to install the exterior drip cap. The drip cap is a piece of metal flashing shaped like a sideways "Z" that sits above the exterior head casing. Once installed, it's covered with the siding and flashes off any water that would otherwise enter at the junction between the siding and the exterior head casing. The drip cap is nailed high along its upper edge with only enough galvanized nails to hold it flat against the sheathing and down against the head casing. Later the siding will be nailed through the drip cap, further securing it.

In general, the setting method described above works well in framed walls with wood, vinyl, aluminum, stucco or brick siding. However, stucco and brick are a little different. In stucco construction, a layer of sisal kraft paper is applied under the nailing flange to protect it from water penetration. Once the window is set, building paper is applied over the flange, sandwiching it and protecting it from water and galvanic effects between the flange and the lath wire for the stucco. A special molding called stucco molding protrudes about $7/8$ in. from the sheathed surface so when

scratch, brown and color coats are applied, the stucco is flush with the window. In brick veneer walls, the veneer is laid first, then the windows are set into the opening. Rather than being nailed to the brick, the window is nailed through its jambs into the trimmers, then caulked to create a tight seal with the masonry.

One last look—If someone else has set the windows, you'll want to check a few things before proceeding. Look to see if the window penetrates the wall fully. Has the nailing flange (or exterior casing) been drawn down tightly to the exterior sheathing? Next, check the side and head jambs for straightness. If they're bowed, remove the exterior casing or flange nails, pry the jamb straight and renail.

I always open and close every window to check its action. If the window has been improperly set, it will show up in the action of the sash. Too much insulation—foam or loose fiberglass stuffed into the gaps—will bow window jambs, and the result is a window that opens and shuts with extra effort, if at all. Dig out the excess insulation with a screwdriver. I also check for light penetration. If I can see daylight I know the air is going to find its way through the same opening. I caulk or insulate rather than count on the casing to stop the infiltration. Occasionally, there will will be a large gap between the rough sill and window sill. Try to fill this gap with a scrap 2x4 or some other filler that will give you good backing for nailing the casing or the apron later on.

One last thing I check is that the jamb edges are flush with the drywall or plaster, as described in detail in Chapter 4. If they're proud of the rock, you'll have to plane them flush. Often the reverse is true, in which case you'll have to add jamb extensions. Jamb extensions are strips of wood (or plywood) fastened to the edges of the window jambs and the sill. They bring the jambs flush with the surface of the inside wall so casing can be nailed on. Depending on the window manufacturer, the juncture of the extension and the jamb can be anything from a simple butt joint to an elaborate splined joint. Some manufacturers make up windows to order so the jambs are as wide as your wall is thick, eliminating the need for extensions. Others make only one width jamb, then provide jamb extensions to match the wall thickness. Much of the time, however, you have to make your own jamb extensions.

Extensions should be of the same wood as the jamb and of the same thickness. Simply rip the wood to the width required to bring the jamb edge flush with the wall, then nail or glue the strips on. Since they'll be covered by the casing, a simple butt joint will suffice where the extensions meet at the corners. Very often, window and wall will be out of kilter to each other so a tapered extension is required. To determine the taper, simply hold your extension stock up to the window jamb and scribe along the face of the drywall. Clamp

Most factory-made windows have a plastic or metal nailing flange or, as shown above, a pre-attached exterior casing. Once a window has been plumbed and leveled, it is nailed about every 12 in. through the flange or the casing into the trimmers, header and rough sill.

Drip-cap detail

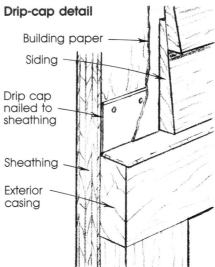

Building paper

Siding

Drip cap nailed to sheathing

Sheathing

Exterior casing

Expanding foam insulation seals gaps between the window jamb and the trimmer, header and rough sill. Don't inject too much, however, or it may cause the jambs to bow.

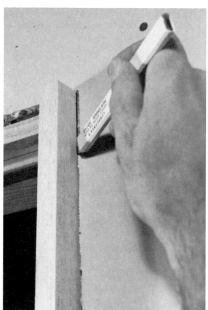

Savage, above, has made up an extension as a complete unit, including the stool. It will be scribed to the jamb edges and nailed to the trimmer. When the jamb isn't a consistent distance back from the surface of the drywall (a common occurrence), jamb extensions have to be tapered. Scribe them first (far left), then cut with a jigsaw or a circular saw. (Photos at left by Jim Hall.)

the board to a bench or sawhorse, then saw the tapered piece with a circular saw, a scrollsaw or a bandsaw. Plane the sawn edge of the extension before you glue and nail it to the jamb.

If very deep extensions are required—say 2 in. or more—I sometimes make them up as a complete unit, nailed and glued at the corners. This way, it's even possible to fit the window casing to the extension before you nail it to the window jamb, as shown in the photo on p. 72 and the top photo on the facing page. If the extension is less than 2 in. deep, the assembly is screwed to the jamb with long screws driven edgewise into the jamb. Deeper extension assemblies have to be nailed to the trimmers with shims slipped in at the nailing points. To get a perfect fit, I make the extension assembly a little wider than it needs to be and then scribe it to fit around the window jamb. If you expect to have trouble fitting an assembled extension, you can make it intentionally larger so as to create a ⅛-in. reveal at the edge-to-edge joints where the extension meets the jamb. I apply a small amount of glue to the jamb extension before nailing or screwing it.

Picture-frame trim

A picture-frame window has four identical casings, each mitered at 45°. Since the miter is used everywhere in trim carpentry, picture-frame trim is a good way to learn and practice it. If you've never trimmed a window before, I'd suggest starting out with a simple, inexpensive molding, say 2¼-in. Philippine mahogany Ranch-style casing. Mahogany is relatively soft, so slightly misaligned joints can sometimes be forced together.

I'm careful to get the height of the window jamb right when I set the window, but if there are minor discrepancies, I want to know about them now so I can hide them by raising one piece of casing a bit or lowering another, or maybe even using wider molding. One more check with the story pole will tell. A quick diagonal measurement across the inside corners of the window frame confirms whether the frame is square or not. If it isn't, I want to know at the outset so I can compensate in the joints.

After checking the diagonals, I lay out the jamb for a constant reveal all around the window. The casing laps over only a portion of the jamb's exposed edge. The reveal is the portion of the jamb that doesn't get covered. The reveal creates a "step" in the joint that's both visually appealing and easier to make than a perfectly flush joint. With a ¾-in. thick jamb, a typical reveal is 3/16 in., but this can be varied. A reveal that's too large forces you to nail near the edge of the jambs and casing, and you risk splitting both. With practice, you can eyeball the reveal but it's safer to use a reveal gauge, shown in the top photo at right. Another way is to set a combination square for the desired reveal and use it as a marking gauge, as shown in the bottom photo at right. Use

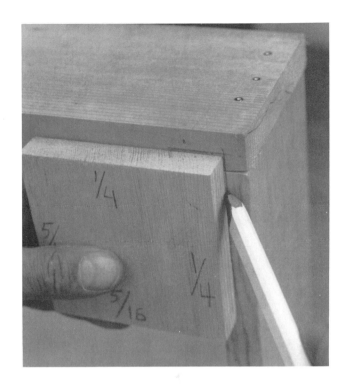

Two tools for marking casing reveals are the reveal gauge, top, and the combination square, above. The reveal gauge is a square scrap block with rabbets milled in all four edges, each corresponding to a common reveal dimension. The combination square can be set to the reveal and used as a marking gauge.

Casing a picture-frame window

Burning an inch means measuring from the 1-in. mark on the tape...

Measure short to short and 'burn' 1 in.

...then subtracting 1 in. from the reading here.

Tape

Head casing length equals 'A' plus twice the reveal. It can also be scribed directly from the jamb reveal marks.

Scribe side casing directly from jambs.

Reveal marks

A

Sill casing goes on last and is cut to fit between side casings. To allow adjustments, don't nail the lower end of the side casings until the sill casing is fitted.

For very long pieces, add to 'A' twice the casing width plus twice the reveal, then measure long to long.

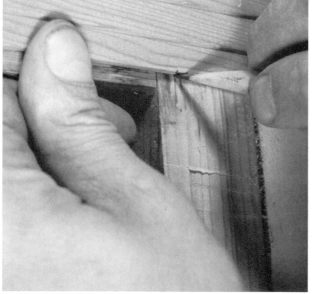

The length of a picture-frame window's head casing can be scribed directly from the reveal marks.

a knife or pencil to mark the reveal with intersecting lines at the corners and along the jamb about every foot or so. Later, the casing will hide these lines.

I start by applying the head casing. You could just as easily start at the bottom or sides, but fitting four miters takes skill and a little luck. The first three joints are simple: they can be cut long and trimmed. The fourth miter is a prayer. Even with a perfect window opening, small bows and twists work against you. My strategy is to get two perfect miters up at eye level where they're most noticeable. The last step is to worry in the bottom casing.

To get the length of the head casing, measure the distance between the two inside faces of the jambs, then add twice the reveal (two times ³⁄₁₆ in., or ³⁄₈ in. in this case). This is the "short-to-short" dimension between the heels of the miters. To transfer a short-to-short measurement, first chopsaw an accurate 45° cut on one end of the casing. With the molding face up on a bench or the floor, align the 1-in. mark on the tape with the short point, then "burn" or add an inch to the required length to mark the piece. Once you've cut one casing, you can set up a stop to cut others for windows of the same size. If each window is of a different size, I sometimes align the precut end with the reveal marks on one end, then scribe the length directly from the reveal marks at the opposite end.

To measure very long pieces, I rely on the fact that a 45° cut is the diagonal of a perfect square. Therefore it follows that adding twice the casing width plus twice the reveal to the inside jamb measurements and then cutting "long to long" will work. The advantage of this method is that you can hook your tape over the long point and measure to the opposite point, which, on long pieces, is a lot easier to do than measuring short to short.

Once you've cut both ends, position the head casing on the jamb. Its inside edge should just cover the reveal marks, and the miter heels should just touch the intersecting reveal marks. Without having to press or twist it, the casing should lie flat along its entire length. If it doesn't, you may have to trim some more drywall or plane down a jamb. If a warped casing is giving me trouble, I don't fight it. I cut the unruly piece into shorter lengths for use elsewhere. If the gods are smiling and everything fits, I nail the casing.

Nail the casing through its face, along opposite edges. Use 3d or 4d nails to anchor the casing to the jamb and 6d or 8d finish nails to fasten the casing through the drywall into the rough header. Thick casings and ⁵⁄₈-in. drywall will require longer nails. I nail the jamb edge first because it tacks the piece securely and positions the short points on the reveal marks. Center the first nail in the casing length, about ³⁄₁₆ in. from the inside edge of the casing. Tap it in, but don't drive it home until you're sure the casing is aligned with the reveal marks and flat against the wall. If it is, drive home the first nail and continue to nail until the jamb edge is locked down. I normally space the nails by eye at equal intervals, between 8 in. and 16 in. Be careful driving the nail near the heel, which is so close to the end that the nail has a tendency to split the casing. If I'm worried about the fit with the next piece, I sometimes leave out the last nail near the heel so that I have some "wiggle" left to align the joint.

With the jamb edge nailed, go on to the outside or header edge. I drive the outside nails at points directly above the 4d nails along the inside edge of the casing. This eliminates visual confusion; as carpenters on my jobs say, "it's for the visual." However, a contractor friend of mine insists that the inside-edge nails not be aligned with the outside-edge nails. He insists that nails should be located on a 45° zigzag across the casing to break up the monotony. He also paints his nail heads to match the woodwork and then sets them flush to the surface with a nail gun, so there's no need to set and putty the nail holes. To each his own.

Apply the side casings next, using the same strategy. Chopsaw a miter on one end of the casing and, holding it flat at the joint with one hand and against the wall with your forearm, examine the fit. Without forcing, the miter should mate with no gaps, and the reveal should remain constant along the entire length of the jamb. If the wall is in plane with the jamb, the miter will touch uniformly across the thickness of the joint. Casing moldings, by the way, have a shallow relief channel cut down the back, which is meant to account for minor out-of-plane difficulties. If the wall is badly out of whack, you'll need to find out what the problem is and fix it. Even when the wall is flat, however, miters often touch at the front or the back and are slightly open at the heel or toe.

Correct the heel-toe alignment first. There are several ways to do this. I try to estimate the size of the gap at its widest point in thirty-seconds of an inch. I've measured it with steel rulers, but it's much easier just to eyeball it. I say to myself "$\frac{1}{32}$ in." and then try to trim off that amount using the chopsaw and paper-wedge method described on pp. 85-87. I form a mental picture of where the gap is so I'll remember to trim the opposite edge, thereby bringing the joint together. Very small gaps are better trimmed with a plane or rasp. I carry a very sharp low-angle block plane in my belt so I can trim small slivers without having to go back to the chopsaw. I know one skilled old pro who does all his trimming with a four-in-hand rasp. A sharp chisel or knife will also work.

If the joint is open but parallel (as in the bottom photo at right), the casings are probably twisted out of plane. Back-cutting will remove material behind the joint line and allow the surfaces to mate. Make the back-cut by placing a wedge under the casing, between the chopsaw table and the molding. It's common to use wedges in both planes to achieve a good fit and, if nec-

A perfect miter fits tightly with no gaps at the heel or toe, as shown in the door casing in the top photo. The miter in the photo above needs to be back-cut in order to fit properly.

Two casing nailing patterns

Nails vertically aligned   Nails at 45° to vertical

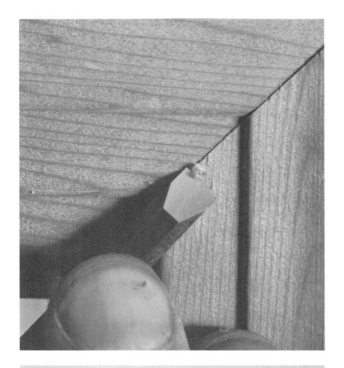

Slightly misaligned casings can be pared flush (top). As a desperate last resort, a wedge driven behind the casing flushes up both parts, above. The wedge is sawn flush, and the gap at the casing's back is caulked over.

essary, two wedges can be used at the same time. Back-cutting with the block plane is also an alternative. Both of these methods are described on pp. 85-87.

When you're happy with the fit, hold the casing in position and mark the point where it intersects the bottom reveal marks. Once the piece is cut to length, test it again for fit, then spread a little glue on both miters before nailing. Glue is cheap insurance against gaps, not because it holds the joint together but because it seals the end grain against moisture migration and subsequent wood movement. Nail the casing from top to bottom, but leave the last few inches unfastened so the casing can be adjusted. With both side casings in place, I move on to the bottom piece.

The bottom piece is always the hardest to fit. Any errors you compensated for in the previous three pieces come home to roost, and you have only one or two chances to make the final cut on the fourth piece. Ever the optimist, I start with an accurate 45° cut on a piece of casing a few inches too long. On the uncut end, the casing necessarily rides up and over the installed side casing. Next, measure the distance between the inside edges of the side casings (or mark it directly on the bottom casing) and use this as the short-to-short dimension. Mark the piece and cut it slightly long of your mark. Now, hold your breath and see if the piece fits.

Since you've left the bottom few inches of the side casings loose, you can adjust some there. If the miter seems to fit but pushes the casing apart, simply trim the piece a bit shorter, using the same chopsaw setting. If there's a tapered gap, trim the casing with wedges, but be very careful to take only minute cuts or shallow passes with the block plane. A joint that requires three or four cuts will probably wind up too short, and you'll have to start over with a fresh piece. But with any luck at all, the bottom joints will spring ever so slightly into place with just enough pressure to squeeze out a hairline of glue.

Occasionally you'll encounter a slightly bowed side jamb. Bring it into line by nailing the trimmer side of the casing first, then pry the jamb so that the reveal is consistent before nailing the casing to the jamb edge.

When things go wrong—I've already described how to adjust miters, which is the principal problem you'll encounter in picture-frame trim. Another annoying glitch occurs when the miter fits fine but one side of the joint isn't flush with the other. You can sand it flush, of course, but sanding scratches the wood and leaves an undesirable surface texture that stain and a clear finish only emphasize. If you're going to paint, it doesn't matter, but a profiled molding that's oversanded will lack crispness. A cleaner way to flush up a mismatched joint is to trim the high side with a sharp paring chisel. This technique leaves a smooth surface suitable for stain or varnish.

When I split a piece of casing, I remove it and cut a new piece. A split always gets worse. Small splits open up and smile at the client six months after the painter filled and sanded them. I find I can cut down on splits by blunting the point of the nail with a hammer before nailing. The blunt point pushes the wood ahead of it rather than pushing it aside. Cutting the points off the nails with wire cutters does the job, too. In extremely hard wood, I drill a pilot hole slightly larger than the nail shank. Otherwise the board may still split when the head of the nail is set, or when the board shrinks tightly around the nail. Another trick is to use a nail as the drill bit. It drills a perfect-sized hole. Simply snip off the nail's head and chuck it into your drill.

Cutting a perfect miter

A miter is a joint formed by two pieces of molding each cut at an angle. Usually, the mitered parts are cut at a 45° angle, half of the right angle formed by the joint. But there are instances when greater or lesser angles are called for.

Miters are commonly used when the moldings are of the same thickness and profile, where no great structural strength is needed and where hiding the end grain is desirable. Typical applications are picture-frame window casings and door casings, but the methods described here are applicable to baseboard miters too.

If you know that the joint will be a right angle, as most are—or are at least supposed to be—the miter angle is simple: 45°. In the real world, however, where window and door openings are generally out of square and walls often lean away from perfect plumb, a miter is usually slightly larger or smaller than 45°. For a joint other than a right angle, however, the most

reliable way of calculating the miter angle is to bisect the joint geometrically, as shown in the drawing at right. You can then transfer this angle to your workpiece (and eventually the chopsaw) with a bevel gauge.

The first step in making a miter is layout, which is done with a miter square and sharp pencil, as shown in the drawing below left. With a square positioned next to the blade, check the chopsaw for square in the vertical plane. To test the 45° settings, cut two scrap pieces and position them as in a finished miter. They should form a perfect right angle. If they don't, adjust the chopsaw by half the amount of the error and try again. Some carpenters set the chopsaw at 45¼°, figuring they'll be trimming the miter anyway. I try to set the saw as close to 45° as I can because I'm trying to create a reliable reference cut.

My chopsaw's table gets pretty chewed up so I put on a new ¼-in. plywood or pine liner when I start a job. Then I make a cut at 90° and at both 45° settings, cutting three crisp kerfs. Aligning the pencil or knifed lines on my molding with the kerf's edge lets me judge precisely the position of the cut. I try to align the molding so the blade's kerf is on the waste side of the line. If you split the line or saw opposite the waste side, the mitered part will be a half or full-kerf width too short.

To make a clean chopsaw cut, keep the work stationary. Hold the molding firmly against the fence with your thumb. Start the saw and

Bisecting a miter angle

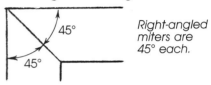

Right-angled miters are 45° each.

Odd-angled or curved casings

First, draw angled parts full size on paper, plywood or particleboard.

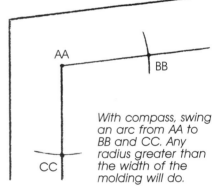

With compass, swing an arc from AA to BB and CC. Any radius greater than the width of the molding will do.

Next, swing arcs from BB and CC.

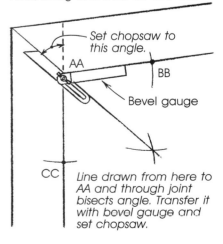

Set chopsaw to this angle.

Bevel gauge

Line drawn from here to AA and through joint bisects angle. Transfer it with bevel gauge and set chopsaw.

Miter marking

Make tick mark first.

Use a miter square to mark face for 45° cut.

To cut the miter, align tick mark with kerf in chopsaw's table. Cut to the waste side of the line.

If for some reason you must remove a piece of casing or reposition it to put some spring into a joint, don't try to pull out the nails with the claw of the hammer. The best method is to drive the nails all the way through with a straight pin punch. Since this doesn't force the nail heads back out of the finished side, you can save the molding for reuse.

Stool-and-apron trim

Even though most of the joints are butted, trimming a stool-and-apron window is more time-consuming than trimming a picture-frame window. If the head and side casings are of identical molding they can, of course, be mitered. But doing so negates the principal advantage of stool-and-apron, which is to combine different mold-

wait for the motor to reach full speed before smoothly lowering the blade into the workpiece to complete the cut. Don't move the wood until the saw has stopped, or you risk marring the work as the saw returns to the up position. Be sure to wear safety glasses and ear protection and check the saw's guard for proper operation.

In casing a window, I usually make one reference cut and then cut the molding to length, testing the fit. "Fit" means that the miter

closes tightly with the casing positioned to produce a consistent reveal. A tight miter rarely happens on the first try, so I make minor adjustments in the miter angle by placing small wedges between the work and the chopsaw's fence, as shown in the photo below. By "small" I mean thicknesses ranging from folded paper to scrap bits of Formica.

How to decide on wedge thickness? I do it by test-assembling the joint and forming a

mental picture of any gaps. The wedges are then positioned between the fence and the molding so when the saw cuts, it will remove material opposite the gap.

If the joint is open but parallel despite compensating cuts, the molding is probably warped or twisted or the drywall or framing is out of true. Back-cutting, as with the butt joint, will remove some material behind the joint line, allowing the surfaces to mate. To make the back-cut, place a wedge

Adjusting a miter angle

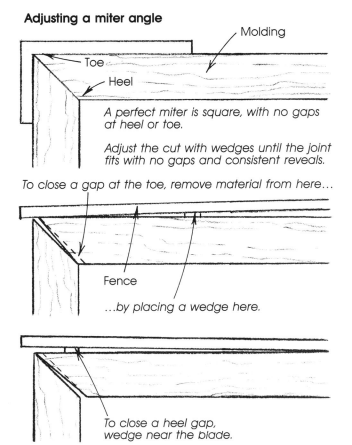

Molding

Toe

Heel

A perfect miter is square, with no gaps at heel or toe.

Adjust the cut with wedges until the joint fits with no gaps and consistent reveals.

To close a gap at the toe, remove material from here...

Fence

...by placing a wedge here.

To close a heel gap, wedge near the blade.

To adjust miter cuts, place wedges between the fence or sawtable and the molding to vary the cutting angle. This is faster than changing the saw's angle of cut.

ings for visual variety. Head and side casings of different shapes or sizes must be joined with butt joints.

Assuming butt joints are to be used, a couple of critical design decisions must be made before starting work. The stool has horns that extend along the wall, usually by a dimension equal to the amount the stool extends beyond the face of the casing, as shown in the drawing at left on p. 88. This dimension is typically ¼ in. to ¾ in. but can vary according to the molding being used. Normally, the head casing is the same overall length as the stool, which means that the head casing also overhangs the side casings by ¼ in. to ¾ in. Again, you can alter this to suit the molding you're using.

under the molding, between the workpiece and the saw table. It's common to usc wcdgcs in both planes at the same time to achieve a good fit.

You can trim a miter with a chisel or plane, as shown in the photo below. Usually, only about a ¹⁄₆₄-in. to ¹⁄₁₆-in. tapered section of wood needs to removed in order to fit a miter. I carry a block plane, with which I can trim the heel or toe of a miter without going back to the chopsaw. Back-cutting—

relieving the back edge of a joint to achieve a better fit—can also be done with a block plane, especially in cases where only a small amount of material has to be removed.

Although it may sound crude, rasps and files will also trim miters. In skilled hands any tool can work. It's the finished joint that counts.

I don't use a wooden miter box very often. Nevertheless, the wooden miter box is a useful tool

and is worth mentioning briefly. The drawing below shows how the box is set up. It can be made of any scrap wood but a hardwood like maple works best. With the molding held firmly against the side of the box farthest from you, start a miter cut with series of short strokes, pushing the saw away from you. Once the cut is started, complete it with full, normal saw strokes. To vary the miter angle slightly, use the wedge method described above.

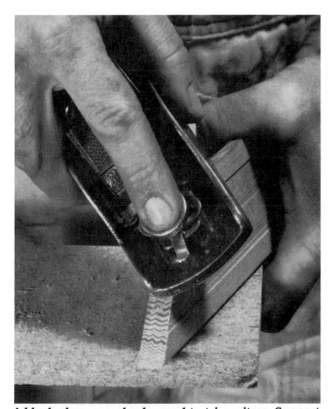

A block plane can also be used to trim miters. Support the molding on a bench or sawhorse and angle the plane across the cut.

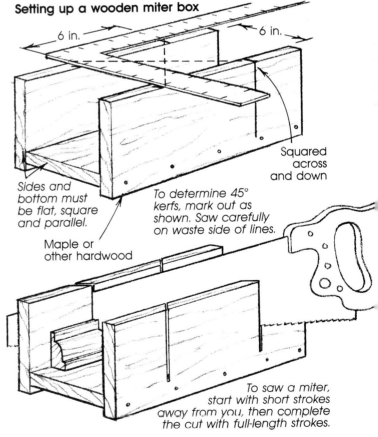

Setting up a wooden miter box

6 in.

6 in.

Squared across and down

Sides and bottom must be flat, square and parallel.

To determine 45° kerfs, mark out as shown. Saw carefully on waste side of lines.

Maple or other hardwood

To saw a miter, start with short strokes away from you, then complete the cut with full-length strokes.

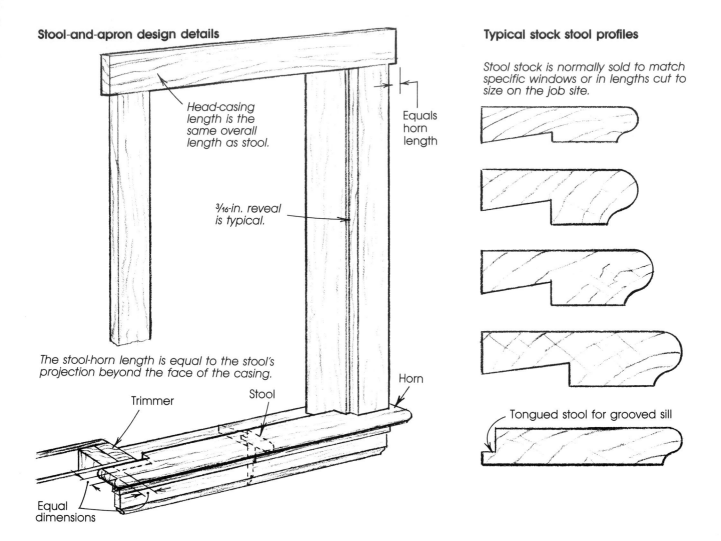

Stool-and-apron design details

Head-casing length is the same overall length as stool.

³⁄₁₆-in. reveal is typical.

Equals horn length

The stool-horn length is equal to the stool's projection beyond the face of the casing.

Trimmer

Stool

Horn

Equal dimensions

Typical stock stool profiles

Stool stock is normally sold to match specific windows or in lengths cut to size on the job site.

Tongued stool for grooved sill

Most lumberyards sell premade stool cap in several profiles, as shown in the drawing above right. They're sold in lengths that correspond to standard window sizes or in longer sections that you cut to length yourself. Traditionally, an angled rabbet was milled into the bottom of the stool so it could fit snugly over the angled sill and still remain level. But as I explained earlier, many modern windows have a flat sill so the stool just butts against the sill, essentially like an oversize jamb extension. Windows with flat sills are sometimes sold with stools that mate to the sill with a tongue-and-groove joint.

Depending on the windows, there are a couple of ways to go about installing stool-and-apron trim. If the window requires jamb extensions, the stool is installed first, just as though it were an extension of the sill. Then the head extension is installed, followed by the side extensions, which "snap" between the stool and head extension. On windows with angled sills, you need to use a stool with an angled rabbet. More likely though,

the window will have a flat sill so the stool can just butt (or tongue and groove, if it's a factory-supplied stool) into the sill. If the jambs are flush with the drywall and no extensions are needed, the stool is still installed first. In this case, however, the stool either butts directly to the sill or is installed on top of it.

Fitting the stool—Begin by cutting the stool to the finished length. This length is equal to the inside distance between the jambs, plus twice the width of the side casing, plus twice the reveal, plus the amount the stool extends beyond the side casing, as described above. Next mark centerlines on both the stool edge and the window frame, as shown in the drawing on the facing page. To establish the horn lengths, hold the stool against the wall at sill level. With your centerlines aligned, place a combination square against the stool and push its blade tight to the exposed trimmer. Scribe a line across the stool, as shown in the drawing. These lines establish the horn lengths.

Scribing and fitting the stool

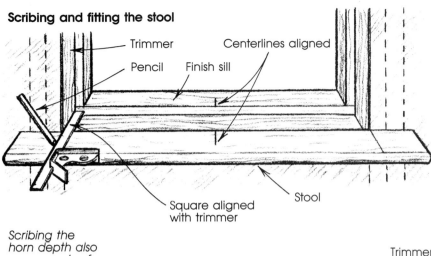

Trimmer

Centerlines aligned

Pencil

Finish sill

Square aligned
with trimmer

Stool

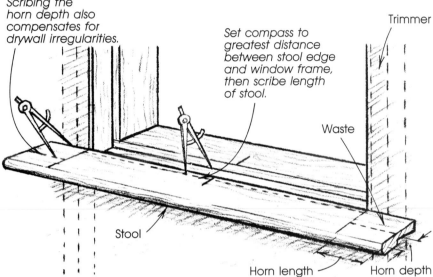

*Scribing the
horn depth also
compensates for
drywall irregularities.*

*Set compass to
greatest distance
between stool edge
and window frame,
then scribe length
of stool.*

Trimmer

Waste

Stool

Horn length

Horn depth

Figuring the horn depth is next. With a compass set to the distance between the inside edge of the jamb sill and the finished drywall (as represented by the edge of the stool), scribe as shown in the drawing above. Occasionally the window frame isn't parallel to the finished wall. If this is the case, set the scribe to the greatest distance between the sill the finished drywall surface. Scribe along the entire length of the stool with the window jamb sill acting as your guide. I cut the horns with a jigsaw. You have a lot of leeway in cutting the horns. When the jamb extensions are installed later, they'll sit on and cover the joint between the stool and the trimmer. Just in case the trimmers aren't square, however, plan to cut inside your scribe lines so you'll have a little extra clearance.

To get a good fit, you may have to plane the mating surface between the stool and the sill or pare the horns where they meet the drywall. With the stool set in the rough opening, I test the fit to see if it is sitting square to the jambs and level in both planes. With the stool

Once the horns have been cut, the stool is fit to the sill. To hold it tightly against the wall, nails are driven through the horn and drywall and into the trimmer. The stool's horns should fit to the wall, with no gaps. (Photo by Jim Hall.)

Apron treatments

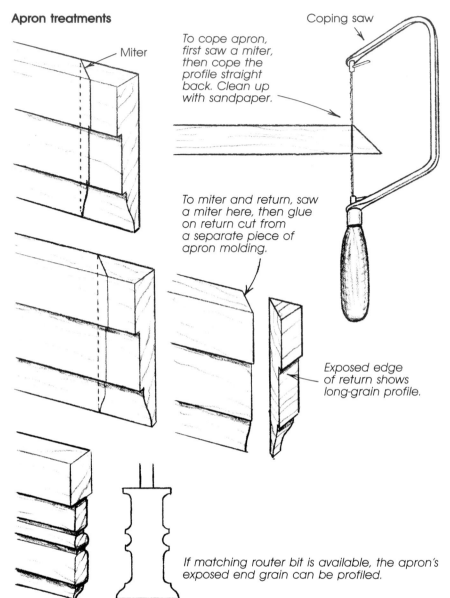

Miter

Coping saw

To cope apron, first saw a miter, then cope the profile straight back. Clean up with sandpaper.

To miter and return, saw a miter here, then glue on return cut from a separate piece of apron molding.

Exposed edge of return shows long-grain profile.

If matching router bit is available, the apron's exposed end grain can be profiled.

This apron has been mitered and returned. Spring clamps hold the returned piece while the glue dries. Returned miters can also be used on casing, crown and base moldings.

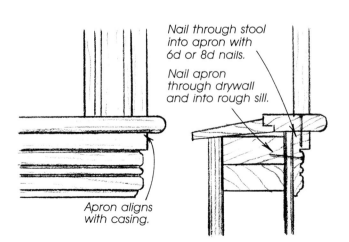

Nail through stool into apron with 6d or 8d nails.

Nail apron through drywall and into rough sill.

Apron aligns with casing.

pushed down tight to the rough sill, your tape (and your eyes) will tell you if the reveal between the top of the stool and the edge of the window frame is consistent. If it's not, you'll have to shim the stool up until it is. If the variation is close to a common plywood thickness, say ¼ in. or ⅜ in., and equal at both ends, I use plywood shims. If the shim space isn't a convenient plywood size or if there are height differences from one side to the other, I use wedged shim pairs. Place the shims so that when you nail through the stool you also penetrate them. If the space between the rough sill and stool is too great for shims, build up the sill with thicker stock, then make fine adjustments with shims.

Once you're satisfied with the reveal and the fit, go ahead and nail the stool. Before doing so, however, the ends of the horns should be shaped in some way. The horns can be rounded off, beveled or shaped to a profile that matches the stool's long edge. The drawing on the facing page shows how the horns can be profiled or even mitered and returned.

I nail through the stool to the rough sill and later, after it's installed, into the apron. Nail the stool with 8d finish nails, 8 in. to 10 in. on center. If I'm trying to hide the nails, I nail where the jamb extensions will cover it, and then blind-nail in the open areas by lifting a wood chip, nailing in the recess, and gluing it back down. On horns more than 3 in. long, I drill a pilot hole and drive an 8d finish nail through the face of the horn, through the drywall and into the trimmer. This nail, positioned 1 in. from the end, keeps the horn from twisting and holds it tight to the wall.

On windows that don't need jamb extensions, you can proceed with casing installation once the stool is nailed down. If jamb extensions are needed, however, install them as shown in the photos on p. 80. Don't forget, though, that the head extension goes on after the stool, followed by the side extensions, which then wedge snugly between the head and the top surface of the stool.

The general method described here works with both flat and angled sills. On angled sills, the stool usually fits right up to the movable sash; it's best to leave a little space so the window will be free to operate. On windows with flat sills, the stool simply butts up the sill, with a reveal. This means that when you're shimming the stool, don't make it flush but adjust to create a reveal of about ⅛ in. to 3/16 in. Windows that don't need jamb extensions should have the stool horns scribed from the inside face of the window jamb, not from the trimmer.

Side casings—A stool-and-apron window that is to have mitered trim can be cased just like a picture-frame window, that is, starting at the top and working down. Instead of a mitered sill casing, though, it will have side casings butted into the surface of the stool. Typically, though, stool-and-apron windows have butted casings the whole way around, so that's what I'll describe here.

Begin casing by cutting a square end on each piece of side-casing stock. These should be a couple of inches longer than the required finished length. Hold one piece in position, square end tight to the stool and aligned with your reveal marks. The casing should mate to the stool with no gaps. If it doesn't, trim as necessary, using a block plane for minor adjustments or the chopsaw-and-wedge method (see pp. 85-87) for larger errors. Hold the piece in place again and mark for the top cut, using your reveal marks to determine the length. To allow for adjustment later, tack the first side jamb in place; then mark, cut and tack the opposite side casing.

After both sides are tacked in place, mark the head casing by measuring the distance between the outside edges of the casing. To this measurement, add twice the head-casing overhang. Another way of determining head-casing length is simply to make it the same as the stool's overall length, horns and all. Position the head casing on top of the side casings, and with your tape, equalize the overhangs. If the butt joints don't fit, remove the side casings and trim as necessary, until the joints are tight and the reveal is constant.

Sometimes the head casing won't lie flat on the wall, because either the wall is twisted or the casing is warped. Some pieces are just too ornery to cooperate so it's best to cut another piece. To help it bridge irregularities in the wall, it's possible (but no fun) to hollow out the back of the head casing with a plane or router. Make sure your hollowing doesn't extend out either end of the piece, though, or it will show. Once the head casing fits, nail it along the jamb edge first, then along the top edge, spacing the nails 10 in. to 14 in. on center. To drive the butt joints together, drive the nails at a downward angle into the rough header. Later, when the house dries out and the joint shrinks apart, you can tap the head piece with a hammer and block, and retighten the joint. That's not possible with a miter joint, which shrinks unequally from top to bottom.

Fitting the apron—The appropriately named apron is a piece placed under the stool to cover the inside edge of the rough framed sill. It also supports the stool and adds visual weight to the bottom of the window. The apron can be made of the same molding as the casing, or it can be of a different profile entirely. However, it probably shouldn't be wider than the casing molding.

Find the apron length by measuring the side casing, outside to outside. This automatically allows for the correct overhang of the stool. Once the apron is cut to length, you have to decide how to finish its ends. There are three choices: profiling, coping or return mitering. The drawing on the facing page shows techniques for all three. If you have the correct router or shaper bit, profiling is the quickest. Simply cut the apron to length, clamp the apron to your bench or sawhorse and rout the profile. Or do it on the router table, using a miter gauge to hold the piece.

Coping and return mitering look the same, except that a coped surface will show end grain and a miter won't. The photo on the facing page shows how a mitered and returned piece is clamped with spring clamps while the glue dries. The spring clamps are available from Woodcraft Supply Co., which is listed in the Resource Guide on pp. 179-181. To get a tight joint between the stool and apron, I plane a slight back-bevel on the top edge of the apron.

To hold the apron tightly against the stool for nailing, I use a "go stick." This is a temporary support sprung between the floor and the bottom of the apron,

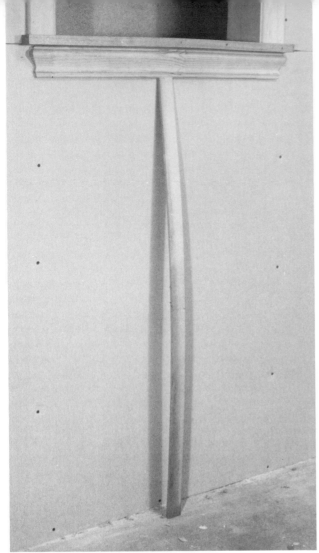

Once the apron is centered beneath the stool, it can be held for nailing with a go stick—a scrap sprung between the floor and the apron. (Photo by Jim Hall.)

as shown in the photo above left. With the apron correctly centered and a go stick or two in place, I nail the apron into the rough sill with 8d finish nails on 10-in. to 14-in. centers. While the go sticks are still wedged tightly, I nail through the stool and into the apron with 6d or 8d finish nails. Setting the nails and filling the holes completes the window.

Variations and unusual situations

So far, I have discussed the basics: simple picture-frame trim and butted stool-and-apron on single windows with rectangular jambs. The real world, however, usually presents the finish carpenter with multiple-choice problems, including cabinet heads, curved head jambs and clients who insist on something out of the ordinary. Here are some tips on how to handle unusual situations.

In butted trimwork, corner blocks are a nice detail. They can be bought commercially or made on site out of the same wood as the rest of the trim.

Corner blocks—One advantage of butted stool-and-apron trim is that corner blocks can be incorporated into the design, much as plinth blocks are used with door casings. You can make your own blocks or buy them (see the Resource Guide on pp. 179-181).

A corner-blocked window is butt-joined, but the blocks themselves are installed after the side casings are installed and before the head casing. As a result, the head casing must fit between the two fixed blocks, not on top of them. It's best to tack the blocks temporarily in place, then fit the head casing, trimming the head as necessary. The photo above right shows some decorative corner blocks.

Corner blocks usually overhang the side casing on both sides, and they're sometimes thicker than the side casing as well. The side overhang can be any dimension that matches the stool overhang, but if the block is thicker than the casings, it should be at least ⅛ in. thicker to look right. Corner blocks are usually nailed with the end grain on the top and the bottom. Be sure to drill a pilot hole for nailing to prevent splits.

Cabinet heads—Cabinet heads are built up of several pieces of molding and give a window a formal, traditional feel. Cabinet heads are usually built in one piece, either on site or in the shop, then installed just like a butted head casing. Simple cabinet heads can be just a molding nailed to the bottom of a flat head casing. More elaborate heads have a series of moldings that rise stair-step style from the bottom toward the top of the head. To produce a finished look, the ends of the moldings are return mitered, as shown in the drawing on the facing page. The Resource Guide on pp. 179-181 gives some sources for premade cabinet heads.

Typical cabinet-head details

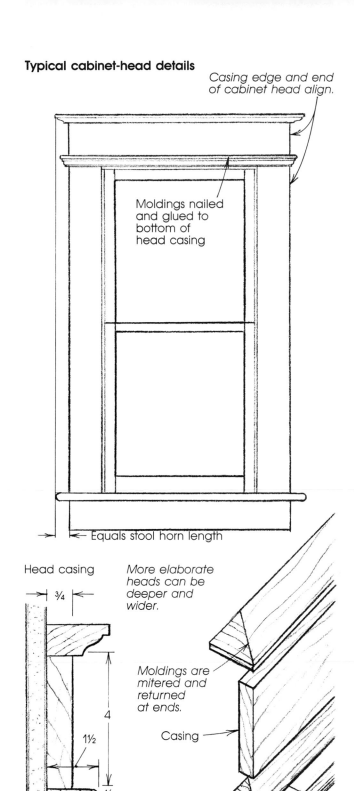

Casing edge and end of cabinet head align.

Moldings nailed and glued to bottom of head casing

← Equals stool horn length

Head casing

¾

More elaborate heads can be deeper and wider.

4

1½

½

1

Moldings are mitered and returned at ends.

Casing

A cabinet head lends a traditional feel to a stool-and-apron window. The cabinet head can be built separately and installed as a unit or built in place on the wall.

Curved heads—Occasionally you may encounter a window with a curved head whose matching curved casing must be mitered to a pair of straight casings. The easiest way to do this is to make a full-sized drawing of the joint on a piece of particleboard or plywood using the moldings as a pattern. On the drawing, scribe across the joint, then transfer the angle with a bevel gauge to your chopsaw and make the cut in the usual way. This method has one disadvantage in that the miter angle it produces, depending on the width and profile of the molding, doesn't always match perfectly because technically the joint should be a slight curve, not a straight line. Sometimes, the mismatch is not noticeable, but if it is, you'll have to experiment, varying the angle until you get an acceptable match.

Because the curved head has no flat edge to use as a reference, you have to eyeball the angle, then cut well away from the line, adjusting the cut to creep up the line. If possible, use wedges between the curved piece and the fence to minimize the chance of its slipping during a cut.

Hanging and trimming a door, the most complex and demanding job the finish carpenter must do, starts with setting and shimming the jamb.

6

Doors

Of all the skills a trim carpenter must have, the ability to hang and trim a door is probably the most important. A correctly installed door hardly draws attention to itself, but each time it's closed, that satisfying thunk is a minor tribute to the craftsman who hung it. A badly hung door, on the other hand, is a constant annoyance. Hinges that creak and bind, bolts that misalign or jambs that stick are a daily reminder of the carpenter's oversight. And they never seem to get fixed, so you have to live with these annoyances.

In some ways, hanging and trimming doors is the finish carpenter's most complex task. The finished door jamb must be plumb and square, an outcome that depends to a large extent on how careful the frame carpenter has been. Hanging and trimming doors quickly takes a lot of practice. But the basics aren't hard to master, and once you understand what happens at each step, I'm sure you'll develop tricks of your own. Most of the skills required for hanging doors also apply to other trimwork, especially windows.

Types of doors

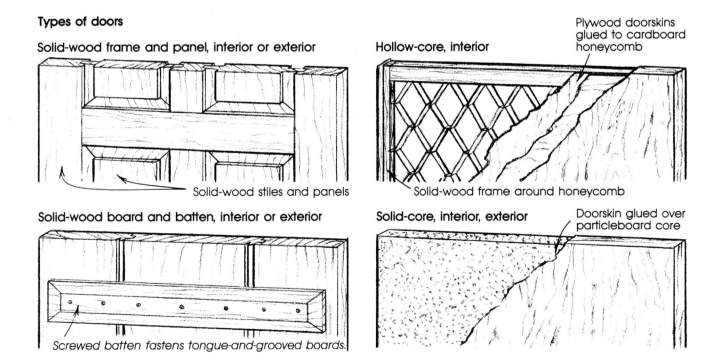

Solid-wood frame and panel, interior or exterior

Solid-wood stiles and panels

Solid-wood board and batten, interior or exterior

Screwed batten fastens tongue-and-grooved boards.

Hollow-core, interior

Plywood doorskins glued to cardboard honeycomb

Solid-wood frame around honeycomb

Solid-core, interior, exterior

Doorskin glued over particleboard core

Door hanging probably requires more finesse and patience than other aspects of trimwork. In framing, you can whack an aberrant 2x4 into line with hard hammer blows, but this approach won't work when hanging a door. More than once I've found myself removing a particularly ornery door from its hinges just one more time to get a perfect fit—and then one more time after that. Ultimately, the extra effort is worth it, though it doesn't always seem like it when you've removed the door for the fifth time.

How a door fits into its frame

For residential use, there are so many types of doors that it's impossible to describe them all here. The drawing on p. 95 shows some of the major types. Despite the variety, however, the principles that apply to one door usually apply to another. Whether the door is a 16-lb. prehung hollow-core or a 200-lb. mahogany frame-and-panel door, it still hangs from butt hinges screwed to a jamb that's nailed or screwed into a rough opening. Trimming the door's rough opening and then hanging the door are two distinct operations. Further, the actual trimming can be divided into two stages, building the jamb and casing the jamb. Hanging the door itself happens between these two steps. When most carpenters talk about trimming a door, however, they are referring to nailing the casing to the jamb, which occurs after the door is hung.

Door construction begins with the rough framed opening. The drawing on the facing page shows a typical framed opening. Although carpenters may do things a little differently, all rough openings must have generally the same components, namely, a pair of king studs to which trimmers are nailed. In turn, the trimmers support a header, which usually—although not always—bears a share of the roof's structural load. King studs and trimmers are 2x4s or 2x6s while headers are at the least doubled-up 2x8s or 2x10s, often with plywood sandwiched between them, as described on p. 63. Headers can also be solid beams, especially in timber-frame work.

The rough opening is sized to accommodate the door to be installed. Manufactured doors most commonly are sold in standard widths beginning at 2-0 (pronounced "two-oh" and representing a 2-ft. door width) and in 2-in. increments up to 3-0. Widths in between are referred to as two-two, two-four, two-six and so on. It's possible to order a door as narrow as 1-3 or as wide as 4-0, but these sizes are unusual. Most residential door heights are 6-8, or 80 in. Exterior doors are normally 1¾ in. thick and interior doors are 1⅜ in. thick, but these dimensions vary.

A rough opening should be sized so it's the width of the door plus twice the thickness of each jamb leg plus ¾ in. The extra ¾ in. allows for ⅜ in. of shim space on either side of the door between the jamb and trimmer

studs. Some carpenters prefer a ½-in. space for shims, which works just as well. Since most doors are 80 in. high, the rough opening will need to be 80 in. plus the thickness of the head jamb, plus ⅜ in. for shims, plus an allowance for the carpet, wood flooring or tile thickness. A safe rough-opening height is 84 in. If more clearance is required, you can always trim the bottom of the door.

The door jamb is the frame that lines the rough opening. It covers the crude 2x4 framing with a finished surface. A door jamb has two vertical legs called side jambs and one head jamb, which spans the side jambs horizontally at the top of the opening. The side jamb that carries the hinges is called the hinge jamb. The opposite jamb is called the lock jamb or strike jamb. The hinges screw into the hinge jamb and take the weight of the door. On a heavy door, the door's hinges are actually screwed through the hinge jamb and into the trimmer so even though the hinge jamb appears to be holding the door's weight, the trimmer is really doing all the work.

Jambs can be bought or made on site out of any clear, straight-grained wood. White pine is a favorite material for paint-grade work, but you'll also see fir and lauan. A jamb is from ¾ in. to 1 in. thick and just slightly wider (about 1/16 in.) than the thickness of the finished wall into which it's set. Door casings are the moldings that tie the jamb to the wall, visually and physically. Casings create the "picture-frame" effect that defines the door. Because they are more prominent than baseboards and crown moldings, door and window casings have great impact on the feel and look of a room.

Besides their decorative job, casings also serve a structural purpose. They act as a gusset or connecting plate that ties the door jamb to the trimmer stud, reinforcing what would otherwise be the jamb's flimsy, exposed edge. This is especially important at the strike plate, where the casing helps transmit the impact of a slammed door from the jamb to the trimmer, which is stiffer and better able to absorb the blow.

You can buy jambs in which the door comes already hung, complete with hinges and prebored for lock sets. There's nothing wrong with prehung doors, although some people think they're cheap and flimsy. I favor factory doors with separate jambs primarily because I can pick the style of casing I want rather than having to accept what comes with the door. The methods for setting prehung doors don't really differ much from conventional door hanging, so the photos in this chapter show both kinds.

The discussion thus far applies to both interior and exterior doors. There are a few differences worth mentioning, however. An exterior door's rough opening is similar to an interior door's rough opening, but exterior jambs are usually wider and thicker than interior jambs, especially in cold climates, where 2x6 framing

Exterior and interior jambs

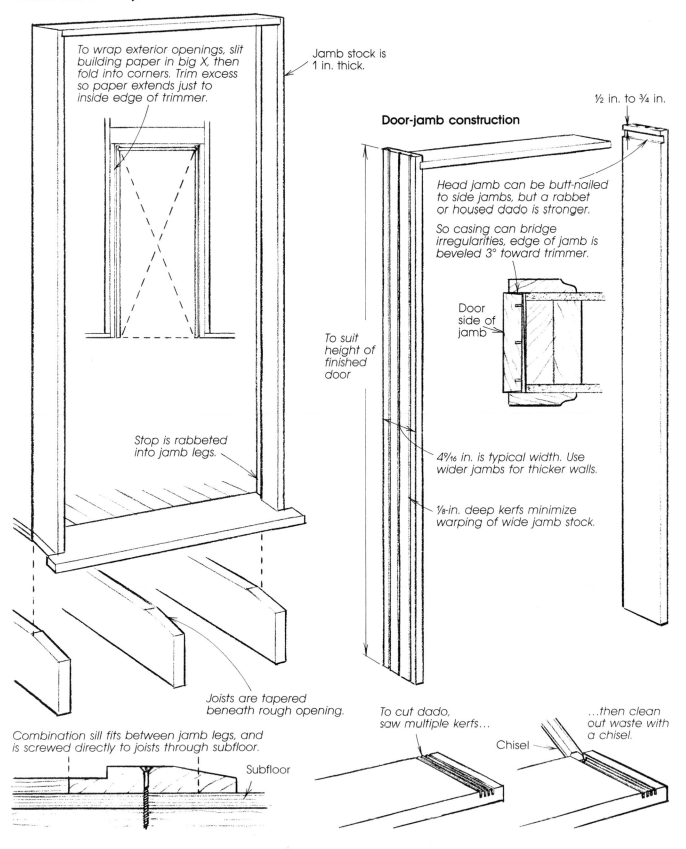

To wrap exterior openings, slit building paper in big X, then fold into corners. Trim excess so paper extends just to inside edge of trimmer.

Jamb stock is 1 in. thick.

½ in. to ¾ in.

Door-jamb construction

Head jamb can be butt-nailed to side jambs, but a rabbet or housed dado is stronger.

So casing can bridge irregularities, edge of jamb is beveled 3° toward trimmer.

Door side of jamb

To suit height of finished door

Stop is rabbeted into jamb legs.

4⁹⁄₁₆ in. is typical width. Use wider jambs for thicker walls.

⅛-in. deep kerfs minimize warping of wide jamb stock.

Joists are tapered beneath rough opening.

Combination sill fits between jamb legs, and is screwed directly to joists through subfloor.

Subfloor

To cut dado, saw multiple kerfs...

...then clean out waste with a chisel.

Chisel

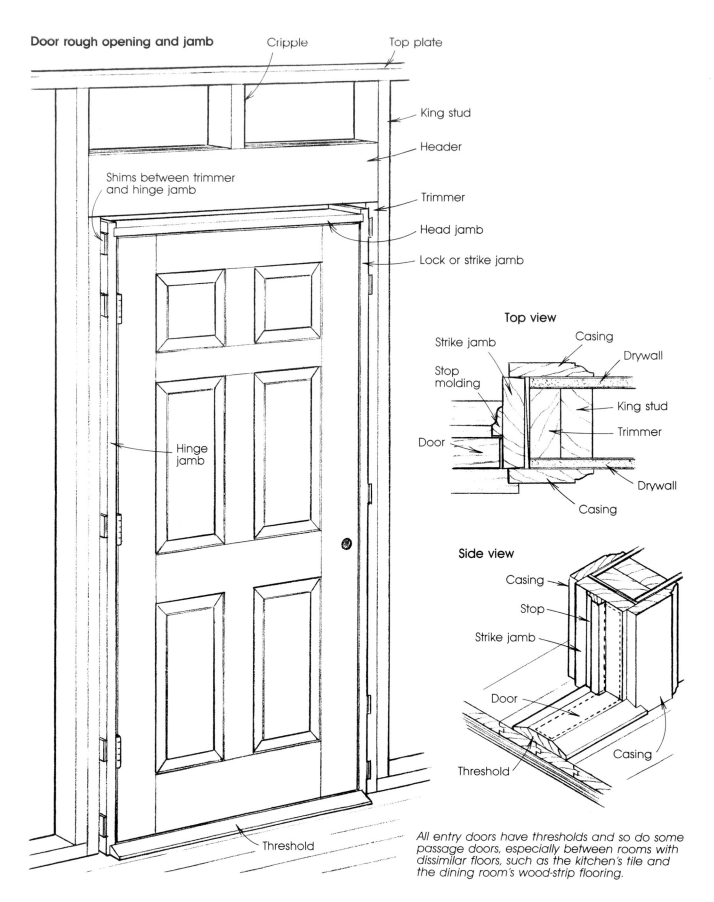

Door rough opening and jamb

Cripple

Top plate

King stud

Header

Shims between trimmer and hinge jamb

Trimmer

Head jamb

Lock or strike jamb

Hinge jamb

Threshold

Top view

Strike jamb

Casing

Drywall

Stop molding

King stud

Trimmer

Door

Drywall

Casing

Side view

Casing

Stop

Strike jamb

Door

Threshold

Casing

All entry doors have thresholds and so do some passage doors, especially between rooms with dissimilar floors, such as the kitchen's tile and the dining room's wood-strip flooring.

is common. A 1-in. thick jamb provides better protection against both the weather and intruders. As a further security measure and weather stop, doorstops are rabbeted into exterior jambs instead of being nailed on, as they are on interior jambs. Also, an exterior door's trimmers should be wrapped with builder's felt, or better yet, one of the high-tech building wraps like Tyvek. This will keep the wind from blowing water behind the exterior casing and into the house.

In older houses, the subfloor was cut away beneath the rough opening of an exterior door and the joists were tapered to accept the door sill. You still see this done occasionally, but it's much more common to use a combination sill and threshold, which is nailed to the bottom of the jamb legs and screwed through to the subfloor without tapering the joists. The drawing on the facing page shows the two methods. Casings on exterior doors are essentially the same as those for interior doors, except that they're occasionally fastened with more nails as a security precaution and caulked to stop drafts.

Getting started: which hand is which?

In a new house, door hanging happens when construction is fairly well along. Before the trim carpenter can begin door hanging, the windows will be set and the drywall will be hung, taped and sanded and perhaps painted. It doesn't much matter if the finish floor is installed—door hanging can proceed before or after this operation. I prefer to have the floors installed after the doors are trimmed so I don't have to worry about scuffing the floors. If carpet is the final floor, I always try to hang the door before the carpet is installed because it's a pain to have to clean up the mess that door hanging makes.

Once the rough openings have been checked and corrected, as described on pp. 64-67, the jambs can be installed. But first, you need to decide on door handing. Handing refers to which side of the jamb the hinges and lock set are located on and, consequently, which direction the door swings. You'd think that this would be a simple matter, but it isn't. Every year I'm in the construction business I learn a new rule to determine handing.

There are really two conventions that establish door handing, one for prehung doors and one for lock sets. For prehung doors, the rules are simple. Imagine the door set into its rough opening with the hinge barrel visible to you. If the barrel is on your left, the door is a left hand; if on it's on the right, it's just the opposite. Easy enough. If you're hanging the door in a jamb of your own construction, the handing will be determined by the lock set. When ordering a mortise lock set, the catalog will present you with four possibilities: right, left, right-hand reverse and left-hand reverse. If you stand facing the door from the outside (the "public side,"

i.e., a hall) and the door swings into the room and away from you, the side that has the hinges is the hand of the door. Order a left-hand lock set if they're on the left. If the hinges are on the left but the door swings toward you, it's a left-hand reverse. Although these conventions are supposed to be universal, it's best to double-check them with the salesman when ordering locks and hinges. Make sure your handing definitions agree.

Confusion about handing always seems to cause problems unrelated to the door itself. Light switches have an uncanny way of ending up behind doors, so it is important to understand handing before you hang the door. For reasons that escape me, exterior doors in the United States swing into the house but in Europe they swing out. My wife, who is Swedish, argues that an outswinging door is compressed more tightly to its stop by the wind, thereby creating a more weatherpoof seal. I respond that it's harder to bolt an outswinging door against intruders. She counters that in emergencies, an outswinging door is safer. Maybe it is, but I can't find outswinging hardware anyway and in the U.S., people just aren't accustomed to outswinging doors, except on commercial buildings, where codes sometimes require them.

Building and installing jambs

With handing decided, you can move on to installing the jambs. I have already mentioned prehung doors, which come with their own jambs and, in some instances, with casings already attached. These are discussed later in this chapter but since I don't use prehung doors very often, I'll concentrate on explaining how to hang high-quality factory or custom-made doors, which don't usually have their own jambs. This presents you with two choices: buy the jambs or make them.

Most commercially made jambs consists of ¾-in. stock, usually pine, fir, hemlock or poplar. Some years back, manufacturers of trim figured that they could minimize waste by finger-jointing together short scraps, and you'll often see paint-grade door jambs made this way. Finger-jointed stock is perfectly suited to the task, as long as it will be painted to hide the variations in color and grain. Standard jamb stock is as wide as an interior wall's thickness, or about 4⁹⁄₁₆ in. This width allows for the width of a 2x4 plus ½-in. drywall on either side. Wider jamb stock is available for thicker walls.

Jamb stock usually has kerfs or grooves milled into its backside. The grooves relieve stresses in the wood and prevent warping and twisting. Also, the edges of the jamb are beveled 3° toward the trimmer, which makes it easier to install casing over slight irregularities in the wall.

Jamb stock is sold in kits or in fixed lengths, which you can cut to length yourself. Kits consist of two side jambs and a head jamb to match the width of the door you'll be using. The head jamb's length should be such that the jamb's interior width is $\frac{5}{32}$ in. wider than the door going into it. This allows a clearance of $\frac{3}{32}$ in. on the latch side plus $\frac{1}{16}$ in. on the hinge side. Some carpenters use a nickel to measure the gap on the strike jamb and a dime for the hinge side.

In the plainest carpentry, the head jamb is joined to the side jambs by a nailed butt joint. Jamb kits, however, are a step up, and are rabbeted at the top to accept the head jamb. Jambs are fastened with 6d casing nails driven through the back of the side jambs and into the end grain of the head jamb. In either case, the jamb is nailed together as a unit, then installed in the rough opening. To hold the assembled jamb rigid during handling, a spreader made from a scrap should be nailed so it bridges the inside of both side jambs. Size the spreader to maintain the correct inside jamb dimension. The top photo on the facing page shows one kind of spreader that is especially useful for assembling the jamb.

I sometimes make my own jamb stock. I use clear, straight-grained wood, pine or poplar. To reduce warping, I kerf the back of the stock with three $\frac{1}{8}$-in. deep saw cuts spaced 1 in. apart. I generally connect the side jamb to the head jamb with a housed dado joint, which is a little stronger than a rabbet. If I'm making only one or two jambs, I cut the dado with a circular saw by setting the depth of the saw equal to half the thickness of the jamb stock. I saw just shy of the layout lines, then pare to the lines with a sharp chisel. If I am making more than two jambs, I set up to cut dadoes on the radial-arm saw, but you could also use a table saw or a router.

As with commercial jamb stock, the jamb legs should be at least as wide and perhaps a little wider than the wall is thick. For a standard 2x4 wall with $\frac{1}{2}$-in. drywall, $4\frac{9}{16}$ in. to $4\frac{5}{8}$ in. or a bit more works fine. It's better to have the jamb stand $\frac{1}{16}$ in. proud of the drywall and have to plane it flush rather than having to flush up the drywall to the jamb, a messy job. Bevel the jamb edges toward the trimmer by ripping the jamb stock at a slight angle or by hand planing the wood before the jamb is assembled. For a light door, $\frac{3}{4}$-in. thick stock is plenty. Heavier doors, such as main entry doors, should have 1-in. or thicker jambs.

When figuring the length of the head jamb, I'm careful to allow for the depths of the dadoes so that the jamb's interior dimensions will be correct. A jamb can be nailed, but I prefer screws. They hold better than nails and since I have my screw gun and drills already set up to do the hinges and lock sets, it's simple to drive screws. In hardwood, I predrill three equally spaced holes across the width of the joint, centering the screws in the thickness of the head jamb. In pine or fir, I drive the screws without preboring. I use a screw that will penetrate the head jamb's end grain at least $1\frac{1}{4}$ in.

The door stop, or stop molding, is the surface against which the door closes. It's applied to the jamb surface after the jamb is built and the door is hung. If the jambs are thick enough, the stop can be rabbeted right into side and head jambs. The stop takes the punishment of the door being slammed and makes a tight seal against sound and weather. Although there's no hard-and-fast rule, an applied stop is used on most interior doors, while exterior doors get rabbeted stops. You can buy stop-molding kits that consist of three pieces of stop premitered to fit into the jamb, or you can buy lengths of stop molding and cut and fit them yourself. It's also fun to make your own stop molding, using a decorative profile that matches trim elsewhere in the room.

Setting the jamb—Once the jamb is built, it's ready to install. Make sure the jamb has a spreader, as described above, before attempting to set it into the opening. Since the jamb's outside dimensions are a little narrower than the rough opening, the jamb fits loosely into the opening. The space between the jamb and rough trimmers will be taken up with wooden shims. I try to get the jamb as plumb, level and square as I can, but if a minor discrepancy occurs, the method I use to hang the door will mask it.

The first step in jamb setting is to decide where the head jamb will be positioned. If the job isn't particularly exacting, I eyeball a $\frac{1}{4}$-in. gap between the top of the head jamb and the bottom of the header. This leaves enough room to maneuver the head jamb up or down to get it level and square to the hinge jamb. If I am working to very exact standards, say, where the casing has to line up with adjacent door or window casing or when a number of identical doors will have the same trim, I mark the height of the head jamb on a story pole (see pp. 76-77) and then use the pole to mark the trimmer. Then all I have to do is line up my mark with the bottom of the head jamb.

With the height of the head jamb set, I'm ready for shimming. I'm particular about shims. When I can get them, I try to use manufactured shims made expressly for the purpose, not cedar shingles the roofer left behind, which tend to split too easily. Given the choice, I like pine shims because they cut easily across the grain without splitting. Once the jamb is installed, the projecting shims have to be sawn flush to the wall, and it's very frustrating to have them split and fall out. If you're industrious, you can bandsaw your own shims from pine scrap.

I begin by shimming the side jambs near the top, or right at the head jamb. I do the same thing at the bottom, wedging the spreader tight in the opening between shims on both the hinge side and the strike side. At this point, I am not concerned about plumb, but I do consider the height of the jamb legs above the floor. If the finished floor is installed—hardwood floor

Until it is nailed into the rough opening, a jamb is relatively fragile. At top, an adjustable spreader is used to hold the jambs during assembly. For installation, another spreader will be temporarily nailed across the jamb legs at floor level, as shown above. The hinge side of the jamb is set first by shimming at the head jamb and at the spreader, as shown at left.

Setting and plumbing the jamb

Step 1

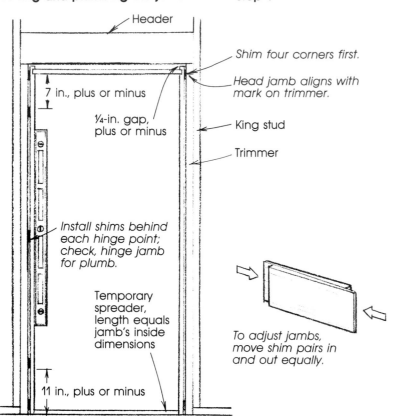

Header

Shim four corners first.

Head jamb aligns with mark on trimmer.

7 in., plus or minus

¼-in. gap, plus or minus

King stud

Trimmer

Install shims behind each hinge point; check, hinge jamb for plumb.

Temporary spreader, length equals jamb's inside dimensions

11 in., plus or minus

To adjust jambs, move shim pairs in and out equally.

Step 2

Jamb should be square to wall.

Jamb   Drywall

Step 3

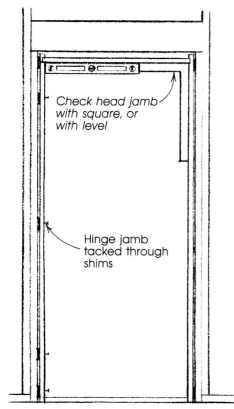

If head jamb is level and hinge jamb is plumb, they're square to each other.

Check head jamb with square, or with level

Hinge jamb tacked through shims

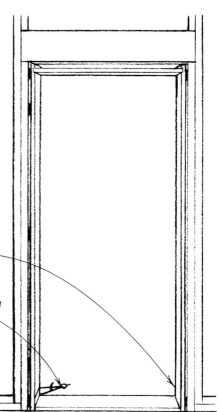

Raise and lower strike jamb until head jamb is level, then shim it plumb and straight before nailing.

If strike jamb seems too long or too short to allow head to be leveled, scribe and trim hinge or strike jamb so both sit flat on floor with head jamb level.

or carpet—simply butt the bottom of the jamb leg to the floor. If the floor is yet to come, use a scrap of flooring to gauge how high the jamb leg should be held above the rough floor. Carpet mechanics can trim right up to the jamb so if there's no carpet yet, hold the jamb legs to within ¼ in. of the rough floor. If the floor is irregular, I scribe the bottom of the jamb and trim it to a perfect fit.

With the jamb wedged at the head and at the spreader, I install wedges directly behind the point where the door's top hinge will be. Refer to the drawing on the facing page to determine this dimension, then measure down from the head jamb and mark the rough center of the hinge. Tack the shims in place with an 8d casing nail driven through the jamb. I center the nail across the width of the jamb by eye. It will later be covered by the stop. Don't set the nails yet because you might need to remove them to adjust the shims.

Before nailing, check that the side jambs' width is centered in the thickness of the wall. Ideally, the jamb will protrude 1/32 in. or more proud of the drywall, but of course this rarely happens. Check by laying a straightedge on the wall across the edge of the jamb, and do your best to split any differences so the jamb protrudes evenly. Also, check to see that the jamb's face makes a right angle with the face of the wall. I use a square for this test, as shown in Step 2 of the drawing on the facing page.

Next, use a 6-ft. level to test the hinge jamb for plumb in the plane perpendicular to the opening. You might have to lean on the level to push out a bow in the jamb, a problem some carpenters overcome by tapping equal-sized wooden blocks at both ends of the level. The blocks bridge the bow but still give an accurate reading at the top and bottom of the jamb. Adjust the jamb for plumb by moving the shims in or out at the bottom. When it's plumb, install wedges behind the bottom hinge point. Lightweight doors have only two hinges; heavier ones have three, four or five hinges. Position shims behind each hinge. Adjust the shims in and out to get the hinge jamb perfectly straight. At this point, the hinge jamb should be plumb, straight and perpendicular to the face of the wall.

The head jamb must now be set square to the hinge jamb. I check it with a carpenter's square, but you could just as easily use a level, relying on the fact that if the hinge jamb is plumb and the head jamb level, they're perpendicular to each other. Using the level, however, there's a slight chance that a minutely out-of-plumb hinge jamb will result in an out-of-square condition. With the square, I'm certain the the inside of the jamb is exactly square, which is more important than its being exactly plumb.

Since the hinge jamb is now firmly nailed, the head jamb must be adjusted by moving the strike jamb. I start by shimming the bottom of the strike jamb, moving it up or down until a square indicates that the

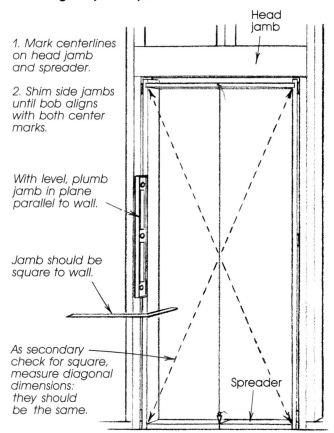

1. Mark centerlines on head jamb and spreader.

2. Shim side jambs until bob aligns with both center marks.

With level, plumb jamb in plane parallel to wall.

Jamb should be square to wall.

As secondary check for square, measure diagonal dimensions: they should be the same.

Head jamb

Spreader

head jamb is square to the hinge jamb. To lock the head jamb in place, I place shims near the top of the strike jamb and tack them. If I've set the hinge jamb and head jamb correctly, the strike jamb must also be parallel and plumb. All I need to do is shim it straight. Again, the number of shims depends on the weight of the door. At a minimum, place shims at the top and bottom and above and below the strike plate. Shims near the strike plate buttress the jamb against impact from slamming. Check the side jambs one last time for straightness, and make sure they are square to the plane of the wall. You can now nail the strike jamb. Finally, shim the head jamb straight (if it isn't already) and nail it.

Sometimes out-of-level floors make it impossible to get the head jamb perfectly level because the jambs appear to be too long or too short. If this is the case, scribe and trim the bottom of either the hinge jamb or the strike jamb until both sit flat on the floor and the head jamb is level.

Two more jamb methods—Every carpenter has some tricks for setting jambs. One clever method, shown in the drawing above, is to level and shim the head jamb

A shopmade sheet-metal clamp holds the door against the jamb for scribing. The drawing below shows how the clamp is made.

Shopmade door clamp

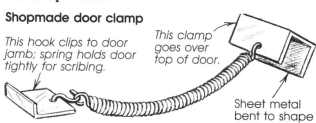

This hook clips to door jamb; spring holds door tightly for scribing.

This clamp goes over top of door.

Sheet metal bent to shape

The door buck is one way of holding a door for planing. This door buck has been padded with carpet to keep it from marring the door.

first, then hang a plumb bob from a centerline struck on the edge of the head jamb. By aligning the tip of the plumb bob with a centerline struck across the spreader board, you know that the four corners are equidistant from the centerline and the jamb is therefore square. Furthermore, if the the header is level, the jambs are perpendicular and therefore plumb. Tap the shims in and out until you get the bob centered, then lock the jambs in place and straighten the side jambs, as described above.

Another jamb-setting technique that is popular in California uses no shims at all. Instead, the jamb is made first, and then the rough opening is constructed to exactly the outside dimensions of the jamb, allowing it to be nailed without shims. In order for this method to work, the framers must erect the walls with the king studs in place but with no trimmers, which are left to the trim carpenter. Also, the framers construct the walls so the sole plate runs right across the bottom of the door openings.

First, the trim carpenter sets one trimmer—it doesn't matter which—by tacking it with 8d nails into the header and the sole plate. The trimmer is plumbed by moving one end in or out, then locking it to the king stud with the clinched-nail method described on p. 63. Once the first trimmer is firmly nailed, the jamb is made in the usual way, allowing for the desired clearance between the door and inside face of the jamb. However, instead of a spreader, a 1x4 gauge block

whose length is equal to the outside width of the jamb is made up. When placed across the rough opening, this gauge block is used to position the second trimmer so that the rough opening will be the exactly the same as the outside width of the jamb. With the gauge placed across the bottom of the opening, the second trimmer is tapped into place and held tightly against the gauge while it's nailed. Next, the gauge is moved to just beneath the header so the top of the trimmer can be positioned and nailed. Because the second trimmer is parallel to the first, it's automatically plumb. All that remains is to insert the jamb, level the head jamb, and nail it in place. No shims are necessary between the jamb and the trimmers but the head jamb should be shimmed immediately behind the points where it's nailed to the rough header.

Just before the jamb is nailed in, the sole plate that spans the bottom of the opening is sawn out, either with a modified circular saw called a sidewinder or with a reciprocating saw.

Hanging the door

Since most of the doors I install aren't prehung, they arrive at the job site in cartons with an equal number of jamb kits. I install them the old-fashioned way, one at a time. There are a lot of "right" ways to hang a door. I've heard my approach called the "California" method, and although carpenters on the East Coast or

The door hanger's bench has clamps to hold the door for planing and holes in the legs for pegs to prop the work at a convenient height. Inside the bench's frame are trays for tools.

in the South might view it skeptically, I believe that any efficient method that produces an acceptable result is fine. In a nutshell, I use a scribe-to-the-opening technique whereby the door is fitted to the jamb before the hinges and lock sets are installed. This way, when the door is hung on its hinges, there is a minimum of planing and fiddling.

Fitting the door is not difficult, though it's sometimes a bit awkward for one person to muscle a heavy door into the jamb. A helper makes things easier. First, place the door against the private edge of the jamb. Since any twisting across the jamb will make one side of the opening a different size from the other, I scribe the door to the side of the jamb the door will actually fit into. To hold the door in place while I scribe, I use a clamp made of two bent pieces of sheet metal with a spring between them, shown in the drawing on the facing page. One part hooks over the door, and the other over the back side of the jamb. As shown in the photo at left on the facing page, the spring pulls the door tight against the face of the jamb.

To allow space for carpeting or flooring that's not yet installed, I wedge the door off the floor until its top edge is just above the inside edge of the head jamb. Once that's done, I center the door horizontally in the opening. Then, with an ordinary pencil (not a carpenter's pencil) held flat against the inside of the jamb, I scribe the jamb's outline onto the door. Held flat, the pencil produces a line just less than 1/8 in. inside the

jamb opening. When I plane the door to size, the next step, I'll plane to within 1/32 in. of the line, resulting in 3/32-in. clearance between the door and the jamb.

Once I'm satisfied with the scribe, I remove the door and clamp it in my door-hanging bench, a temporary door jack, a Workmate® or any other surface that will hold it securely for planing. Professional door hangers use a bench, shown in the photo above right, that's really a complete work station. It's about 6 ft. long and 30 in. wide. The top is covered with carpet scraps so a door can be laid on it without scratching. There's no real tabletop for tools, but there are slats that allow sawdust to fall through and an outlet bar to plug in several hand tools. The legs of the table have holes drilled in them to accept closet rod. The rod is moved up and down to adjust the door that sits on them. The point is to have some way of holding the door securely for marking and mortising. One other way of holding the door is the carpenter's door buck, shown in the photo at right on the facing page.

I use a Porter-Cable power plane to trim to the scribe lines; a sharp jack plane will work just as well, if more slowly. Both sides of the door are beveled; the hinge side to keep the hinges from binding, and the latch side so that it clears the jamb as the door swings open. On the hinge side I set the plane to a 1° bevel with the short side of the bevel toward the public side. On the latch side I set the plane to 5°, with the bevel also to the public side. In both cases, plane down until the

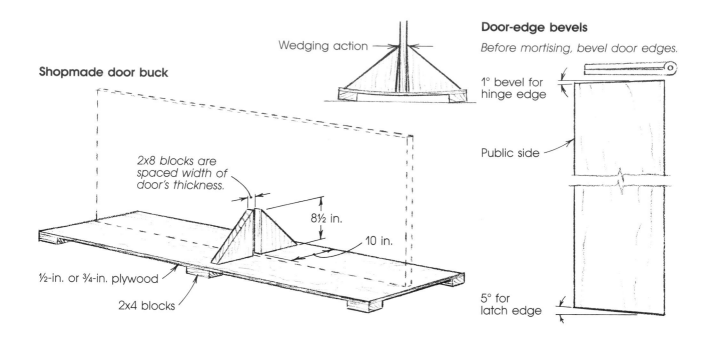

Shopmade door buck

Wedging action

2x8 blocks are spaced width of door's thickness.

8½ in.

10 in.

½-in. or ¾-in. plywood

2x4 blocks

Door-edge bevels

Before mortising, bevel door edges.

1° bevel for hinge edge

Public side

5° for latch edge

To trim small amounts of wood off the end of a door, a cut-off jig is handy. It's made of a straight scrap of ¼-in. plywood; a wooden fence, positioned away from the jig's edge by a dimension equal to the distance between the blade and the edge of the saw's baseplate, guides the cut.

scribe lines disappear, then try the door for fit. As I said earlier, use a nickel for spacing on the strike side, a dime for the hinge side.

Because it's difficult to plane end grain, I cut the top (and the bottom, if it needs it) of the door using a cut-off jig and my circular saw, as shown in the photo at left. The saw is equipped with a planer blade, which minimizes splintering. To use the cut-off jig, you simply place the edge of the jig on the scribe line, clamp it in place and run the saw along the guide. When the door is planed and cut to length I put it back in the opening and test the fit, reinserting the wedges at the door bottom. When you're learning door hanging, it's best to remove a small amount of wood, then test for fit several times. However, if I'm doing several doors and feel up to speed, I go right ahead and install the hinges without checking the fit.

Hinge mortising—As explained on pp. 107-109, butt hinges are the most common type for residential entry and passage doors. (Full-surface or half-surface hinges might be a better choice when a wood door is hung in a steel frame, but these are beyond the scope of this book.) Full-mortise hinges are mortised into both the door and the jamb. These days, there are two ways to do the mortising: by hand with a chisel or by router with or without a template. I'll describe both methods.

The first step is positioning the hinges correctly. The chart on p. 108 shows hinge layouts for various size doors. For a standard 80-in. door, the uppermost edge of the top hinge is mounted 7 in. from the top of the door and the lowermost edge of the bottom hinge 11 in. from the bottom. If the door has three hinges, the middle one is centered between the other two.

In addition to correct vertical alignment, each hinge has to be installed in the door's thickness so that the casing won't interfere with the door's opening to its full 180°. This is called hinge backset, and it's the measurement between the front face of the door's public side and the front of the mortise (the edge opposite the barrel). Backset varies with hinge size and door thickness, but a good rule of thumb is to use backset that will place the hinge barrel flush with the face of the casing. This will allow the door to swing fully open without levering itself off the hinges.

I mark out the hinge mortises with a sharp knife. First, for the backset I mark a pencil line slightly longer than the length of each hinge and about ¼ in. from the public face. This is a good general-purpose backset for ¾-in. thick casing. You'll need more backset for thicker

How to select hinges

The local hardware store or lumberyard is the last place I'll go to buy hinges. In my experience, retail stores stock a limited selection of hinges, and what they do have may be a bit too pricey for the quality. Check the Yellow Pages under the Hardware–Builder's listing. Even a small town will have one or more suppliers of high-quality commercial-grade and architectural-grade hardware. These companies generally deal wholesale to the trade but will sometimes sell over the counter—cash and carry. If you can't find a local supplier, the Resource Guide on pp. 179-181 lists some mail-order sources.

There are dozens of hinge types on the market. It's easy to narrow the choices: virtually all residential doors, passage or entry, are hung on butt hinges. The exceptions are surface-mounted hinges for metal and some wood doors and/or pintle hinges for period reproduction work. Butt hinges are made in several design variations, finishes, sizes and weights. As an alternative to butt hinges, you can buy what are called half-surface and full-surface hinges, but I won't go into detail about them because they aren't often used in residential work. The major manufacturers also make two distinct lines of hinges, one for residential, one for commercial applications. Residental-grade hinges are what you usually find on prehung doors and in most retail hardware stores. I can't say

Types of hinges

Full-mortise

For wooden residential doors hung in wooden jambs, butt hinges are mortised flush with surface of jamb and door edge.

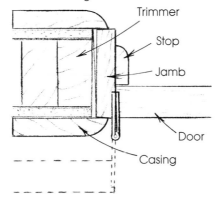

Half-surface

For wooden doors hung in metal jambs, half-surface hinges are attached to surface of door and let into premade mortises in jamb.

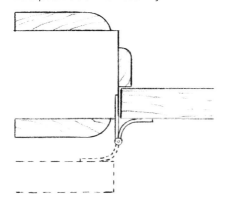

Full-surface

For hollow metal doors and hollow metal jambs, hinge is mounted on surface of both. Jambs and door are usually predrilled and threaded.

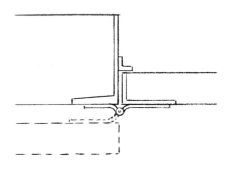

Raised-barrel

For doors set deeply into a wide jamb, raised-barrel hinges allow sufficient clearance for full opening.

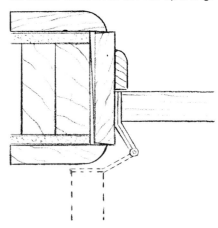

doors or casings. To save measuring at each hinge location, I set my combination square so that ¼ in. of its blade projects, then I use it as a gauge. Next, I hook my tape over the top end of the door and stick the point of my knife in the edge of the door at the 7-in. mark. Without removing the tip, I push the end of the hinge up to the blade, and with the hinge aligned to the backset marks, I scribe lightly around the leaf. I deep-en these scribes using the combination square as a guide. Then I repeat this process to mark the top and center hinges.

To determine the mortise depth, scribe a line on the face of the door, using the hinge as template. One way to speed up marking out is to use a device called a butt gauge, made by Stanley. The butt gauge is a hinge-shaped template with a sharp cutting edge embossed

they're all junk, but I much prefer commercial-grade hardware. Commercial-grade hinges have thicker leaves and a better finish.

In selecting hinges, a number of factors must be considered, including handing, the door and jamb material, the weight and thickness of the door, whether it's an entry door or passage door and how many times the door will be opened and closed each day. The chart at right tells how to take these into account when you shop for hinges.

Full-mortise butt hinges are the usual choice for wooden residential jambs and doors. As described on p. 106, these hinges are mortised flush into both jamb and door. They are also swaged, which means that the leaves are bent in slightly at the barrel so when the hinge is closed, there's a space of about ¹⁄₁₆ in.

For light to medium-weight doors that won't be opened frequently—hollow-core and lightweight frame and panel, for example—plain-bearing butt hinges are suitable. A plain-bearing hinge pivots the door on a steel pin driven through the knuckles of the hinge barrel. The vertical weight of the door is borne by the knuckle surfaces, which are solid brass or brass-plated or chrome-plated steel. A pair of 4-in. commercial plain-bearing hinges costs about $10, and residential-grade hinges usually cost about $5 or $6. The price difference is just too slight to matter, so I always buy commercial-grade hinges.

Heavy doors or those that will see a lot of use should be hung on ball-bearing, full-mortise butt

Determining hinge height and width

Hinge dimensions are always quoted by height followed by width. Height is the dimension parallel to the pin; width is the dimension across both open leaves. Use the chart below to determine height, and the following formula to calculate width. Hinge width = (Door thickness minus backset) × 2, plus required clearance, plus inset (if any). If the calculated total equals a non-standard, use the next standard hinge width.

Door thickness	Door width	Hinge height required
1⅜ in.	to 32 in. over 32 in.	3½ in. to 4 in. 4 in. to 4½ in.
1¾ in.	to 36 in. 36 in. to 48 in. over 48 in.	4½ in.* 5 in.* 6 in.*
2 in. to 2½ in.	to 42 in. over 42 in.	5 in.** 6 in.**

* Doors opened frequently—main entry doors or commercial building doors—should be hung on heavy-duty plain or ball-bearing hinges.
** Use heavy-duty or ball-bearing hinges only.

Calculating hinge width

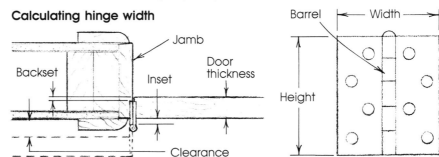

hinges. In these hinges, the vertical load is carried by two or more ball-bearing assemblies pressed into the hinge barrel. Ball-bearing hinges have less vertical and horizontal play and will carry heavier loads than plain-bearing hinges. They'll also last longer. Some ball-bearing hinges have concealed bearings; others have bearings visible as delineated segments in the hinge barrel.

Which hinge you choose is a matter of taste. I happen to like the action of ball-bearing butt hinges so I use them even on light doors. Depending on the size, ball-bearing hinges sell for between $20 and $30 a pair. Regardless of weight, any door that's equipped with an automatic door closer should have ball-bearing hinges.

The major hinge makers, like Stanley and Lawrence Brothers

on one face. It's available in 3-in., 3½-in. and 4-in. lengths. As shown in the photo on p. 110, the gauge is placed against the edge of the door or jamb at the desired location and struck with a hammer, producing a perfect outline of the hinge.

For hand mortising, I rely on my trusty (not rusty) Stanley tang butt chisel, the one that's at least as wide if not wider than the mortise. Start with shallow cross-grain cuts that deepen the knife lines. Make sure the chisel's bevel is toward the waste side of the line, or it will tend to enlarge the mortise beyond the lines. At this point, the chisel cuts shouldn't go to the full depth, just define the line. Next, move the chisel toward the opposite end of the mortise about ¼ in., and with the blade inclined at about 40°, give the chisel a smart whack, driving it the full depth of the mor-

Hardware stores sell inexpensive hinges, such as the butt hinges shown at left. Commercial-grade hinges, although more expensive, are available in ball-bearing models, right. The bearings, shown in the foreground, give the door a smoother action. Note that the hinge pin at right also has a ball-bearing detent to keep it from rising.

Hinge-tip types

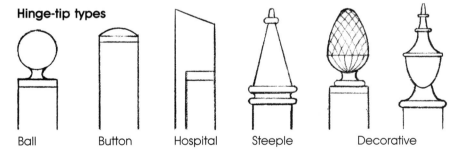

Ball   Button   Hospital   Steeple   Decorative

Inc., sell hinges with several styles of pins. One annoying problem with cheap hinges is that the pins tend to back out or rise as the door is used, occasionally requiring resetting. Better-quality butt hinges can be ordered with non-rising pins fitted with a small, spring-loaded ball-bearing that engages a groove inside the barrel or a knurled section whose friction keeps the pin from backing out.

Sometimes a door has to be hung so it swings out, leaving the barrel on the public side. In these cases, to keep an intruder from gaining access by yanking the pins, buy hinges with non-removable pins (usually abbreviated NRP) held in place with a tiny setscrew. Stanley sells hinges with both non-removable pins and a device called a security stud. The stud is mounted to one leaf and projects into a hole in the mating leaf so the closed door can't be removed, even with the pins out. For a temporary security hinge when NRPs aren't available, remove one screw from each of the hinges on both the jamb and door. Drive 8d finishing nails into the jamb-side holes so they're proud about ⅜ in. When the door closes, the nails will project into the opposite holes, preventing removal of the door even if the pins are taken out.

Pins can be bought with various kinds of tips, as shown in the drawing at left. Flat button tips are considered standard since they fit into practically any kind of decor, but ball tips are a close second. Hospital tips are smoothed over so that bed clothes and gowns won't snag on them. In addition to deciding on pin styles and tips, you can choose butt hinges with either square corners or radiused corners for use with hinge-mortising jigs. If you order rounded corners, make sure the radius of the rounded corner matches your router bit.

Each hinge manufacturer offers its own line of special-application butt hinges. The Lawrence Brothers catalog has a full selection of plain-bearing and ball-bearing hinges, and also a friction hinge fitted with special leaves that permit the door to be held open at any angle. For doors that have to be hung deep into a very wide jamb, Lawrence Brothers and Stanley make a raised-barrel hinge that clears the sides of the jambs, letting the door swing fully open. Strictly speaking, these aren't butt hinges, but they can used in some of the same applications.

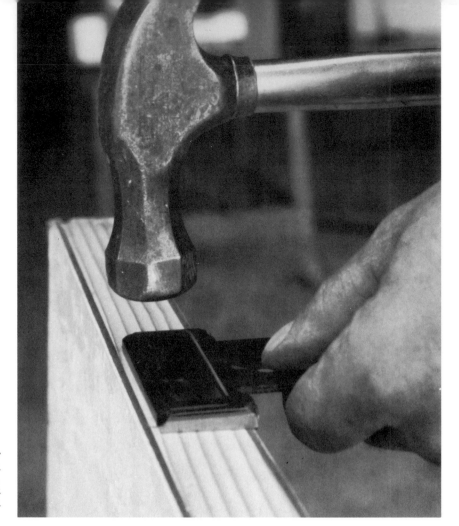

Hinges can be marked with knife or pencil lines, using the hinge as a template, or with a butt gauge. Struck with a hammer, the butt gauge marks the mortise with a deep, incised line.

tise. Make more of these cuts at ¼-in. intervals inside the two end cuts that define the length of the mortise. With the chisel angled back toward the end scribe lines, make a deeper back-cut and remove the waste. The ends of the mortise are now cleaned out, and the center waste is chopped into manageable strips. To finish the job, deepen the knife lines along the back of the mortise, then clean out the rest of the waste by paring cross-grain, toward the back of the mortise. (The drawing and photos on the facing page show the sequence of cuts.) Test the mortise depth by tapping the hinge in place. After a few tries you'll be amazed at how fast you can mortise a hinge by hand.

Mortise the door for all three (or more) hinges before moving on to the jamb. The jamb mortises are laid out and cut in the same way, except that the top hinge is 7⅛ in. down from the inside edge of the head jamb instead of the 7 in. on the door. This creates a ⅛-in. gap between the door and the head jamb. The remaining hinges are positioned by measuring exactly—and I mean exactly—the same as they are spaced on the door. To get the 7⅛-in. measurement, I burn an inch, putting the 1-in. tape mark on the edge of the head

jamb and marking at 8⅛ in. Once the top hinge is located, I measure the distance between the hinges on the door, again burning an inch. I transfer the hinge measurements to the jamb, then lay out and mortise as before. Don't forget to allow for hinge backset, as described above.

Chopping the mortise on the jamb is more difficult because of the awkward angle at which you have to work. Also, the jamb bounces a bit when you strike it with the chisel. The solution is a sharp chisel and patience. If the jamb is particularly bouncy, extra shims or a block tapped temporarily behind the jamb might help. As with the door, check the mortise depth and overall size by inserting the hinges. Some carpenters "prehang" the door, chopping the mortises in the jambs before they're installed.

Router mortising—If I'm doing a lot of doors I use a router template to mortise. Templates ensure that all the mortises will be spaced exactly the same distance apart and at the same depth. You can buy templates (see the Resource Guide on pp. 179-181) that are adjustable for any size door and hinge combination. Basi-

Mortising by hand

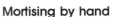

1. Begin by deepening layout lines at ends of mortise.

2. Chop toward center of mortise to full depth.

3. Upon reaching opposite end, reverse bevel so it faces waste side of mortise.

4. With shallow cuts, deepen layout lines along back of mortise.

5. Remove waste by paring toward back of mortise.

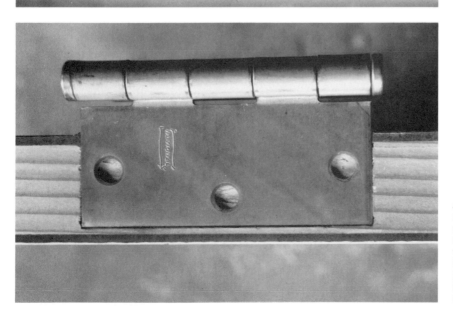

A sharp chisel makes for crisp hand-cut mortises. First (top), a series of angled cuts is made along the length of the marked-out mortise. The waste is cleaned with a series of paring cuts toward the back of mortise (middle photo). In the bottom photo, the hinge is tapped into the mortise to test the fit.

Making a router mortising template

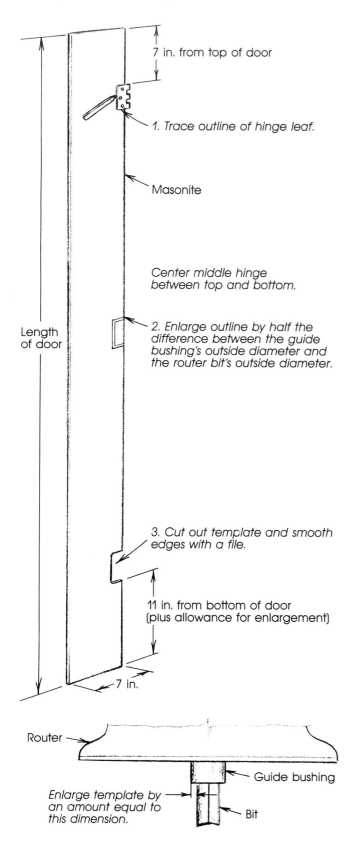

7 in. from top of door

1. Trace outline of hinge leaf.

Masonite

Center middle hinge between top and bottom.

2. Enlarge outline by half the difference between the guide bushing's outside diameter and the router bit's outside diameter.

Length of door

3. Cut out template and smooth edges with a file.

11 in. from bottom of door (plus allowance for enlargement)

7 in.

Router

Enlarge template by an amount equal to this dimension.

Guide bushing

Bit

cally, these templates are metal or plastic guides fastened by way of a track to a long fence. The fence is clamped to the door (or jamb), and the guides are slid along the fence and locked into place at the hinge location. The mortising itself is accomplished with a router fitted with a template bushing that follows the guide. Since the template produces a round-cornered mortise, you can buy hinges to match or, if you prefer, square the round corners with a chisel.

I suppose there are good arguments for owning a commercially made template (there are at least five brands) but I've found it more sensible to make my own. For one thing, I always manage to lose the knobs and gizmos on the commercial models, and it's never made much sense to me to carry around a single-purpose tool that's used infrequently. I make my own templates on the job site, using a router. They're made of a piece of ¼-in. Masonite or plywood as long as the door or, alternatively, of three separate pieces joined to a wooden stick that's as long as the door or jamb. One other version consists of a single-hinge Masonite template that's simply nailed to the door at the point where the mortise will be. My shop-made butt template is used with a 1½-hp router, a ½-in. straight flute bit and a ⅝-in. O.D. template bushing attached to the base of the router. You can, of course, adapt the templates to whatever router and bushing combination you happen to have, including a ¼-in. shank router.

Here's how I make a butt template. With a scrollsaw and a chisel, I make a Masonite template to the exact shape of the hinge for the guide bushing to ride against. Since I'm using a ½-in. router bit and a ⅝-in. O.D. guide bushing, the template's overall size must be larger than the hinge by half the difference between the bit and the bushing, or 1/16 in. First, I cut a piece of ¼-in. Masonite 7 in. wide and as long as the length of the door. I draw out the template's shape by placing the end of a hinge 7 in. from one end of the Masonite, scribing the hinge shape onto the Masonite. Next, I enlarge the layout lines by 1/16 in. to account for the bushing, then scrollsaw the pattern. I carefully clean up to the lines with a chisel, filing if necessary to get the lines straight.

As shown in the drawing at left, the pattern should be at least 1 in. wider than the hinge to allow the router to start its cut outside the edge of the door. Test the template by tacking it with small brads and mortising a scrap. If a hinge fits tightly make two more templates. If the mortise is too small, enlarge the pattern with a chisel; use tape to shrink it if the mortise is too large.

To set the mortise depth, turn the router upside down (unplugged, of course) then, using a scrap of template stock and a hinge as a depth gauge, set the router cutting depth, as shown in the top photo on the facing page. After testing the depth on the scrap, go ahead and mortise the door. Begin by securing the template with C-clamps or tack it to the door right

To adjust a router's depth of cut for hinge mortising, use the actual hinge as a gauge, left. Set the bit so it's flush with the bottom of the hinge. Savage makes his own router mortising jig, below, using Masonite for the templates. (Photo at left by Stephanie Johnson.)

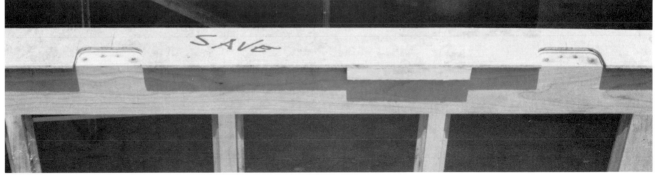

through the Masonite. Then mortise with the router, as shown in the photo above. Always move the router against its rotation or left to right (clockwise in the template) to keep it from grabbing and ruining the mortise. As you work, check both the depth and overall size of each mortise by inserting a hinge.

To mortise the jamb, place the template on the hinge side of the installed jamb. I place a nickel between the top of the head jamb and the template to establish the ⅛-in. gap between the door and the jamb. You could just as easily make a mark and set the template to it. Don't forget this offset, or your door won't have a gap

at the top. Clamps aren't always practical on the jamb side, so you'll have to tack the template during mortising. Again, check each mortise as you go to make sure that the template hasn't slipped and that the router isn't cutting too deeply.

Once mortising is complete, you can move on to installing the hinges. I install them in the door first. Pay close attention to the hinge-pin direction (the head should be up). Nothing is more frustrating than to mortise and install hinges with the pins upside-down. I bore holes for the screws with a Vix bit, a self-centering, spring-loaded bit that is available for screws in two sizes. Whether you use a Vix bit or not, the holes for the hinge screws should be drilled so they're slightly offset toward the back of the hinge. This will pull the leaf tightly into the mortise with less chance of its getting cocked out of alignment when the first screw is driven. I drive the screws closest to the back of the mortise first to pull the hinge back tight against the shoulder of the mortise.

Hanging the door—As with mortising, every carpenter has a preferred way of hanging a door. Most remove the pin, split the hinges and install the leaves on the door and jamb. Mating the hinges and driving in the pins complete the job. Other carpenters leave the hinges assembled, install them in the door first and then position the door so the jamb leaves can be screwed in. Splitting the hinges seems less awkward to me, so that's the method I use. Traditionally, the door is hung by carefully aligning the knuckles of the top hinge, then angling the door downward to engage the other hinges. However, if you used a mortising template, it's safe to make the leap of faith that both door and jamb leaves will mate. With that in mind, I align the bottom hinge first, set its pin and then pivot the door into the opening in a gentle slamming motion. This forces the remaining hinges to mate, even when there are four or more, as in a 10-ft. door.

If you've done everything right, the door should theoretically fit perfectly in the opening. It should open and close with no sticking or binding, and there should be an even space (about ⅛ in.) between the top of the door and head jamb and between the side jambs and the edges of the door. With the door held closed, its face should be perfectly flush with the edges of the jambs, with no twisting or warping. Keep in mind, however, that the door-stop molding isn't yet installed so if the door is pushed too far into the opening, it will appear to bind. The stop molding will alleviate the problem.

I don't think many carpenters claim to get a door hung perfectly the first time. I certainly don't. But I do measure my skill as a door hanger by my ability to diagnose and solve problems. Here are a few dodges I've picked up:

Sticking: If the door sticks, find out where and why. If the hinges are secure and the opening isn't racked, the door is probably slightly too big for its opening. Locate the sticky point and plane it down with a jack plane. Normally, planing a shaving or two off the hinge edge or slicing ¹⁄₁₆ in. off the top will cure a door that seems generally sticky. During the winter, plane off a little more to allow for swelling during the summer. Conversely, don't plane too much in the summer or the gap will be too big when the door shrinks in the winter.

Sag: A door that sags probably has worn or loose hinges. One trick is to exchange the bottom hinge with the top hinge. Another is to insert a piece of metal rod about ³⁄₁₆ in. in diameter between the leaves of the bottom hinge and gently lever the door over it. This will bow the hinge slightly, in effect kicking the door bottom out and relieving the sag. If these tricks don't work, mortise the top hinge deeper or, if more adjustment is still needed, slip a paper shim in the mortise of the bottom hinge.

Hinge bind: Hinge bind is a common problem that occurs when the hinges close but for some reason the door doesn't. The cause is almost always hinge mortises that are too shallow or hinges that aren't set flat in their mortises. The fix is to check that the screws are seated flush with the surface. If they aren't and tightening the screws doesn't help, remove the hinges and deepen the mortises.

Misalignments: If the hinges don't align, a judicious tap on the end of the barrel with a hammer, up on one half of the hinge and down on the other half (splitting the difference) will usually align them. If they still don't align you need to move one of the hinges up or down by increasing the length of the mortise. Remove the hinge, plug the screw holes with wooden plugs and remortise. If the mortises are too deep, the common fix is to use cardboard to shim the hinge out flush. Out-of-plumb jambs will sometimes cause the door to creep open or closed. One fix is to let one hinge in deeper, then shim out the opposite one. Plane the strike edge of the door, if necessary, so that it fits correctly against the strike jamb.

Trimming out: installing the casing

Casing the door is the next step, unless you prefer to install the lock set first. It's really up to you. If you do the lock set first, you'll have a little more room to maneuver tools, since the casing and door stop won't be in the way. On other hand, the casing ties the jamb to the trimmer, which reinforces it against the impact of mortising for the strike plate and bolt. I've done it both ways, but I generally install the casing first.

Casing gives the door its finished look, and it protects the jamb and rough opening against the dings and dents of everyday life. As with window casing, discussed in Chapter 5, door casing should fit flat and tight against the jamb and the finished wall. It should have crisp details and tight joints where it meets other trim elements.

If you've done your prep work well and the rough opening is reasonably accurate, casing proceeds quickly and smoothly. In principle, door casings are very similar to window casings. The chief difference is that there's no sill and hence no bottom casing. As shown in the drawing at left on the facing page, door casings can be butted, mitered, or butted with corner blocks at the head casing and plinth blocks at the floor. In all these cases, the joinery methods are the same as with windows but the order of events is different. Some carpenters install the head casing first, then fit the side

Some typical casing designs

Simple butted casing

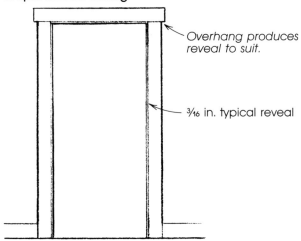

Overhang produces reveal to suit.

³⁄₁₆ in. typical reveal

Butted casing with plinth and corner block

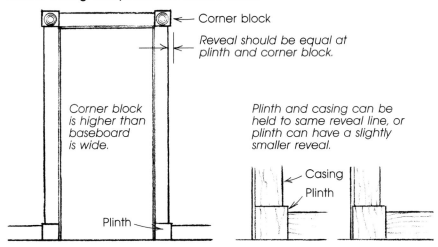

Corner block

Reveal should be equal at plinth and corner block.

Corner block is higher than baseboard is wide.

Plinth and casing can be held to same reveal line, or plinth can have a slightly smaller reveal.

Casing
Plinth

Plinth

Mitered picture-frame casing

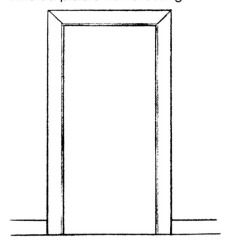

Typical casing profile

Molded casings can't be butted to each other but must be mitered or butted to plinth and corner blocks.

Simple square casings can have a separate piece of molding called a backband. Backbanded moldings are generally mitered, although the casing itself may be butted.

A butt joint that fits

When butting two moldings, back-cut to achieve a better fit at front of joint, where it's most visible.

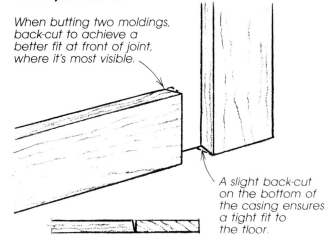

A slight back-cut on the bottom of the casing ensures a tight fit to the floor.

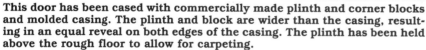
This door has been cased with commercially made plinth and corner blocks and molded casing. The plinth and block are wider than the casing, resulting in an equal reveal on both edges of the casing. The plinth has been held above the rough floor to allow for carpeting.

casings. This method ensures tight fits and obviates having to tack and remove pieces. I do it the other way around, however. I scribe the casings to the floor first, cut them to length and then tack them into place. Then I fit the head casing, trimming the side pieces as necessary. Use whichever method seems more comfortable to you.

Butted casings—Casing begins by marking the reveal on the side and head jambs, just as with windows (see p. 81 for a detailed explanation). Next I cut the side casings a little long and hold them in place so they're aligned with the reveal marks. If the floor is out of level or the jamb is out of plumb (minor variations are inevitable), the casing won't sit flat on the floor and will need to be scribed, then trimmed. If a hardwood floor is yet to be installed, slip a scrap of flooring under the casing and scribe to it. If carpeting is to come, just hold the casing ¼ in. above the floor and don't worry about scribing. Once the casing is marked, saw its

floor end with a slight back-cut so it will fit the floor tightly, as shown in the bottom drawing on p. 115. Don't back-cut too much, however, or you'll have a gap on the sides of the casing. Again, hold the casing in place and mark the point where the head-casing reveal line intersects the edge of the side casings. If you're using butt joints, go ahead and trim the casing, using a slight back-cut. For mitered casings, refer to pp. 81-84 and the discussion below.

The head casing is next. For butted head casings, simply center the head casing atop the side casings, cut it to length and nail it in place. Make sure it sits flat on top of the side casings. If it doesn't, remove the side casings and trim them as necessary, either using the wedge method described on pp. 86-87 or with a block plane. If the head casing tilts toward or away from the wall, you may have to make a compound cut on the tops of the side casing. Do this by placing a wedge between the chopsaw table and the molding and taking very small, careful cuts. It may take some trial and error to achieve a perfect fit. Once you do, drive and set the nails, using the same strategy as with windows, explained on pp. 82-83.

The method described above will work with any butt-joined casing system, including those with corner blocks and/or plinth blocks. When I use corner blocks and plinth blocks, I work from the bottom up. I install the plinth blocks first, then the two side casings, followed by the corner blocks and the head casing. As described on p. 127, a preacher is handy for marking the length of the head casing so it fits snugly between the corner blocks. If you've used a small reveal between casing and jamb, install the plinth and corner blocks to align with the inside edge of the casing. The blocks can be wider than the casing, however, to create a small reveal, as shown in the photos on the facing page.

Mitered casing—When I miter casings, I use the same general strategy described on pp. 81-84. If I'm doing a lot of doors, I mark the reveals all at once, going from door to door, production-line style. I start by trimming the head casing to length and tack it in place so the miter heels are exactly on the reveal intersection marks. Nail through the head casing into the jamb with 3d or 4d casing nails spaced about 10 in. apart. Keep the nails 1 in. or so from the mitered end to avoid splits. Predrill the casing if you need to nail closer to the joint but don't drive the nails flush so you'll have some leeway when fitting the side casings. Now nail through the top of the head casing and into the rough header with 6d or 8d finishing nails. Again, don't set the nails or drive them too closely to the joint until the side casings are installed.

Next, the side casings are cut to length and nailed to the trimmer stud and the jamb edge. On a production job, where all the doors are similar, I miter all of the side casings at once. If the house is to be carpeted, this cut also trims the piece to length, since I have ¼ in. of slack at the bottom of the casing. For wooden floors, I cut the side casings a little long and scribe the bottom of the casing to the floor. Then I place the casing on the floor and mark the heel of the miter where it intersects the heel of the head casing. On production jobs, some carpenters stand the miter end on the floor (or on scrap representing the floor) and mark the casing where the long point of the previously installed head casing and the edge of the side casing intersect. This establishes the square crosscut for the bottom of the side casing.

Once the miters are complete, check for a tight fit and consistent alignment with the reveal marks. Problems with the way the miter fits can be cured using the fixes described on pp. 84-86. The side casing is ready to nail only after the miter fits without being forced. I remove the casing, dab a little glue on both sides of the miter and reassemble. I start nailing at the miter with the intention of locking the joint with the first few nails. Then I nail the casing on the jamb side with 3d or 4d finishing nails, followed by 6d or 8d nails on the trimmer side. I cross-lock the miter with two 2d finish nails driven into into the side and top edge of the casing. To avoid splitting the wood, it's best to predrill these holes.

One problem that complicates casing a door is jambs that are bowed into or away from the opening. If the bow is really bad, reset and adjust the jamb with shims. Slight bows can be handled by splitting the difference, bowing the casing a little and letting the reveal run out a little. Be sure to lock the miter with cross nails and nail close to the joint before you attempt to bow the casing. Otherwise, the miters might open up.

The last step: lock sets and stop moldings

I've always found installing lock sets to be a frightening experience, probably because at this stage, a slip can ruin the entire door with a gaping hole in the wrong place. If there's ever a time to measure twice and cut once, it's with lock sets.

Prehung doors come with their own lock sets, but custom wood doors can have tubular latches or the old-fashioned and more expensive mortise lock sets. I don't normally use mortise lock sets so I'll limit my discussion to tubular latches. Tubular latches are sold with paper, plastic or cardboard templates that tell how and where to locate the holes for the latch, lock and doorknob assembly. However, if you've got a lot of doors to hang, try to get a lock-set jig from the lock-set manufacturer. This is simply a guide that accurately positions your drill bit for boring the necessary holes.

Most doorknobs are set so their centers are 36 in. above the finished floor and backset either 2⅜ in. or 2¾ in. from the edge of the door. Other backsets are available, but these two dimensions are the standard. Begin by marking on the door a horizontal line 36 in. above the floor and an intersecting vertical line to represent the center of the backset. Bore for the knobs first, then the latch, using the paper template or boring guide to locate the holes.

Once the latch plate is mortised and installed, the hard part comes: aligning the strike plate on the jamb with the latch's centerline on the door. This operation is critical if the door is to close against the stop molding with good action and a satisfying click. I locate the strike by closing the door and, with a square, carrying the centerline of the latch across to the edge of the jamb, then to the face of the jamb.

If you're dealing with an interior door, the stop molding won't be on yet. Just bore a hole for the strike plate that will position it so the door closes flush with the jamb edge. Later, the stop will be positioned for a good fit against the door. Exterior doors will probably have the stop rabbeted into the jamb, so you'll have to position the strike plate so the door closes snugly against

A lock-set boring guide takes some of the anxiety out of fitting doors with lock sets. The model at top is available from Schlage Lock Co. and is listed in the Resource Guide (pp. 179-181). On the typical lightweight, two-hinge prehung door at right, the casing has already been installed on one side of the jamb.

the stops. You can make minor adjustments in latching action by bending the tongue inside the strike plate in or out with a screwdriver.

Stop moldings—The stop molding is nailed (or screwed) directly to the jamb. Usually, the molding is a very simple rectangular section but it can be more elaborate, as shown in the top-view drawing on p. 97. Rectangular stop molding can be butted at the inside corners, but stop molding with any kind of profile will have to be mitered. Coping is another option, albeit one that's a lot of work for the sake of hiding what little wood movement is likely to occur across the stop's relatively narrow width.

Of critical importance is the stop's position in the jamb width. This will determine the door's closing action. If the stop molding is installed improperly, the door will rattle in its jamb with all the tightness of an old pickup-truck door. With the door closed and the latch pushing tightly against the strike, I position the latch-side stop molding so that it's tight against the door at the top and bottom but bows out slightly less than $\frac{1}{16}$ in. near the latch. This minute bow means that when the bolt slips into the strike, the door is held in slight tension against the stop, giving a positive feel and reducing the chances of rattling. On the hinge side, the stop is nailed so that it's evenly about $\frac{3}{32}$ in. away from the door. This keeps the door from binding when it swings open.

Install the head-jamb stop first. First, latch the door closed. Pushing the door tight against the latch, scribe a line along the head jamb. Do the same along the latch jamb. Now open the door and tack the head stop in place along the line. Then tack on the latch-side stop, bowing it slightly away from the line at the latch, as explained above. Close the door and check for a good feel. Adjust the stop, if necessary, then set the nails. I install the hinge-side stop last. To get the spacing correct, I insert a cardboard shim (the hinge box top is perfect) between the door and the stop, then nail it in place.

If you're hanging an exterior door, you'll need to install weatherstripping and/or a weatherproof threshold. There are many kinds of weatherstripping. Some types attach to the stop, others to the door.

Notes on prehung doors

So far, I've limited my discussion to site-built jambs and factory or shop-made doors. In doing so, I don't mean to suggest that prehung doors aren't a suitable choice for some applications. Prehung doors are shipped to the job site complete and ready to hang, with a spreader nailed across the bottom of the jamb to hold it together. In dealing with a prehung door, you first have to set aside your prejudices about doing things right by doing them by hand. I know carpenters

who think that prehung doors are synonymous with cheap construction and that they can't ever be properly hung. While it's true that the cheapest doors usually are prehung (sometimes as little as $25 for a door), it's possible to buy prehung doors of reasonable quality and to install them with good results.. I don't use prehung interior doors much but in Idaho, prehung exterior steel insulated doors are virtually standard equipment for new houses and renovations. This is because they are far more energy efficient than wooden doors.

Nothing special is required to prepare a rough opening for a prehung door. Again, plumb, level and square will make things go more smoothly. There are several ways to approach installing a prehung door. I remove the door from its jamb, then figure on using the door itself as a template to adjust the jamb for a good fit in the rough opening. There's nothing particularly radical about this. If the door fits the jamb while both are leaning against the wall, it can be made to fit when the jamb is nailed into the opening.

After checking the opening for true, as described earlier in this chapter and on pp. 64-67, I remove the door from its hinges and install the jamb into the rough opening, using the same basic strategy described earlier but nailing only the hinge side of the jamb. Once you know the jamb is plumb, install the door. Be careful, though, because the assembled jamb is attached only on the hinge side and is liable to twist. Use the door as a guide for setting the rest of the jamb. I usually adjust the top of the latch-side jamb first. That way I can examine the gap at both the side jamb and the head jamb simultaneously. I install shims along the length of the latch-side jamb until the gap between the door and the jamb is an even $\frac{1}{8}$ in. I also check the gap at the head. It should also be $\frac{1}{8}$ in. If both gaps are correct, I drive an 8d finish nail through the jamb and the wedges and into the trimmer.

There are a couple of things to look for when you're wedging the jamb. Tap each wedge in an equal amount so you're creating a parallel shim behind the jamb. That way you won't cause the jamb to twist. As with a site-built jamb, the jamb should be square to the plane of the wall. Shim out ever so slightly more than is necessary so that the nails, when set, will compress the shims slightly for a tight fit. When you're satisfied with the gap all around the door, set the nails.

Some prehung doors come with the casing already nailed to one side of the jamb. Some carpenters will hold the entire assembly in the rough opening and using a nail gun, secure the door by nailing through the casing. They use the door as a template, moving the jamb in or out before shooting a nail. The jamb is then shimmed from the side without the casing, trued and nailed. Finally, the casing is nailed on both sides. This is the fastest method I know of hanging a door. It's also the shoddiest. To get good results with even an inexpensive door, take your time and do the job right.

Crown molding gives a finished look to the juncture of wall and ceiling. It can be installed by itself or combined with other moldings to create a formal cornice.

7

Base and crown

So far, I've discussed trim for windows and doors, which carpenters and millwrights call standing trim. Once it's installed, however, it's time to turn to the other major trim type: running trim. Running trim refers to the horizontal molding in a house—the baseboards, chair rails, picture rails and crown moldings. The original purpose of baseboard and crown was to seal up cracks and keep out the weather. Chair rails kept the furniture from bashing up the walls, and picture rails provided a convenient way to hang paintings. In a modern house, horizontal moldings are largely ornamental; they give a room a particular feel.

Where piecework carpentry prevails, some mechanics joke that the term "running molding" refers to the way it's often installed: by carpenters running through the house with air nailers drawn. Actually, its name probably comes from the fact that these moldings are "run" (and sold) in standard or random lengths through a machine called a sticker. They are not sold as sets, as most standing trim is. Every style of house has running trim, some more than others. A Georgian reproduction has lots of it, beginning with multi-part baseboard through chair rail to an elaborate crown molding at the ceiling. A Modernist cube, on the other hand, might have no standing trim at all, but it's almost certain to have at least a simple baseboard.

Running trim is usually the last to be installed. Doors, windows, wainscoting and their associated standing trim are first. By then, it's a good idea to have baseboard heaters, registers and electrical outlets in place so the trim carpenter can work around them. Once the running trim is in place, all that usually remains is the painter's work and the general contractor's final punch list. I'll cover all forms of running trim in this chapter, but because baseboard is common to virtually all houses, I'll deal with it more fully.

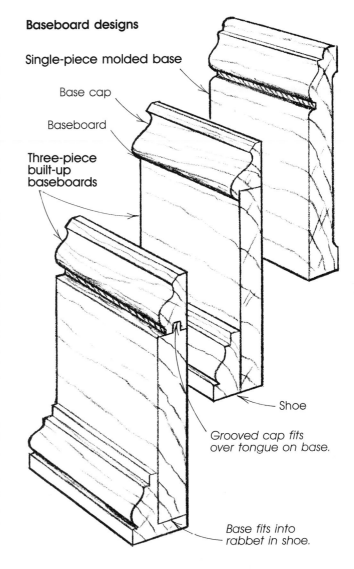

Baseboard designs

Single-piece molded base

Base cap

Baseboard

Three-piece built-up baseboards

Shoe

Grooved cap fits over tongue on base.

Base fits into rabbet in shoe.

Single-piece baseboard can be coped, butted or mitered—or joined by a combination of these joints. The flat portion of this molding has been butted, while the profiled top section has been mitered.

What baseboard does

Baseboard, variously called skirt, skirting board, base plate, mopboard, washboard, scrub board or simply base, visually anchors the wall to the floor. It gives your eye a place to start in assessing a room's interior texture. Baseboard also protects the drywall or plaster against damage from errant furniture or a two-year-old having fun with pots and pans.

Baseboard designs are of far greater variety than any other kind of running trim. I like to think of baseboard as having two broad categories: single-piece and built-up. Single-piece baseboard, as its name implies, consists of one piece of wood. In section, it can be flat, chamfered, rounded, elaborately molded or even carved, but all of the shaping is done on a single board. Single-piece molded baseboard is commonly from 3 in. to 12 in. wide and from ¾ in. to 1⅛ in. thick. Built-up baseboards consist of two or more separate moldings combined, as shown in the drawing on p. 121. Their widths and thicknesses vary with the kinds of moldings used.

In most cases, single-piece baseboard is faster to install since you're dealing with just one piece. But a wide, single-piece molding can be difficult to fit to an irregular wall. The thickness and width of the molding make it harder to draw tight to the wall between studs. Of course, in paint-grade work, the painters can hide the gaps with caulk. On stained work, you'll need good backing so the gaps can be drawn in with nails. Also, wide single-piece baseboard will cup more than the equivalent width made with several moldings. You can minimize warping in paint-grade or stain-grade work by spraying or brushing a coat of finish on the back of the molding before you install it.

There's no end to the profiles you can develop by building up a baseboard with two or more moldings. The drawing on p. 121 shows some typical examples. Built-up baseboards usually consist of three pieces: the baseboard itself; a cap; and a shoe, sometimes called the sub-base. A three-piece baseboard is fussier to install, but it will follow wavy contours a little more readily, especially a floor. And if the floor is really bad, a small shoe is easier to scribe to irregular contours than a wide, single-piece baseboard.

Visually, the shoe adds a "base to the base." Traditional shoe-molding profiles, as described in Chapter 1, are often based on classical elements. Robust curves give weight to the base of the wall, creating the impression of a sound foundation. In modern construction, quarter-round molding is the most popular kind of shoe molding, but other profiles are possible. Where wall-to-wall carpet will be installed, the shoe molding is sometimes left off. Caps serve as a decorative top to the baseboard. Also, a cap is easier to scribe or bend to irregular walls than is a wide baseboard.

The baseboard itself is nailed through the wall into the sole plate or, for wider styles, into backing installed for the purpose. The shoe and cap are installed next. The shoe is nailed to the floor rather than to the baseboard. This way, when the baseboard or the floor shrinks (as it always will), an ugly gap won't open up between the shoe and the floor. There are two schools of thought on how to nail the cap. Some carpenters nail it to the top edge of the baseboard, reasoning that when the baseboard moves with moisture changes, so does the cap, thus preventing a gap. Unfortunately, nailing the cap to the wall is the best way of closing up gaps between the cap and a wavy wall. Of course, when the baseboard shrinks, the cap stays put on the wall and...you know the rest. I have no foolproof advice, so you'll have to decide for yourself.

In very elaborate work, you sometimes see a three-piece baseboard whose cap is joined to the baseboard with tongues and grooves. One way to do this is to cut a tongue along the top edge of the baseboard and a groove into the cap molding, as shown in the drawing on p. 121. Similarly, the baseboard fits into a rabbet milled into the shoe molding. This configuration is time-consuming to install, but it's better at disguising wood movement. Occasionally cap molding is compound-joined to door casing that has a profile similar to the cap molding. The lower section of the cap butts to the plinth, and the upper section miters to an outside molding on the casing.

Running baseboard

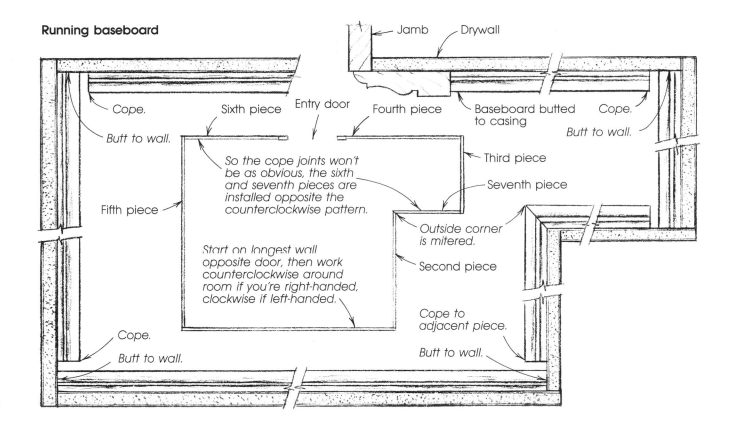

Jamb

Drywall

Cope.

Sixth piece

Entry door

Fourth piece

Baseboard butted to casing

Cope.

Butt to wall.

Butt to wall.

So the cope joints won't be as obvious, the sixth and seventh pieces are installed opposite the counterclockwise pattern.

Third piece

Seventh piece

Fifth piece

Outside corner is mitered.

Start on longest wall opposite door, then work counterclockwise around room if you're right-handed, clockwise if left-handed.

Second piece

Cope to adjacent piece.

Cope.

Butt to wall.

Butt to wall.

Baseboard strategies

Of all the running trim, baseboard is usually saved for last so it can be joined to the standing trim and the finished floor. When possible, I prefer to install baseboard after the wood floor is laid (and finished, if appropriate). Otherwise I have to leave a space beneath the baseboard so the flooring can be slipped underneath. If the flooring is to be laid after the base, scraps of flooring should be used to gauge the space. It's possible to nail the baseboard on first and then butt the floor (wood or tile) to it, eliminating the need for a shoe molding. But with wood flooring, this is bad construction practice. As the floor swells in humid weather, it will have no room to expand and will either buckle or crush the baseboard. In dry weather, the floor will retreat, opening up a gap.

You will encounter three distinct situations when running baseboard: fitting it between two walls, fitting it from an inside corner to an outside corner, and fitting it between two outside corners. The joinery you use depends on the molding and on how much time you've got. Flat baseboard (that is, base with no decorative profile) can simply be butted at the corners and it will look fine, although a demanding eye might find such a joint unappealing. If a cap and/or shoe molding will be added, it doesn't matter what joint you use since the top of the joint will be covered. In this case, use a butt joint.

Molded base will have to be coped or mitered at inside corners and mitered at outside corners. In paint-grade work, it's tempting just to miter all the joints and fill the gaps with caulk, but coping is the better way to go. One other choice for baseboard that has both a molded section and a flat section is to miter the molded part and butt the flat parts, as shown in the photo on the facing page. This joint is sometimes called a half-lap miter.

Before I begin running base, I try to figure out a logical order of events, based on the joinery I've decided to use. If I'm coping the corners, I pick the longest wall and butt the baseboard tight between the side walls. That way, I don't have to worry about chumping my longest boards, and the shorter pieces (which need to be coped) will be easier to handle.

I also try to arrange the cuts so as many joints as possible are out of the direct line of sight as you enter the room. In other words, I want the part of the cope that goes under the mating piece to be at right angles to the line of sight. That way, if the joint opens up, it won't be noticeable.

As the drawing above shows, I try to work counterclockwise around the room, chiefly because I am right-handed and this makes the joint easier to see and scribe. To make the cope joints less conspicuous, however, one or two pieces usually have to be installed opposite the pattern.

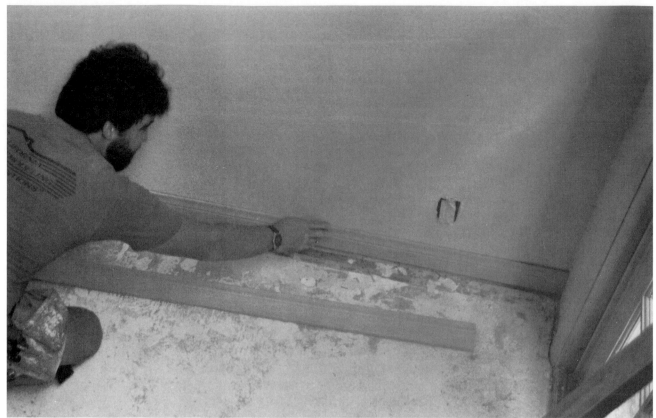

Start running baseboard on the longest wall, then work clockwise or counterclockwise, whichever you prefer. If joints are to be coped, the first piece is simply butted to the opposite walls but cut a bit long so it 'snaps' into place.

On small jobs, you can work from one location in the house, making your cuts and walking from room to room. In a whole house, I usually move the chopsaw from room to room and complete one room before moving on to the next one. California piecework carpenters fill the house with baseboard. A helper rough-cuts the base and lays it out along every wall, ahead of the installer. The installer carries a nail gun and a lightweight, manual miter box or miter trimmer and literally crawls from cut to cut. If you're using a table saw or radial-arm saw and benches, set them up where convenient.

Even if you've bought the finest molding available, some pieces are nicer than others. Use the best stuff in the most conspicuous places. Lesser-quality wood goes in closets, halls and bedrooms. I always start on the long walls. That way, if I miscut I can use the chumped pieces later, step-down fashion, for the next longest job. If you don't have long enough molding for long walls, scarf shorter pieces together with nails and glue. Make sure the scarf falls over a stud or elsewhere where there's plenty of backing to nail into.

I start my working day in a closet or secondary bedroom so that I can get my joinery up to speed where it won't show. It's better to ruin a small poor-quality piece in the closet than a long perfect piece in the entry. Save the very best molding and your finest joinery for the bathrooms—nothing encourages scrutiny of the trim more than sitting on a toilet.

Straight, flat walls (if you are lucky enough to find such a thing) make installing baseboard much easier. As explained on pp. 64-67, the most meaningful preliminary work happens before the drywall goes up. As best you can, make sure the walls are plumb, the floors level and the rooms square. Check to see that floor plates are on their snap lines and that any misaligned plates have been chiseled or sawn flush. Baseboard wider than 5 in. will need continuous backing, especially at the corners, so that there will be plenty of material to nail into. See pp. 68-69 for an explanation of how to install this backing. Backing for narrower baseboard can be a double bottom plate or blocking between studs. Drywall corners—both inside and outside—seem always to be a problem. Metal outside corners are rarely exactly 90°; heaped-up drywall compound in an inside corner causes similar problems. Clean the inside corners as best you can with a sharp putty knife; trim the outside corners with a rasp or Surform plane.

Nailing strategies

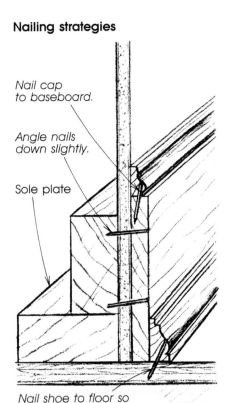

Nail cap to baseboard.

Angle nails down slightly.

Sole plate

Nail shoe to floor so when baseboard shrinks, no gaps will appear.

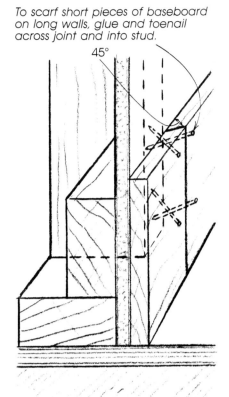

To scarf short pieces of baseboard on long walls, glue and toenail across joint and into stud.

45°

Getting started—Let's assume we're working with single-piece baseboard and that we'll be coping all of the joints. Step one is to butt the first piece tightly between two walls or between a wall and a door casing. I measure with a 20-ft. tape or with pinch sticks if I'm being paid to be careful, then add ¹⁄₁₆ in. As with any butt joint, I undercut to a slight point on both sides, so when the overlong piece is installed, it "snaps" into position, forcing the slightly undercut points into the plaster or drywall mud. It's not important that this joint fit at the bottom—that is, that the molding be flush against the wall across its width—since the next coped piece will cover any gaps.

With a block of wood, I tap the molding into place against the floor and wall and then nail it with two nails per stud. For softwood, I nail on 16-in. centers, two nails per stud, ¼ in. from the top and ½ in. from the bottom, into the bottom plate. Wide hardwood base that gets a cap molding should have only one nail in its center, or it may split when it shrinks. For hand nailing, I use 6d finish nails for thin baseboard and 8d for thicker molding. It's especially important to nail near the corners; otherwise the mating piece might displace the first, creating a gap.

Whether you are using a nail gun or hammer, the object is to draw the moldings tight to the wall so the joints won't open up. This is especially true of outside miters. I try to get a nail as close to the joint as possible without splitting the piece. It's a judgment call, and you'll have to develop a feel for what you can get away with. Generally, softwood moldings split less than hardwoods. Consequently, you can nail within 1 in. of the end and within ½ in. of the edge of a softwood molding without disastrous splits. A nail gun shoots a thinner nail that rarely splits the wood, so if you enjoy tempting fate, you can nail a little closer.

Hardwood baseboards are a different story. I always predrill near the ends and edges with a bit that just allows the nail to slip through. The nail itself, in fact, makes a good bit. The head of the nail is really doing the holding, and the slight slop around the nail will let the molding shrink without splitting later. With hardwood or softwood baseboards, I try to angle the nails down slightly so that if I have to tighten the base to the floor later by tapping it with a block, I won't have to fight the nail angle, and the piece will be pulled toward the wall. The drawing above shows general strategies for nailing baseboard.

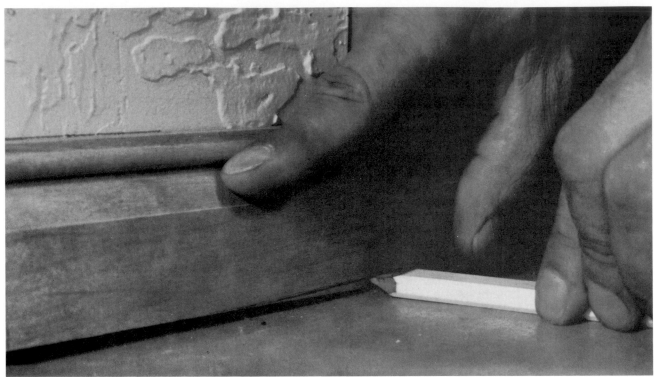

Irregular floors are more the rule than the exception. To scribe a baseboard to the floor, use a carpenter's pencil or a compass set to span the largest gap. Then scribe toward the smallest gap, as shown. Plane down to the line with a block plane, then test the fit. A narrow molding can sometimes be bent around irregularities, without scribing.

For inside corners, a cope is the most durable joint. Although it's more time-consuming than a miter, it's less likely to open up with seasonal movement.

Using a preacher to mark the baseboard directly for the cut automatically compensates for an out-of-plumb plinth or casing.

Once the first piece of baseboard is installed, measure for the second piece. Cut the second piece a bit longer than your measurement. Then cope the joint, as described on pp. 128-129. If the floor is irregular or out of level, you'll have to spring the piece in place as best you can and scribe the baseboard before cutting the cope. The cope profile can come from a 45° cut or, if the mating wall is out of plumb, from a direct scribe. In any case, when the joint fits, cut it slightly longer than the exact length needed and "snap" it into place. On very wide baseboards or when the casing is out of plumb, mark the cut with a preacher, as shown in the photo at bottom right on the facing page. If the preacher won't fit around a very deep casing, scribe the base directly, as shown in the photo at right. Of course, when scribing one end into a corner like this, the opposite end will have to run long so it can be trimmed to a miter, butt or cope.

The miter is the only joint that will turn an outside corner cleanly, without exposed end grain. Whether you're using copes or butts at the opposite end, you'll still need crisp miters at the outsides. Fitting an outside miter would be a cinch if walls met at exactly 90°. They rarely do.

Making an outside miter begins with marking the baseboard length. Since the outside corner is exposed and easy to scribe, it makes sense to position the piece to mark the length directly off the wall. To establish the length of the cut, I use scraps of baseboard held in the corner, and I scribe along their outside faces to mark two intersection lines on the floor, as shown in the top drawing on p. 128. This intersection represents the heel (short point) of the miter. Next, after the opposite end of the baseboard is fitted with a miter, cope or butt, I hold the actual piece to be mitered in position with its fitted end snugly mated. I mark the back of the molding, both where the wall's corner touches the top edge of the base and where the intersection line touches the bottom of the base. By extending 45° lines across the top and bottom edges and connecting them, I've marked a miter that automatically compensates for a skewed wall. If the wall is square in both planes or if I'm working in paint grade and minor gaps at the top of the base can be caulked, no remedial work is needed. Sometimes, if I'm in a real hurry, I mark the base only at the intersection lines and then extend it with a square.

In either case, I saw the marked-out miter on my chopsaw, cutting well away from the line on the waste side so I can judge how much I'll have to wedge the

A baseboard that butts to an exceptionally deep casing or a blind wall can't be marked with a preacher. Instead, the baseboard can be scribed directly with a pencil, as shown. The same method works for a cope joint that must mate to a badly out-of-plumb molding.

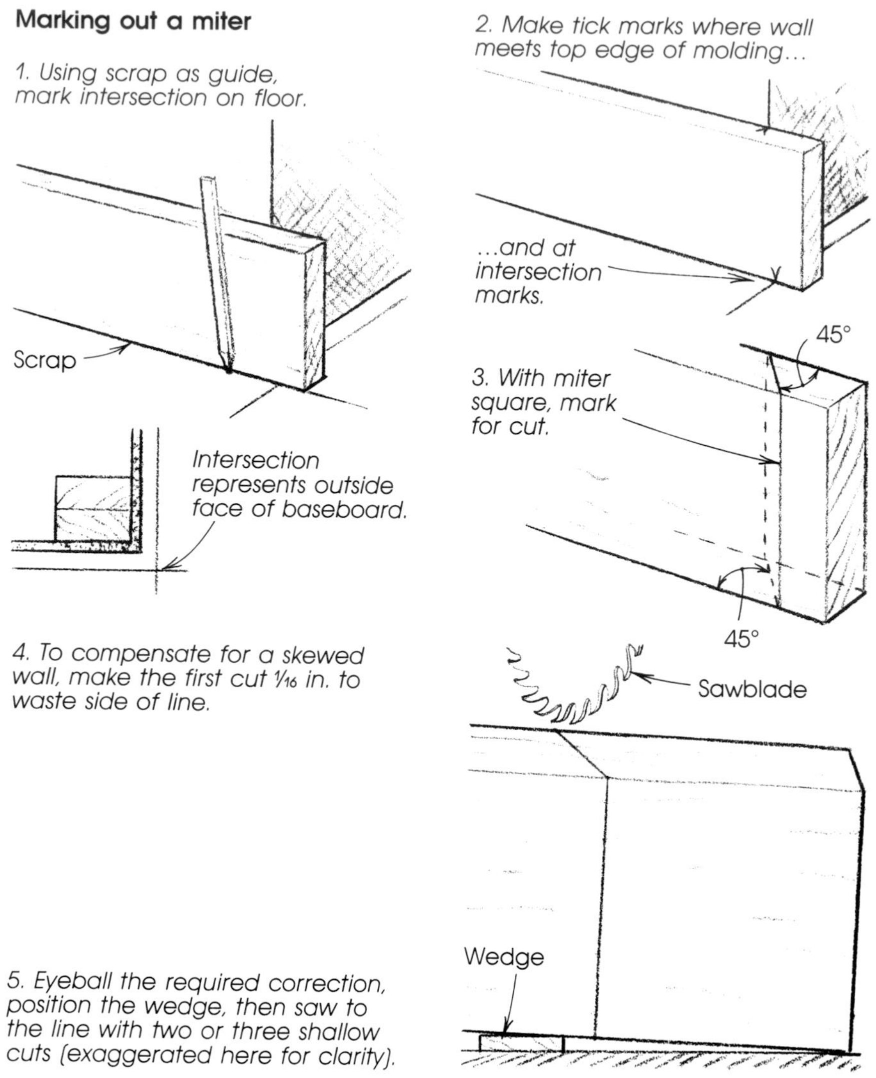

Marking out a miter

1. Using scrap as guide, mark intersection on floor.

Scrap

Intersection represents outside face of baseboard.

2. Make tick marks where wall meets top edge of molding...

...and at intersection marks.

3. With miter square, mark for cut.

45°

45°

Sawblade

4. To compensate for a skewed wall, make the first cut 1/16 in. to waste side of line.

5. Eyeball the required correction, position the wedge, then saw to the line with two or three shallow cuts (exaggerated here for clarity).

Wedge

molding away from the table to compensate for any out-of-squareness. Relatively narrow molding can be positioned vertically and mitered by holding the back of the molding against the saw's fence. With your hands well away from the blade, slowly lower the saw into the wood to complete the cut.

If the molding is very wide, it has to be cut on a 14-in. chopsaw or horizontally on a table saw or radial-arm saw. With mitering, you get one cut so if anything, make the piece a little longer than your marks indicate. You can always trim it. Fit the mating miter using the same marking method, sawing it a hair long, then trim to a tight joint. As explained on pp. 86-87, adjust the fit with the chopsaw or a block plane.

On some occasions where a short section of base has to wrap around a freestanding partition wall, I make the miters on a box form whose size and shape represent the wall. The pieces are nailed and glued, then in-

stalled as a unit. In this case, I nail through the miters in addition to nailing the base to the wall.

If possible, the last piece of base put in a room should have a coped joint on one end and a butt joint on the other, either to a wall or to a door casing. With the preacher, the butt joint is easy to scribe to length and nail in place. If this isn't possible, you'll have to cope or miter both ends. To cope both ends, measure carefully and cut a little long. If you're cutting two copes, remember that the length of the piece will be determined by measuring between the heels of the miters you saw to reveal the profile, not the toes. Make the piece a little long and snap it into place, trimming where necessary if it's too long.

Finishing up—Once all the base is down, I move on to the cap molding. Some carpenters prefer to install the shoe molding first, but I can't imagine that it makes

The cope joint

A cope joint is used to join baseboard, crown and other moldings where they meet at inside corners. Coping has several advantages over mitering. For one, it hides the effects of seasonal wood movement. Since wood shrinks and swells across the grain with changes in moisture, miters tend to open and close with the seasons, regardless of how well they fit at the outset. However, both parts of a coped joint move in unison so the effects of movement aren't as noticeable. Also, a well-made coped joint is "sprung," meaning that parts are cut minutely overlong and forced into place, compressing the joint.

Where the wall surface is rough and irregular, the cope is a bit easier to fit than a miter. Since the wall gives a bit as you nail against it, one side of a mitered joint inevitably opens up or slips past its mate. A cope is less likely to do this. On the down side, however, the cope takes longer to make.

The actual cope itself is cut only in one of the two pieces forming the joint. To develop the cope's profile, first cut a miter so the length of the part is about 1/16 in. longer than required. The miter is cut so it slopes toward the corner of the joint, as it would in an inside miter, rather than away from it, as it would in an outside miter joint. Thus, the heel of the miter represents the profile that will ultimately be an exact mirror image to fit over the mating piece. Cut the miter as any other miter, with a chopsaw or miter box. The smoother the cut, the sharper the profile will be and the easier it will be to cut the cope. The profiles of intricate moldings may be hard to see, especially in poor light. Highlight the profile by rubbing the side of a pencil along the miter's edge. I've used chalk or a lumber crayon for the same purpose.

To cut the joint use (what else?) a coping saw. The coping saw is a delicate tool that does its work effortlessly. It takes a carpenter as

Coping a joint

First, cut a miter to expose end grain.

Cut to profile with coping saw with saw held 90° or more to molding.

To make a cope cut with a scroll-saw, hold the saw's blade at 90° to the face of molding and nibble down to the profile line with a series of sideways scraping cuts.

Once the profile of the trim has been coped with a coping saw or scrollsaw, clean up the cut and adjust the fit to the mating piece with a rattail file.

close to sculpture as most will ever get. With the coping saw, saw along the profile developed with the miter cut. I start the cut at 80° to the back of the molding, but this angle changes as the saw moves across the profile. Where a thick profile results in a thick cut, I hold the saw nearly perpendicular to the molding's face. For a thinner cut, angle the saw back as much as 60°. The idea is to produce a continuous back-cut so that only the tip of the original miter remains, creating a crisp profile that fits tightly around the mating piece.

When you finish sawing, try the joint—it usually needs some fine tuning. In tight radii where it's hard to get a steep enough back-cut, I pare the molding back with a knife or wood rasp. Any wood-shaping method you're comfortable with works fine for fitting a cope. Rasps (four-in-hand or rattail) are accurate, but tedious. I've also seen a small disc sander used.

The scrollsaw is the machine version of the coping saw. It can be used to cope the most complex profiles and is a little easier, if not faster, than doing the job by hand. As with a coping saw, first miter the molding to establish the profile. Next, holding the scrollsaw to cut a 60° or so back-cut, saw to within 1/16 in. of the profile. Next, with the saw's blade perpendicular to the molding face, carefully pass it back and forth in a raking action across the profile, working right up the profile line. This operation works best if the molding is clamped at an angle so a back-cut results. As with the hand method, try the joint first. Then pare away the high points to a perfect fit.

Compression and spring in the molding keep a coped joint tight. Nails are necessary only to fasten the molding to the wall. Glue makes a slightly sloppy coped joint look better, but not much. And since copes butt end grain to long grain (and not much of it, at that) glue doesn't improve the joint's strength at all.

much difference. Cap moldings are coped or, if they are very small, mitered on both inside and outside corners. They can be butted only where they meet door casings or terminate against other pieces of trim.

Cap-nailing strategies differ according to the design. If the cap is tongue-and-grooved to the baseboard (a rarity), nail it through the wall and into the backing. If it simply rests on top of the baseboard, nail it to the top of the baseboard rather than to the wall. Like caps, shoes are coped or mitered on inside corners and mitered on outside corners. Sometimes the thickness of base and shoe, when combined, makes the shoe stick out beyond the casing or plinth block, in which case simply beveling the shoe is an acceptable solution, as shown in the drawing on the facing page.

Dodges, tricks and fine points—Even in that rare room with plumb walls and flat floors, your best baseboard miters and copes just won't fit sometimes, for no apparent reason. Fortunately, trim carpenters have invented lots of dodges to make baseboard (and other moldings) look correct. If I suspect I'm going to have problems, I try to plan the trim so that the joints are out of plain view. I also orient a problem joint so that if it does open up, the gap will be in a plane that's hard to see. Here are some common baseboard problems, and their fixes.

Wavy walls: Plaster and drywall may look flat to the client, but baseboard always shows up the smallest hills and valleys. Sometimes, judicious nailing will "suck in" the gaps, other times not. The best solution is accurate framing and drywall, plus plenty of backing for close-spaced nailing. Another solution is to use three-piece baseboard when you can. Then the cap molding can be scribed to irregular contours if it appears that nailing won't close the gaps. This is a tedious process but well worth it, especially in an old house, where settling may have twisted the walls. When working with stain-grade molding that can't be caulked, a three-piece baseboard is often the only solution. If, no matter what, molding and wall just won't meet, call the painter, who will caulk and paint over the gap. Or you can do it yourself, as described on pp. 166-167.

Out-of-square corners: Outside corners that don't meet at 90° are a common problem. The easiest fix is simply to measure the angle with a bevel gauge and protractor, then divide by two to arrive at the miter angle. You can also eyeball the first cut and get a perfect fit with subsequent trial-and-error cuts. Inside corners can be handled in the same way, but they are generally less troublesome because they can be butted or coped.

Baseboard around an outlet box: Occasionally, baseboard passes over an electrical box installed near the floor. To mark the box's exact location, I first fit the baseboard to the wall, then mark the exposed edges of the outlet box with chalk, lipstick or even spit. When the base is pushed back against the wall, the box's out-

line is transferred to it. I drill holes at the four corners from the back; then, just as the bit is about to punch through, I turn the molding over and finish the hole from the front. Connect the holes with a jigsaw, then smooth with a file. If your baseboard is thick, you may have to pry the outlet box loose and remount it so it projects through the hole you sawed in the baseboard.

Baseboard around a heat register: Wall heat registers are usually higher than a baseboard is wide. This presents a problem because the molding must stop and start. There are three solutions to the dead-end moldings. One is simply to butt the molding to the register frame. Another is to cope the end of the baseboard to the same profile that's on the face of the molding. Finally, if you're really fussy, return miter the ends, as shown in the drawing on the facing page, and rip off the molded section and carry it around the register with miters.

Curved baseboard: Curved walls aren't common, but occasionally you might have to run baseboard around one. The traditional method of doing this for an outside radius is to saw a series of kerfs in the back of the molding. This removes enough wood fiber to make the molding flexible. The tighter the bend, of course, the closer the kerfs have to be spaced. Start with 1/8-in. kerfs spaced about 1/2 in. apart. The disadvantage of this method is that the kerfs are visible along the top edge of the molding. In paint-grade work, the kerfs can be covered by a cap molding or filled, sanded and painted, once the bend is complete. For outside curves, kerfing will accommodate only mild bends. Tighter curves will require custom curved pieces made up by a millwork shop, either in solid wood or from a form-laminated blank.

At least one company makes a flexible polyester molding bendable in any plane (including compound bends). This material can be nailed just like wood. The moldings are sold in paint grade and stain grade and are available in custom profiles. One company that sells bendable trim is Flex-Trim, whose address is listed in the Resource Guide on pp. 179-181.

One other situation you might encounter from time to time is a wall with a rounded outside corner. A neat way of handling this is to make up a curved plinth block by lathe-turning a cylinder of wood whose outside diameter matches the required radius. Bore a hole through the center of the cylinder to match the rounded corner, then bandsaw the cylinder lengthwise into four segments. The bottom right photo on p. 132 shows this method.

Ceiling moldings

As the name implies, ceiling moldings are found at the junction of the ceiling and wall. Modern ceiling moldings are largely ornamental, although they're sometimes used to disguise unsightly interior structures such

Some solutions to baseboard problems

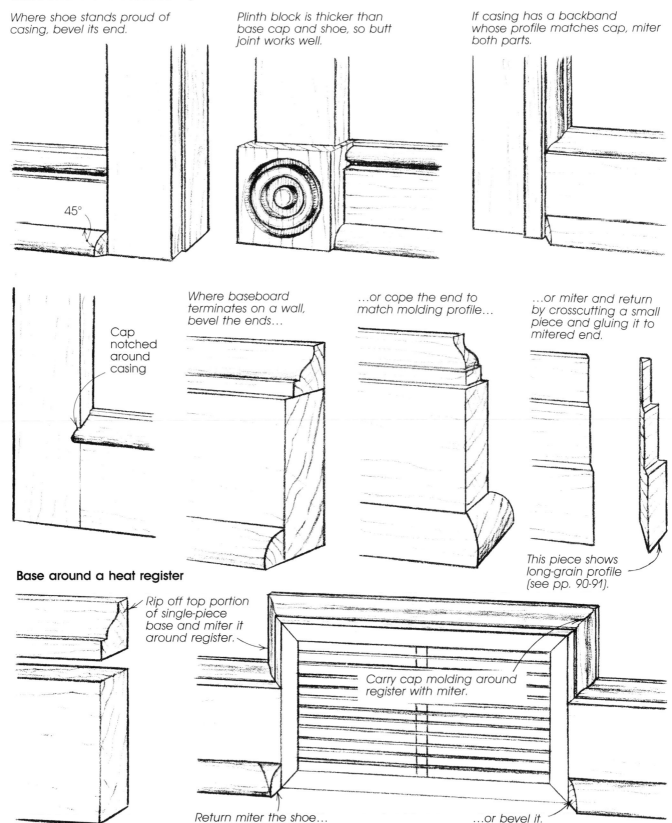

Where shoe stands proud of casing, bevel its end.

45°

Plinth block is thicker than base cap and shoe, so butt joint works well.

If casing has a backband whose profile matches cap, miter both parts.

Cap notched around casing

Where baseboard terminates on a wall, bevel the ends...

...or cope the end to match molding profile...

...or miter and return by crosscutting a small piece and gluing it to mitered end.

This piece shows long-grain profile (see pp. 90-91).

Base around a heat register

Rip off top portion of single-piece base and miter it around register.

Carry cap molding around register with miter.

Return miter the shoe...

...or bevel it.

131

Bending molding

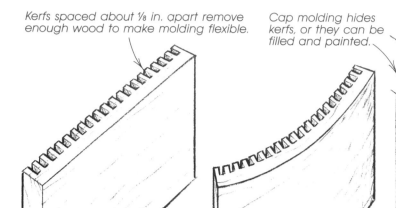

Kerfs spaced about ⅛ in. apart remove enough wood to make molding flexible.

Cap molding hides kerfs, or they can be filled and painted.

To curve molding, simply kerf the back of the molding, then bend it into place, as shown in the drawing at the top of this page. In this photo, the kerfs are just visible beneath the cap molding. Later, they can be filled with glue, epoxy cement or caulk and then painted over.

Baseboard can be taken around a wall with outside radii with curved corner blocks made from lathe-turned cylinders. The cylinders are bored with a hole matching the wall's outside radius. Then the blank is bandsawn lengthwise to produce four corner blocks.

as beams or pipes. The drawing at right shows some typical ceiling treatments possible with off-the-shelf moldings, including a formal cornice you'd expect to see in a period home.

Flat moldings—The simplest ceiling moldings, which I call flat moldings, are little more than upside-down baseboards. Flat moldings install flat on the wall with their top edges either touching the ceiling or kept just below it, the gap covered by another molding. Traditionally, flat moldings aren't used by themselves but in combination with other moldings, usually crowns and beds. However, in Arts and Crafts style houses, you'll often see a wide band of flat molding used to trim the ceiling or to top off a wall of wood paneling.

With their simple profiles, flat moldings are normally coped or mitered at inside corners and mitered at outside corners. But in certain instances, they can be fit with a butt and cope, too. In any case and whether the molding is used by itself or in combination with others, I try to assemble the joint so it's hard to get a view of it that might reveal a gap.

Sprung moldings—Sprung moldings are made of wide, thin material that's inclined away from the nailing surface. When installed, there's a hollow space behind a sprung molding. Almost all crown moldings, regardless of profile, are sprung. Crown moldings are normally made so they're 45° to plumb when installed, but some are at 32° and some are at 35°. Crown molding at 45° appears sharper and of higher relief than crown molding at the shallower angles, which look subtler and less intrusive. Which you choose is a matter of personal preference. Bed moldings—miniature versions of crown that are used in conjunction with it—are also sprung at 45°, 35° or 32°.

As with flat moldings, crown moldings can be used by themselves or in combination with other profiles, usually flat moldings and/or bed moldings. Crown and bed moldings are available in dozens of profiles in wood as well as in veneered wood, plastic and even metal. (See the Resource Guide on pp. 179-181 for suppliers.) It's even possible to buy premitered crown (for outside corners) and precoped crown (for inside corners) that scabs onto longer pieces, making the trim carpenter's life a breeze.

Installing crown molding

Installing ceiling molding can be as simple as running baseboard with butt joints or as complicated as building an entire cornice. If you are installing only flat moldings, use the same general procedure as for installing baseboard. The chief difference is that with ceiling molding, you have to work from a scaffolding or ladder. For sprung moldings, the best inside-corner joint to use is the cope, with miter joints at outside

Ceiling-molding treatments

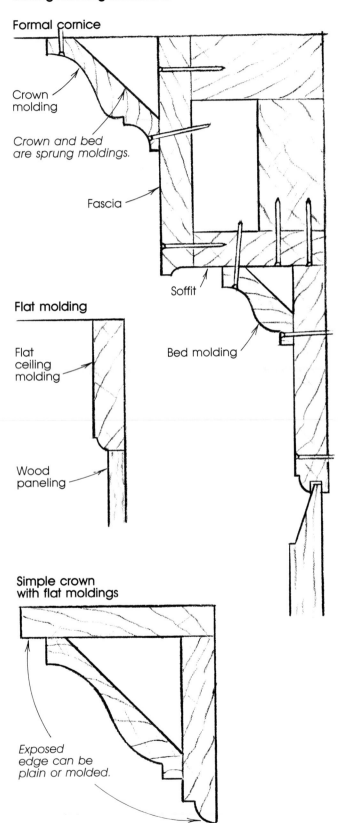

Formal cornice

Crown molding

Crown and bed are sprung moldings.

Fascia

Soffit

Bed molding

Flat molding

Flat ceiling molding

Wood paneling

Simple crown with flat moldings

Exposed edge can be plain or molded.

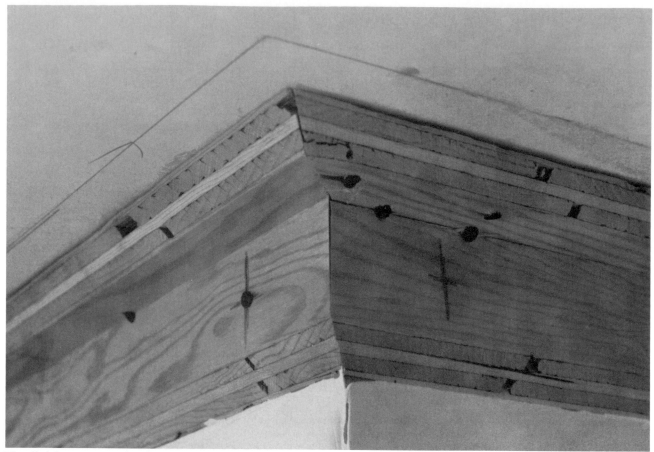

The finish carpenter is often called on site after the drywall is hung, too late to install proper backing for really wide crown molding. One solution is to nail or screw plywood backing outside the drywall.

corners. This is time-consuming, tedious work, but it produces the best results.

To keep this discussion in the real world, I should say that most finish carpenters take the fast way out: they miter both inside and outside corners. The inevitable slop in the miter joints is taken up with wedges or by filling and caulking the open joints, then covering the mess with paint. The miter method I'll describe here will work with both inside or outside miters but because I'm convinced that inside joints should be coped, I'll concentrate on describing that method. Also, I'll explain some tricks I've used to make this difficult joint. But first, some notes on preparation.

For a simple one-piece crown molding not more than 4 in. wide, the top plate, studs and ceiling joists will provide sufficient backing for nails. Where ceiling joists run parallel to walls, an extra piece of backing should be nailed to and cantilevered over the top plate, as shown in the drawing on p. 69. In most circumstances, however, the drywall backing will be enough. If it isn't, you can add backing outside the drywall, as shown in the photo above.

One aspect of preliminary work unique to crown molding is the need to have a flat and straight ceiling. Due to settling, ceilings sink in a shallow parabola toward the center of the room. There are three ways to deal with a curved ceiling. One is to ignore it and hope that moldings that follow the curve won't be noticed. This method is acceptable only if the ceiling's run-out is ⅜ in. or less. Crown-molding patterns have a relieved edge where the molding touches the ceiling, so that a shadow line is created between the ceiling and the molding. The shadow line disguises irregularities.

The second method is to scribe the top of the crown to the curve of the ceiling, then plane off wood so the molding runs straight along its bottom edge. This works fine as long as you don't have to remove too much wood. The third solution is my favorite: install the molding level, holding it to a predetermined lowest point, then have the drywall contractor float the ceiling with drywall compound, leveling the corners and fairing out the curve.

Unless the room is very small, I "shoot" the ceiling elevation with my builder's level (or a transit) to deter-

Installing crown molding on an out-of-plumb ceiling

Dimension D

Ceilings usually sag toward the center of the wall (exaggerated here for clarity).

Align bottom edge of crown molding to level line.

From lowest point in ceiling, measure down dimension D, then strike a level line with builder's level or 6-ft. level.

Dimension D

Where the crown molding doesn't touch the ceiling, float drywall compound to cover gap.

Crown molding order of events

Cope. 3 Butt to wall.

Butt to wall. Cope.

Install first piece on longest wall, opposite door.

4

1

Door

Butt to wall. Cope.

Cope. 2 Butt to wall.

Nailing crown

Nail through flats, into backing.

Stagger nails.

mine whether it's level. By holding the tip of a tape to the ceiling and sighting through the level I can establish just how out of level the ceiling is. If you don't have a builder's level, you can accomplish the same thing, albeit with more effort, using a line level on a string or an 8-ft. level.

In a room with a badly out-of-level ceiling, shoot several locations to establish the ceiling's lowest point, which will then serve as a reference point. If I'm using 4½-in. crown, for example, I know that it will extend down from the ceiling 3⅝ in., so, at the low point, I mark this distance on the wall. Next, I use my level to establish several marks elsewhere on the wall, all in the same plane. Connecting the points with a straightedge or chalkline produces a level reference line to which the bottom of the crown molding is aligned.

Running the first piece—To begin running crown, I pick the longest wall and one that will also create an inconspicuous joint in case the copes open up later. I push the tape into one corner (on long walls, a helper will be needed) and read the length. This measurement is then transferred to a piece of crown and the length is butt cut with a very slight back-cut. I usually cut the piece ¹⁄₁₆ in. too long and snap it into place. The back-cut points should dig into the wall a tiny bit, just as with baseboard.

With the molding aligned to the level mark, I nail it with a nail long enough so that at least half the nail length penetrates into the backing. This requires long nails—12d or 16d, sometimes. Nail through the flats where the molding meets the wall and ceiling and around the corners to pull the molding tight to the wall so that butting pieces won't move it.

If you're holding the crown to a level line and the ceiling is radically curved, it will be touching the ceiling at only one place. At the other nailing points, you may have to put thin shims between the ceiling and the molding to keep the crown from bouncing during nailing. These will be hidden later when the drywaller floats the ceiling.

The second piece is coped to the first piece on one end and butt joined to the wall (or mitered if it's an outside corner) at the other end, using the coping

Measuring crown molding

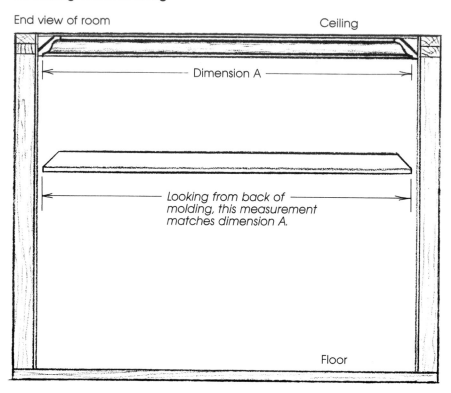

End view of room

Ceiling

Dimension A

Looking from back of molding, this measurement matches dimension A.

Floor

method described on p. 128-129. To determine the length of the second piece and each subsequent piece, use your tape or pinch rods to measure the dimension shown in the drawing above. Then cut your molding a bit long so it will snap into place.

I said earlier that the cope is the most forgiving joint, and it is. However, because crown molding is sprung, the angled cut that reveals the profile is more difficult to make since the molding has to be held securely while it's cut in the chopsaw. If you are cutting on a standard chopsaw (one that won't cut a compound miter), hold the crown just as it will be on the wall, with the flats against the saw table and the fence. However, keep in mind that positioned this way, the molding is really upside-down and backwards. In other words, the surface that fits to the wall rests on the saw table, while the fence represents the wall. You may have to install a plywood extension to the fence for very wide crown molding. Otherwise, you'll have insufficient support for safe cutting.

Usually it's practical to hold the molding firmly with your hand well away from the blade. For extra security, you can tack a strip of wood along the saw table to hold the crown at the proper angle. Remember, however, that the miter angle slopes toward the corner in a cope, not away from it, as in an outside miter. This cut needn't be as accurate as a miter, but it does have to

be at least 45°. It won't matter if you remove too much wood; you're simply making a point so the molding's profile can be coped. When you back-cut, the profile revealed will fit over the mating piece.

Cope and fit one end of the joint first, then move on to the opposite end. With very long moldings, have a helper hold one end while you fit or measure the other. If the crown is coped at one end and mitered at the opposite end, fit the cope first. Cope-to-cope crowns should be measured as shown in the drawing above, then cut a tad long so they'll spring into place. Nail as you go, but don't drive the nails flush in case you have to remove a chumped piece.

Outside corners—Crowns at outside corners have to be joined with miters. In this case, I start by carefully marking on the wall the position of ceiling joists and wall studs. These might not be where you think they are, so it's best to locate them by driving in a 6d finishing nail at points where the finished molding will cover the holes. Miters need better backing than copes because coped joints are held together by the spring action. Outside miters depend on nails.

Outside miters are tricky to perfect. It's best to cut them long and trim once or twice until they're right. If the opposite end of an outside mitered piece goes to an inside corner, I try to make it a butt joint so I can

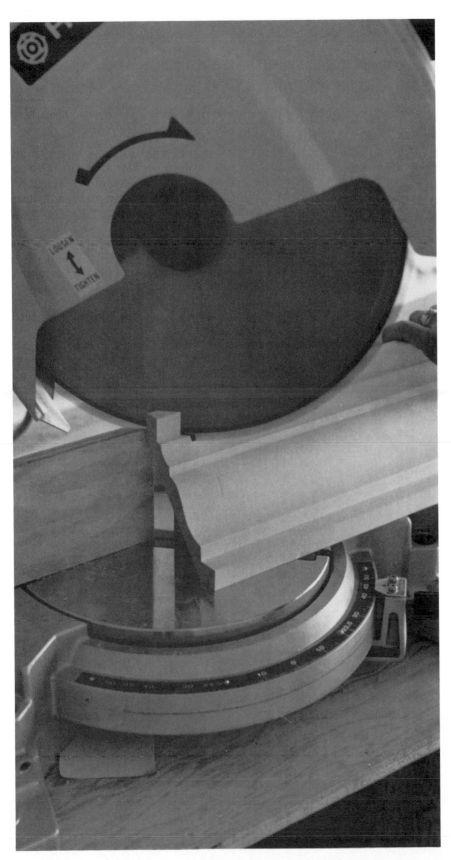

To expose a profile for coping, the crown has to be mitered first. The trick is to position the molding on the saw just as it will go on the ceiling, then saw a miter whose end grain slopes away from the molding's show surface. Hold the molding with its flats firmly against the saw's table and fence. The saw's guard has been removed here to show the direction of cut.

Once the molding's profile has been exposed, a coping saw cuts right to it. Because crown molding is so wide and angled to the wall, a radical back-cut (more than 45°) is sometimes needed to ensure a good fit.

fudge the length and hide the gap with a cope later. To mark the length, hold the piece in place with a bit of extra length flying by the corner. Mark the bottom edge where it intersects the corner of the wall. This will be the heel of the miter. Sometimes, it's awkward to use this as your index for the cut because the saw won't adjust to that side or won't cut deep enough. In this case, I use the same method as with baseboards, using scraps to mark an intersection on the ceiling. The intersection marks the toe of the miter, which can then be marked on the molding.

Two pieces of mitered sprung molding (45° to both wall and ceiling) meet at a compound angle. It's possible to figure the compound cut with a complex formula that mathematically defines a four-sided staved cone, a pyramid. This formula can come in handy when you are dealing with walls that intersect at odd angles or if you want to cut crown molding on a table

saw or radial-arm saw or on a chopsaw capable of compound cuts. I've included the formula here as a matter of reference.

$$\text{Chopsaw angle} = \cos^{-1}\left\{\frac{1}{\sqrt{1+\cos^2 C\ \tan^2\left(W/2\right)}}\right.$$

$$\text{Blade tilt angle} = \tan^{-1}\left\{\frac{\sin C\ \tan\left(W/2\right)}{\sqrt{1+\cos^2 C\ \tan^2\left(W/2\right)}}\right.$$

Where C = 90° - crown molding's spring angle
Where W = joint angle, usually 90°

Frankly, though, I find the empirical method more expedient—I simply jig the molding in the saw to make the cut, then adjust by trial and error. For this seat-of-the pants method to work, you have to be able to visualize the molding as it will be installed on the wall and

Crown molding turns outside corners with a miter joint. If possible, try to avoid finishing off a room with two outside miters. A cope or butt at one end will be more forgiving.

then position it correctly for the cut. In the saw, the cut will be made with the molding upside down and backwards from the way it will be on the wall. The cut is made just like the cope, except that the miter slopes away from the joint instead of toward it.

Between the reversal of the saw working across two planes—the wall and the ceiling—there's lots of need for idiot-proofing the process so a lot of good wood won't get ruined. For this reason I always keep short scraps of trim around to test each cut, then try them in position for correct fit. This means trudging up the ladder with the test piece and eyeballing the thing to make sure that the miter slopes in the correct direction and that I've got the angle close enough to achieve a decent fit. If you're cutting and fitting very long pieces, have a helper steady the molding for marking and cutting. And remember, cut long and trim to a perfect fit.

Troubleshooting crown—The most common crown problem is an out-of-square room (a room where the ceilings are not square to the walls). In this situation, you'll have to scribe the cope joint. I usually take a scrap piece and hold it in position and then scribe it. Then I use the test piece to make fine adjustments in the chopsaw angle (or use the wedge method described on pp. 86-87) for the actual cut.

To scribe a cope, chop the miter in the mating piece, then hold it in the position it will occupy when installed. With a scribing tool, follow the profile of one piece and transfer it to the mating piece. Recut the miter to the scribe line or simply cut to this line when you make your back cut. Then adjust the cope to fit in the usual way.

Minor gaps in outside miters can be corrected using the strategy described in the drawing on p. 141. It's best to work out the size of the wedge with a scrap be-

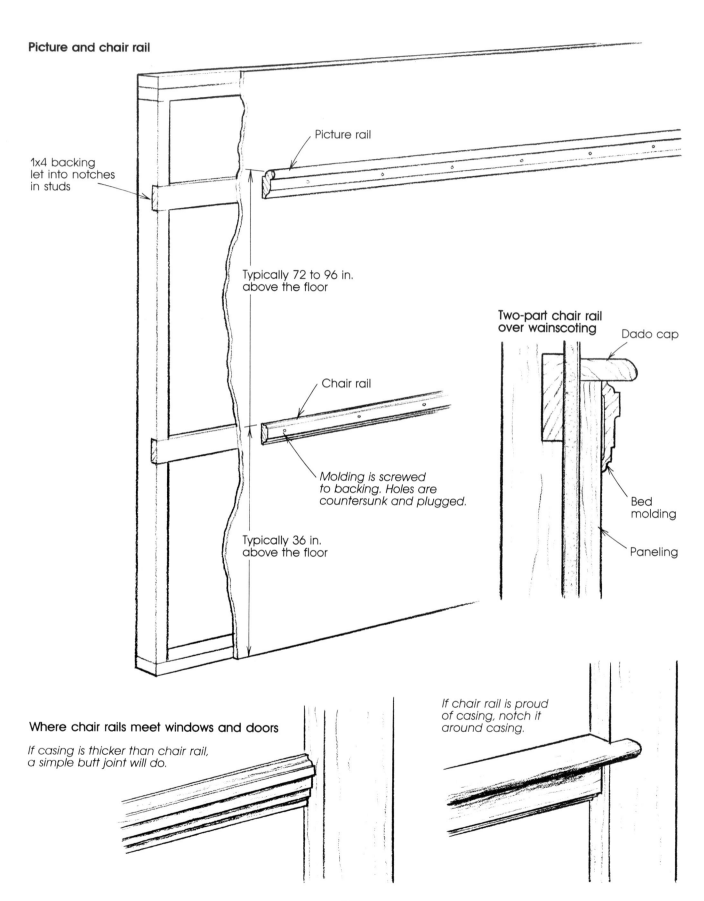

Picture and chair rail

Picture rail

1x4 backing
let into notches
in studs

Typically 72 to 96 in.
above the floor

Chair rail

*Molding is screwed
to backing. Holes are
countersunk and plugged.*

Typically 36 in.
above the floor

**Two-part chair rail
over wainscoting**

Dado cap

Bed
molding

Paneling

Where chair rails meet windows and doors

*If casing is thicker than chair rail,
a simple butt joint will do.*

*If chair rail is proud
of casing, notch it
around casing.*

140

Correcting gaps in outside miters

If gap in crown molding tapers, place a wedge between the saw table and the bottom edge of the molding to adjust the cut.

Evenly open joints should be corrected by adjusting the saw's angle of cut.

If there is a gap at the toe of the miter, increase the cutting angle slightly. Gaps at the heel won't show and can be ignored.

fore making corrective cuts on the actual piece. Crown molding is expensive, and it's by far the easiest molding to chump.

Chair and picture moldings

In addition to base and crown, there are two other kinds of moldings that can be installed on interior walls. These are chair-rail and picture-rail moldings. Depending on the aesthetic effect you wish to achieve, you might use either of these (but probably not both) in combination with baseboard and crown moldings.

Chair rail is installed horizontally on the wall about one-third of the way between the the floor and ceiling. Originally, chair rails were meant to protect the plaster wall or the paneling against marring from chair backs. Chair rails still serve that purpose, but today, they're primarily decorative. Off-the-shelf chair rail is likely to be a rather undistinctive reverse ogee paired with beads or fillets. A traditional chair rail, however, consists of a small, thin flat molding, often with a chamfer on the lower edge, capped with a projecting torus that gives the rail the appearance of receding from top to bottom. It can be made and installed in one or two parts. In any case, the element of the rail that projects farthest from the wall should be softly rounded, since it takes the brunt of abuse from the furniture.

Obviously, chair rails are found in dining rooms, but the style can be carried into other rooms as well, including libraries, dens and hallways. The chair rail serves as a divider for decorative purposes, with wallpaper or paneling below or above rail. The drawing on the facing page shows some typical chair-rail profiles and dimensions. Chair rail is installed following the same general procedures as for baseboard. Two-piece rails with a flat section and a rounded section can be

mitered and coped respectively at inside corners and mitered at outsider corners. Backing for chair rail should be installed before the drywall. I like to let 1x4s into notches cut into the studs. This helps straighten any bows in the walls and give me plenty of material to nail into.

One design problem you'll encounter when installing chair rail is mating it to window and door casings. Normally, the chair rail stands proud of casings so a simple mitered return looks fine. Another method is to notch the rail over the casing, as shown in the drawing at bottom right on the facing page.

Picture rail—Picture rail is probably a relatively recent invention, since it's not found in well-preserved early period homes. Picture molding is mounted just below the juncture of ceiling and wall. Its purpose, besides decoration, is to provide an attachment point for wall hangings. The molding is shaped to accept rounded metal hooks to which wires can be attached to support the wall hangings. The hooks are attached without tools, and they can easily be repositioned along the picture rail's length. If the room is to have a large crown molding, the picture molding can be part of the frieze, in which case it's installed immediately below the crown or bed molding.

Since picture rails are high up on the wall, they usually run continuously around the room, with no breaks for windows or doors. So the rail will be straight and level, I snap a chalkline to points established with a builder's level or from measurements taken from the bottom edge of the crown. On a long wall, the chalkline is the bottom line, and I just cover it up with the bottom of the molding. As with crown and base, inside corners should be coped, outside corners mitered. Picture rails with very deep profiles will be awkward to cope and should be mitered instead.

Picture rails are nailed into the studs using the same strategy as with baseboard. However, picture rails project as much as 2 in. from the wall, so they'll require nails through the outside miters to lock them against opening. Plugged screws will do an even better job. Picture moldings may be called upon to hold a lot of weight if large wall hangings are to be displayed. For that reason, it's better to use too many nails than too few or to screw the molding into the studs, then plug the holes.

Solid-wood wainscot is usually associated with period homes, but with restrained use of molding in paint-grade woods, it lends itself nicely to contemporary interiors.

8

Wainscoting

The word "wainscot" has had several meanings throughout the history of building. Used in Europe as early as the Middle Ages, "waynscottes" referred to well-seasoned boards imported from the Baltic countries and intended for use as wall coverings. In Colonial America, wainscot referred to the superior-quality oak boards used for partition walls inside First Period timber-frame homes. Time has broadened the definition so that today, wainscot, or wainscoting, is considered to be any kind of wooden wall covering, especially paneling that is applied to the lower portion of an interior wall.

Because wainscoting reached the height of popularity during the mid-18th century, it's often considered a period architectural treatment. Made of pine and painted, traditional wainscoting was usually installed in rooms where one wall had been paneled from floor to ceiling. Period wainscoting is still quite popular in New England, especially in authentic restoration work. In my own work, I have occasionally been asked to make contemporary interpretations of wainscoting. These usually consist of a frame-and-panel system trimmed with a simple, shallow relief molding and a baseboard. The panels can be solid wood, veneered plywood, painted medium-density fiberboard or even cloth-covered plywood.

Another type of wainscoting is called tongue-and-groove or, out West, tongue-and-groove paneling. It's not really paneling at all, but simply narrow boards into which a profile has been molded. Tongue-and-groove was very popular around the turn of the century and is enjoying a bit of a comeback. As with paneled wainscot, tongue-and-groove can be stain grade or paint grade. Besides having an entirely different look from frame-and-panel wainscot, tongue-and-groove requires fewer tools and takes less time to install.

Tongue-and-groove wainscot is commonly available in pine or, as shown here, fir. Trimmed with a simple molding and finished clear, it can be used to create a contemporary aesthetic.

Wainscoting details

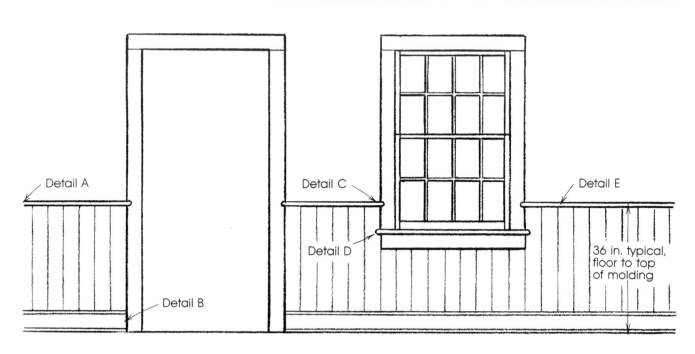

Detail A

Detail B

Detail C

Detail D

Detail E

36 in. typical,
floor to top
of molding

Detail A: Inside corners

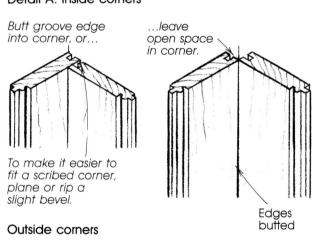

*Butt groove edge
into corner, or...*

*...leave
open space
in corner.*

*To make it easier to
fit a scribed corner,
plane or rip a
slight bevel.*

Edges
butted

Outside corners

*Rip off grooved sections,
butt, glue and nail...*

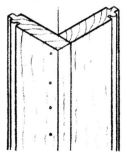

*...or miter the corner
lengthwise, glue and nail.*

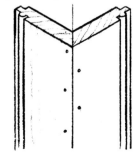

Detail B: Where wainscot meets door casing

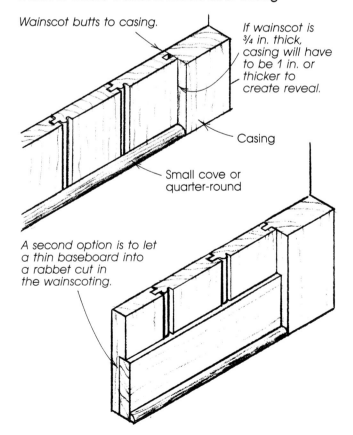

Wainscot butts to casing.

*If wainscot is
¾ in. thick,
casing will have
to be 1 in. or
thicker to
create reveal.*

Casing

Small cove or
quarter-round

*A second option is to let
a thin baseboard into
a rabbet cut in
the wainscoting.*

Detail C: Where wainscot meets window casing

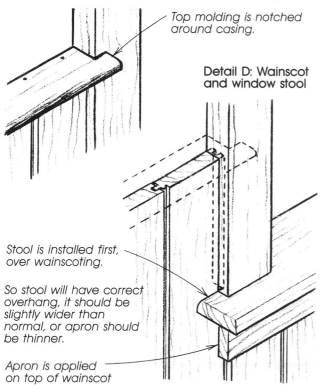

Top molding is notched around casing.

Detail D: Wainscot and window stool

Stool is installed first, over wainscoting.

So stool will have correct overhang, it should be slightly wider than normal, or apron should be thinner.

Apron is applied on top of wainscot

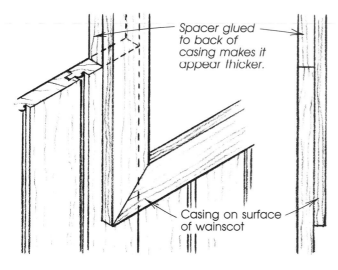

Spacer glued to back of casing makes it appear thicker.

Casing on surface of wainscot

Detail E: Top-rail treatments

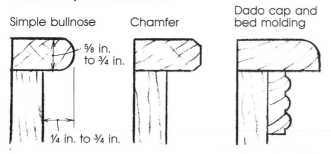

Simple bullnose

⅝ in. to ¾ in.

¼ in. to ¾ in.

Chamfer

Dado cap and bed molding

Wainscoting: when and where

In my opinion, a little wood paneling goes a long way. If you have the budget for it, it's tempting to panel an entire room, but you run the risk of creating an uncomfortable, busy look. This is especially true in libraries and private offices, where too much paneling makes for such visual chaos that it's impossible to read or to find space between the frames and panels for shelving. In an authentic period house, you expect to see lots of elaborate molding, but restraint is the theme in contemporary architecture.

I tell clients who want paneling to consider paneling one wall floor to ceiling and then integrating the other walls with simple wainscoting or even just a chair rail running around the rest of the room. If the paneling is to be stain-grade wood (my usual preference), wainscoting around the entire room will be plenty of wood.

Living rooms, dining rooms, libraries and dens are the typical locations for wainscoting, but it can also be installed to good effect in halls and even kitchens. Whether painted or stained, wainscoting tends to make a room appear smaller and busier. This is especially true in rooms with low ceilings. Similarly, rooms with lots of windows are already visually broken up, and wainscoting adds yet more detail. In these cases, it might be better to forego the wainscoting in favor of a simple chair rail, as described on pp. 140-141. One other problem with lots of windows is contrast. When bright light streams into a room paneled in a dark wood, the eye has a difficult time adjusting.

In new construction, you'll have some choice of what kind of wall the wainscoting will be applied to. In remodel work, you'll have to work with the existing walls. In general, the more backing a wall has, the easier it will be to attach wainscot. This goes for both tongue-and-groove and frame-and-panel wainscot. In new work, you can apply wainscot right over the drywall, which should be taped but not fine-sanded or painted.

Make sure that you've installed plenty of backing behind the drywall. One method of backing for wainscot is to let 1x4s or 1x6s into notches cut in the studs, as explained on pp. 68-69. It's possible to attach paneled wainscot directly to the studs, but check the local building code first—some codes require that drywall, not solid wood, be installed to studs.

Old drywall or plaster can be a problem surface. If you can locate the studs and mark them, nail or screw the wainscoting directly to the framing. In remodels, I've seen drywall, plaster or plywood paneling covered with ½-in. medium-density fiberboard, which then serves as a backing for the wainscoting.

Tongue-and-groove wainscot

Tongue-and-groove wainscot consists of individual boards sold in random widths or in standard widths, typically 2½ to 5 in. wide. One edge of each board has

Wainscot order of events

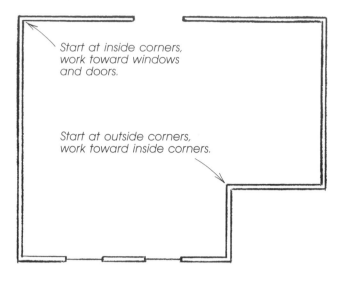

Start at inside corners, work toward windows and doors.

Start at outside corners, work toward inside corners.

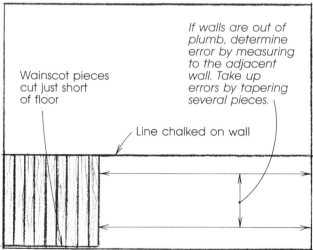

Wainscot pieces cut just short of floor

If walls are out of plumb, determine error by measuring to the adjacent wall. Take up errors by tapering several pieces.

Line chalked on wall

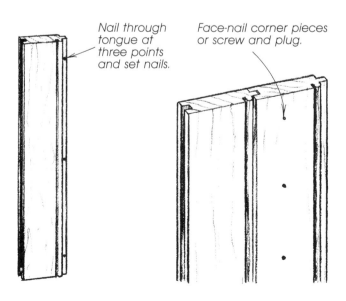

Nail through tongue at three points and set nails.

Face-nail corner pieces or screw and plug.

a tongue, the other edge a groove. Both edges usually have some sort of decorative profile such as a bevel, a bead or a fillet. Some lumberyards stock tongue-and-groove wainscot in pine or other softwoods or will make it to order in any species. Because of the close resemblance, some yards sell tongue-and-groove flooring as wainscot stock, usually in oak. It's an acceptable substitute, so long as you like oak and don't mind your walls looking like floors.

Wainscot is sold by the piece or the bundle and is typically ⅜ to ¾ in. thick. If you use ¾-in. material, the wainscoting will end up flush with the door and window casings. In this case, I'd suggest 1-in. thick casings to create a ¼-in. reveal where the wainscot butts to the casings.

Tongue-and-groove wainscot is simply nailed to the wall so it's very important to have plenty of backing, as described above and on pp. 68-69. The drawing on pp. 144-145 shows a typical application for tongue-and-groove wainscot, as well as some methods for handling door, window and baseboard details.

To begin installing tongue-and-groove wainscoting, chalk a level line on the wall to indicate the height of the wainscoting. All of the pieces can be cut ahead of time to a length that stops them just short of the floor. The resulting gap will be covered by the baseboard. The drawing at left shows some strategies for starting the runs on each wall. If there are no outside corners, start at the inside corners and work toward the opposite walls or toward the door and window casings. When there are outside corners, try to start with them and work toward the inside corners or toward the window and door casings. That way, it'll be easier to fit the outside corners, which are more conspicuous.

As shown in Detail A on p. 144, the inside corners can be handled in several ways. One is just to butt the groove end of the piece into the corner and not worry about the fact that the adjacent piece will create an uneven reveal. Normally, this isn't noticeable. If you want an even reveal, hold the first piece away from the wall by a distance equal to the thickness of the wainscot, then butt the mating piece. This will create a hollow space in the corner, but it will be covered by the chair rail. Outside corners are simply butted and nailed or, if you want a crisper corner, mitered lengthwise. Cut the miter on a table saw.

Assuming no outside corners, begin by nailing a full piece butted into an inside corner. Nail the wainscot through the tongue at three points, as shown in the drawing at left. Set the nails so the next piece will slip over the tongue. Each subsequent piece is slipped over the tongue of the previous piece and then, in turn, nailed through its own tongue. To allow for wood movement in very moist climates, leave a gap of about ¹⁄₁₆ in. between the shoulder of each tongue and the adjacent piece. A scrap of Formica makes a good spacer for judging the correct gap.

If you want to finish the wall with a full-width piece in the corner, you will have to do a bit of planning ahead of time. After I have installed about five or six pieces, working out from one corner toward the opposite wall, I lay out seven or eight pieces on the floor, then carefully measure the combined width. This gives me a good sense of how many pieces will be needed to complete the wall and how close I'll come to finishing with a full piece.

If the measurement indicates I'll fall short by a dimension greater than the width of a full piece, I can take up the slack by increasing the spacing between pieces to $\frac{3}{32}$ in. If it indicates I'll end up requiring less than a full piece, I can plane a bit (up to $\frac{1}{4}$ in.) off the width of as many pieces as necessary to make up the difference. This small difference in width won't be no-

Tongue-and-groove wainscot

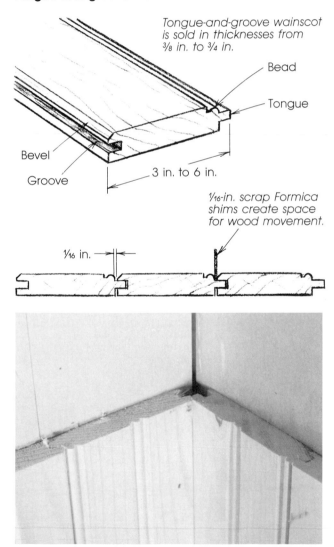

Tongue-and-groove wainscot is sold in thicknesses from $\frac{3}{8}$ in. to $\frac{3}{4}$ in.

Bead

Tongue

Bevel

Groove

3 in. to 6 in.

$\frac{1}{16}$-in. scrap Formica shims create space for wood movement.

$\frac{1}{16}$ in.

To achieve an equal reveal on both pieces, wainscot is nailed at the corners, left, leaving a small gap that will be covered by the chair rail. Working from the corners out, slip the groove of each piece over the tongue of the previous piece.

Check the wainscot for plumb about halfway through the run, as shown at left. Correct errors by tapering one or more pieces. To correct for an out-of-plumb wall at the outset, mark a plumb line on the wall about a wainscot's width from the corner. Then scribe the mating piece so it's both parallel to the line and tight to the corner, as shown above.

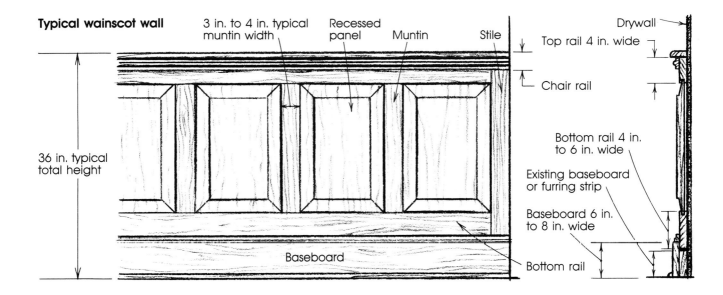

Typical wainscot wall

3 in. to 4 in. typical muntin width

Recessed panel

Muntin

Stile

Drywall

Top rail 4 in. wide

Chair rail

Bottom rail 4 in. to 6 in. wide

Existing baseboard or furring strip

Baseboard 6 in. to 8 in. wide

36 in. typical total height

Baseboard

Bottom rail

ticed in the finished wall. To make things easy, plane the grooved edges of the wainscot, then re-bevel the edge to match the original, if the grooved edge has a bevel. The last piece on the wall may have to be slid in from the top, and if there's no room to nail through the tongue, you can nail (or screw) right through the face of the piece.

A more difficult challenge is installing wainscot on out-of-plumb walls. Often, one wall will be canted one way, the other the opposite way. In this case, start the wainscot in the usual way but when you're four or five pieces away from the adjacent wall, measure into the corner you're headed for from the top and bottom edge of the last piece installed. This will tell you if the wainscot will end up parallel to the wall. If it won't, taper the last few pieces slightly to take up the error. If the error is slight, say ¼ in. or so, you can ignore it, so long as the run of the wall finishes up with close to a full piece.

Another way of correcting for out-of-plumb walls is to mark a plumb line on the wall about a board's width from the corner you're coming out of. Then, with a piece held parallel to this line, scribe as shown in the photo at right on the facing page to taper the piece. Even if the walls appear to be plumb, it's a good idea to check the wainscot run for plumb about halfway down the wall, then correct any errors by tapering the remaining pieces.

Where wainscoting meets door casings, it can simply be butted to the casing, as shown in Detail B on p. 144. Windows are a little trickier, though, because the casing has to bridge the different planes between the wainscoting and the wall. If the window is trimmed picture-frame style, the easiest solution is to install the casing first, then butt the wainscoting right to it. Make sure, however, that the casing is thick enough to

stand proud of the wainscoting so that you will have an attractive reveal. Another method is to install the casing on top of the wainscoting; then, to make the casing appear thicker, glue and nail a spacer behind it, as shown in Detail D on p. 145. The spacer fills up what would otherwise be a gap where the casing bridges the wainscot.

With stool-and-apron style trim, it makes sense to leave the casing off until the wainscoting is installed, then fit the casing over the wainscoting. Again, you can use the spacer trick to take up the gap behind the casing. A more elegant if somewhat involved solution is to let the wainscoting into the casing by cutting a small notch on the backside of the trim, as shown in Detail C on p. 145. The notch should be as deep as the wainscot is thick.

One last window-trim element that you will have to deal with is the apron. Because the apron is nailed to the surface of the wainscot and not the wall, the amount the stool overhangs the apron will be reduced. This means the stool will have to be wider to compensate or the apron thinner by an amount equal to the wainscot thickness.

Detail E on p. 145 shows molding treatments for the top of wainscot. These are really chair rails and can be applied using the methods described in Chapter 7. However, the molding should be nailed down through the top and into the end grain of the tongue-and-groove paneling.

There are several ways to handle baseboard with wainscot. If the boards have been held above the floor, you can simply nail the baseboard to the wainscot and attach the shoe and base cap in the usual way. Another method is to let a baseboard into a rabbet cut along the bottom edge of the wainscoting, as shown in Detail B on p. 144.

Paneled wainscot is a common feature in 18th-century homes, such as the example below in the Silas Deane historical house in Wethersfield, Conn. The paneling is topped with a typical high-style Georgian chair rail, right.

Paneled wainscoting

As the drawing on p. 149 shows, paneled wainscoting consists of solid wood or veneered panels let into grooves cut into rails and stiles. The frame is constructed just like a frame-and-panel door, with molded rails (the horizontal members) and stiles (the vertical members) joined by mortise-and-tenon joints. To allow them to shrink and swell with seasonal changes in moisture, the panels float loosely in grooves milled into the rails and stiles. Usually, the frames are constructed in the shop as completed sections and then taken to the job, where they are nailed or screwed to the wall. If you have the equipment, of course, you can build the frames on site instead.

Paneled wainscot looks more formal than tongue-and-groove wainscot, and by manipulating the dimensions of rails, stiles and panels, it's possible to achieve wide variations in style. Traditional wainscot has raised and fielded panels, a wide baseboard and a formal chair rail, as shown in the photos on the facing page. Contemporary wainscot, on the other hand, tends toward simpler moldings and panels with lower relief, as shown in the photos on pp. 142-143. In fact, the panels shown on p. 142 are actually recessed well behind the plane of the rails.

The first step in designing a paneled wainscot wall is to determine its overall dimensions. I start by snapping a level line at 36 in. above the floor (or whatever height the paneling will be). If the frame is to fit, you need a very accurate way of measuring the walls in both planes, but especially horizontally since the wainscot frame usually has to fit between two walls. I normally use pinch sticks or rods for this purpose. These are described on pp. 48-49. I check the walls with a level too, so I know ahead of time if they are out of plumb.

I carefully measure the location of doors and windows along the wall and record these in a notebook as well as marking them on my story pole. Next, I decide on the width of the stiles, rails and muntins, the intermediate vertical members that run between the two rails. The bottom rail of wainscot paneling seems to look best if it's about 6 in. high. If the rail will double as a baseboard, which is often the case, refer to Chapter 7 for ideas on molding profiles. The important thing is that the bottom rail be wide enough to act as a visual anchor for the rest of the paneling and that there be some way to fasten it securely to the wall. The top rail should be narrower than the bottom rail: 3 in. to 4 in. is a good starting place. The top drawing on p. 152 shows some typical top-rail treatments and dimensions. Stiles should be about the same width as the top rail, but muntins can be 1 in. narrower.

With these dimensions in mind, I sketch out an overall elevation of each frame on ¼-in. grid graph paper. Next, I determine how many panels the wall will have, without worrying about their exact size just yet—

Panel-joinery methods

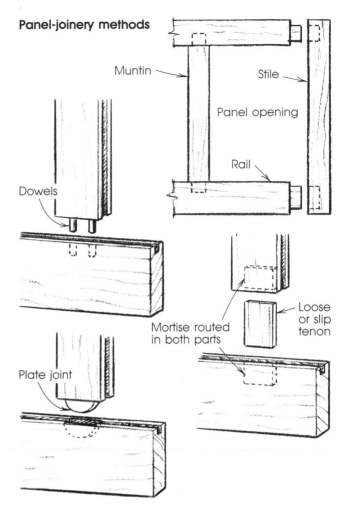

Muntin
Stile
Panel opening
Rail
Dowels
Mortise routed in both parts
Loose or slip tenon
Plate joint

In high wainscoting, a plate rail is an attractive top treatment. This example was built by California contractor Rodger Whipple. (Photo by Steve Morris.)

151

Paneled-wainscot top-rail and baseboard treatments

Top rail

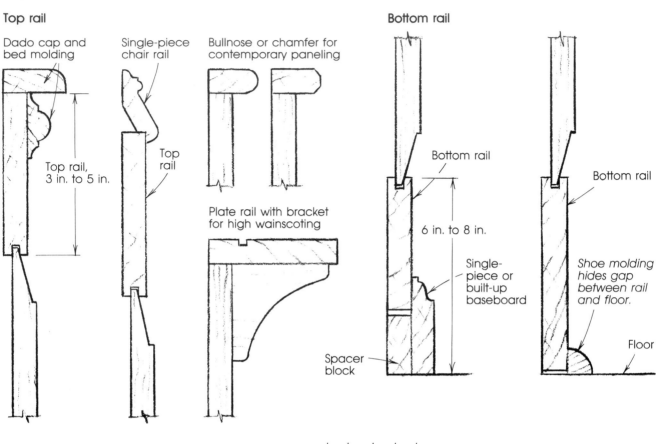

Dado cap and bed molding

Top rail, 3 in. to 5 in.

Single-piece chair rail

Top rail

Bullnose or chamfer for contemporary paneling

Plate rail with bracket for high wainscoting

Bottom rail

Bottom rail

6 in. to 8 in.

Single-piece or built-up baseboard

Spacer block

Bottom rail

Shoe molding hides gap between rail and floor.

Floor

Door and window treatments

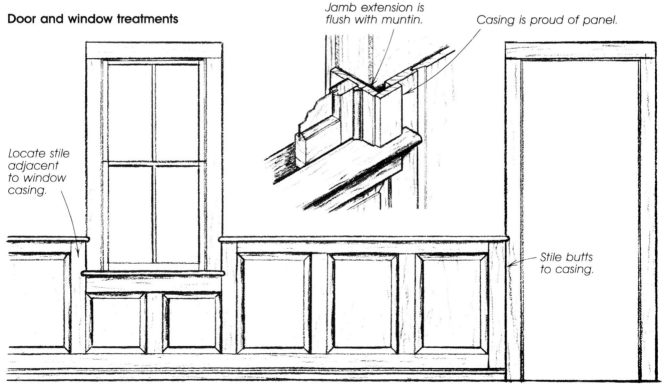

Locate stile adjacent to window casing.

Jamb extension is flush with muntin.

Casing is proud of panel.

Stile butts to casing.

at this point, I'm just wanting to see what's possible. To do this, I figure out the total space available for panels by adding up the widths of all the stiles and muntins. By subtracting this total from the length of wall to be wainscoted and dividing the result by the number of panels, I arrive at an approximate panel width. Panel height is figured the same way: add the width of the top and bottom rails, then subtract it from the total height of the frame. Later on, I refine my panel dimensions to allow for grooves in the rails and stiles, but for now, I can draw my frame-and-panel system to see how the panel proportioning will come out.

Proportioning the panels is probably the hardest part of designing wainscot. If you're after a period look, I recommend that you look at photos of existing rooms and copy these proportions as closely as you can, within the limitations of your room size. The Further Reading list on p. 181 gives some examples of books to look at, as well as some contemporary design sources.

Early architectural texts often cite proportioning systems based on the mathematical proportions of classical Greek and Roman architecture, or the so-called golden section. The golden section states that ideal proportion results from dividing a line such that the smaller part is to the larger part as the larger part is to the whole, a ratio of about 5 to 8. By applying this logic to a rectangular panel, you'll come up with a golden rectangle, a panel that's five units by eight units. Unfortunately, in the real world, panels that are golden rectangles might not work out evenly on the wall you happen to have.

I usually experiment with proportioning by drawing the paneling to scale on graph paper, dividing the panels evenly to fill up the space. If no pleasing proportions seem obvious, the golden section might be a starting place. I strive for visual balance and for pleasing proportion in the panels. This doesn't necessarily mean all of the panels will be of the same size. In fact, it sometimes looks better to vary the panel width within a wall, combining narrow, strongly vertical panels with squarish shapes. Sometimes small panels on one side of a room will help balance busy shelving on the other. Because every room is different, there aren't any universal rules. The best approach is to keep drawing until you get a design that works. Your drawing will also have to allow for doors and windows. The bottom drawing on the facing page shows some approaches to mating paneling to door and window casing.

Layout—Once the drawing is done, you'll have to refine its dimensions enough to lay out and cut stiles, rails and panels. It's possible to do this by very careful measurement with a tape or pinch rods, but a story pole, as described on pp. 48-49, is more accurate. Actually, two poles are needed, one for horizontal dimensions, one for vertical. Cut the horizontal pole the exact width of the wall to be paneled, and mark it directly with all the relevant dimensions. The vertical pole

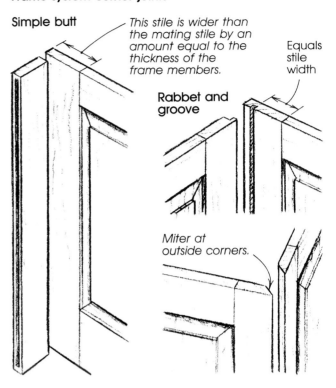

Frame-system corner joints

Simple butt

This stile is wider than the mating stile by an amount equal to the thickness of the frame members.

Equals stile width

Rabbet and groove

Miter at outside corners.

should be long enough to reach about 1 ft. above the top of the paneling.

Use your drawing to mark out rail and stile locations on the pole, along with the locations of windows, heating registers, electric outlets and any other features that affect layout. Sometimes it's easier to use pinch rods, since they can be readily adjusted to compensate for out-of-plumb walls. The vertical pole records dimensions in the vertical plane. Use the poles like a notebook, noting any measurements or information that might be useful when you start layout. Although the wainscot can be assembled in place right on the wall, I prefer to build it on site or in the shop and install it as a unit on the wall. If I'm working in the shop, I won't be able to check my measurements as I go, so I double-check the poles before I start cutting wood.

When it comes to layout, there are a couple of considerations. First is the type of joint to be used where the frame systems join at the corners. If you're paneling only one wall, this is no problem. The frames simply butt to the walls. But if there are two or more walls, you have the choice of the joints shown in the drawing above. The best of these is the rabbet and groove, because it hides wood movement. A butt joint usually works well enough, as long the stiles aren't too wide. Outside corners can be mitered or butted. Applied moldings, the base shoe (if any) and chair rail, can be joined as described in Chapter 7.

Mitered and coped rails and stiles

Molded rails, stiles and muntins require coped joints...

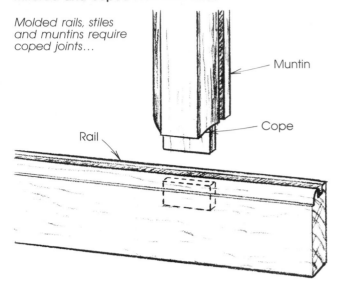

Muntin

Cope

Rail

...or miter this section of molding.

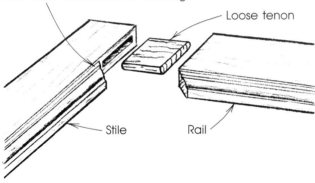

Loose tenon

Stile

Rail

An easier way is to use unmolded frame parts, then nail on molding after assembly...

...or capture panels with bolection molding nailed to surface of frame.

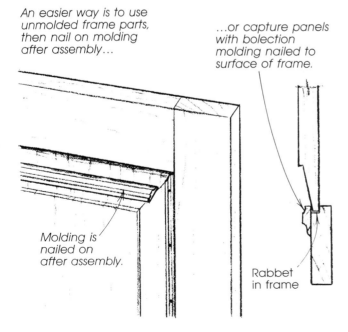

Molding is nailed on after assembly.

Rabbet in frame

The second consideration is the frame joinery. Mortise-and-tenon is the traditional method, and it's what I use. However, doweling, plate joints such as the Lamello system and lap joints are also practical. I use a slip-tenon or loose-tenon method, which greatly simplifies construction. This is descibed in detail on p. 156.

Step one in layout is to determine the frame's overall size, starting with the length. I build the frame to be slightly (¼ in. or ⅜ in.) longer than the distance between walls. This allows for scribing and an exact fit into the corners. If one or both of the walls is out of plumb, I try to compensate for it by making the end stiles a bit wider so I'll have extra wood for scribing. In any case, stiles that butt to another stile in the corners should be wider by the thickness of the framework. That way, all the corner stiles will appear to be the same width.

Once overall dimensions are determined, the individual rails and stiles can be ripped to width and cut to length. If you're using conventional mortise-and-tenon, don't forget to allow extra length for the joints. With loose tenons or plate joints, you can cut the parts to their exact lengths.

Next, use the story pole or careful tape measurements to establish the location of stiles and muntins. I usually do this by dry-clamping the top and bottom rails between the end stiles on a bench or a clean floor. Using my story-pole layout, I mark with a centerline where each vertical member joins the rails. Later, I'll measure to either side of the centerline to mark for joint cutting. Double-check your measurements before cutting the joints. Grooves for the panels can be cut before or after the mortises, but I usually do it before mortising. The grooves should be about ⅜ in. to ½ in. deep and wide enough to accommodate your panel design. Grooving can be done with a dado head on the table saw or a slotting cutter in the router. The latter method is slower but safer.

Assembling the frame—If you have the tools and skill, traditional mortise-and-tenon joinery is probably the best choice for wainscot framework. Mortised frames are extremely strong, and the joints will remain tight for many years. With a very simple plunge-router setup, however, I make a loose tenon that's just as strong and far easier to make.

Frames that have a stuck-on molding will have to be coped or mitered where rails and stiles join, an added level of complication. Mitering just the molded portion of the rail and stile is not difficult, but it is time-consuming. To speed it along a little, I use the router setup shown in the photos on the facing page. A large chamfering bit or V-groove bit mounted in the router table, as shown in the top right photo, cuts an accurate miter. As shown in the bottom right photo, the miter can be trimmed to a perfect fit with a chisel and a shop-made guide block.

Before they're molded and joints are cut, rails and stiles should be grooved for panels. This can be done on a router table, as shown here, or on a table saw.

Molded stiles must be coped or mitered. One way of mitering is to use a chamfer bit in a router table to make a 45° cut. (Photo by Charles Miller.)

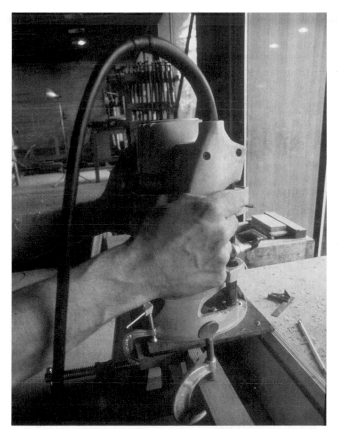

To cut mortises, Savage uses a plunge router and the shopmade jig shown above and in the drawing on p. 156. Stiles are clamped in the jig horizontally. Rails and muntins are held vertically. (Photo by Charles Miller.)

After mitering, the joint is trimmed to fit with a shop-made jig block and chisel. (Photo by Charles Miller.)

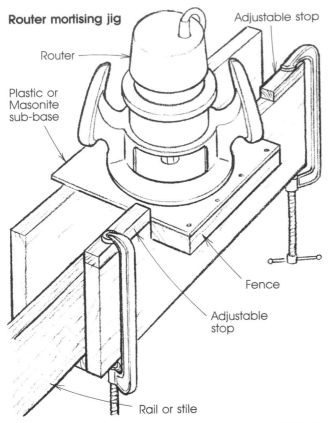

Router mortising jig

Router

Adjustable stop

Plastic or
Masonite
sub-base

Fence

Adjustable
stop

Rail or stile

A completed rail-to-stile joint with its molded section mitered. Although more difficult to make, a coped molded section better hides the effects of wood movement. (Photo by Charles Miller.)

One way of avoiding the extra work of mitering is to make the frame parts without molding, then nail it on after the frame is assembled. Another way of skinning the cat is to let the panels into rabbets cut in the frames. Surface-mounted moldings called bolection moldings are then nailed to the surface of the frame and mitered at the corners, capturing the panels, as shown in the drawing on p. 154. There's yet another way that's easier still: skip the molding entirely. Contemporary designs look just fine with no molding at all. Save the decoration for the baseboard and chair rail. If you absolutely insist on molded rails and stiles and don't want to bother mitering the molded sections, you should invest in a shaper or one of the cope-and-stick router sets listed in the Resource Guide on pp. 179-181. Any of these sets will make a tight-fitting, coped mortise-and-tenon.

To begin cutting joints, I measure equally on either side of the centerlines I marked earlier to establish the length of the mortise, then use this measurement to set the stops on the router jig. I cut joints in the rails and the end stiles first, as shown in the photo series on p. 155. I cut the mortises with a plunge router and a ⅜-in. dia. steel spiral end mill. This bit has cutting edges on both its sides and bottom and can be plunged into the work in a series of ½-in. deep cuts, producing very clean, accurate mortises. To guide the router during the plunging operations, I use the jig shown in the bottom left photo on p. 155 and in the drawing above left. The jig consists of a plywood box that holds the work firmly and two stops that limit the router's horizontal travel. The mortises should be at least 1 in. deep for a total loose-tenon length of 2 in.

Once the mortises are cut, I make the loose tenons in 2-ft. or 3-ft. lengths, then saw them to the required finished lengths. To make tenons, first thickness-plane the wood to the exact width of the mortise, just thick enough for a slip fit. Then rip the stock to a width equivalent to the length of your mortises. The mortise's radiused ends present a minor dilemma: should you round the tenons or square off the mortises? I round the tenons with a roundover bit in the router. Cut the tenons a hair shorter than full length to allow a little space for glue.

Test-assemble the frame system and clamp it tightly enough to check each joint for a tight fit. Also, check the overall frame as well as each panel opening for square. Any errors will show up now. With loose tenons, it's easy to correct a mistake. Just glue a loose tenon into the misplaced mortise, saw it off flush and start over again.

If there are no problems with the frame, I measure each panel opening carefully to determine the overall panel size. Measure the inside dimensions of each opening with a tape, then add the depth of the panel grooves. Size the panels so there's a little room at the bottom of the groove for seasonal expansion and con-

Panel designs

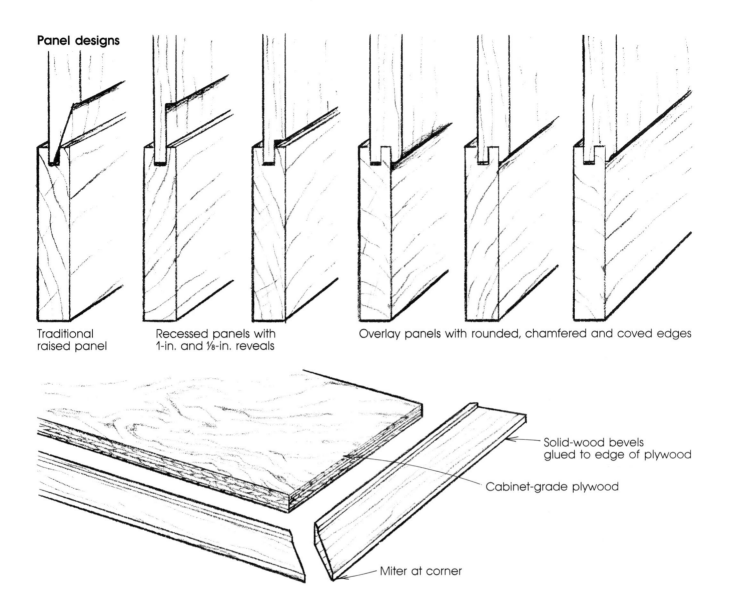

Traditional raised panel

Recessed panels with 1-in. and ⅛-in. reveals

Overlay panels with rounded, chamfered and coved edges

Solid-wood bevels glued to edge of plywood

Cabinet-grade plywood

Miter at corner

traction of the wood. The amount of clearance you'll need depends on the season. During the winter, if the groove is ⅜ in. deep, the panel should penetrate the groove at least ¼ in., leaving ⅛ in. on each side for expansion. In summer, when the wood's moisture content is high, you can get by with half as much clearance, unless the panels are very wide.

Making the panels

With the panels' overall size determined, I next decide on the construction method. The panels themselves can be made of solid wood or a stable, man-made board such as plywood or medium-density fiberboard. Medium-density fiberboard makes a perfectly adequate panel material. It's cheap and dimensionally stable, and it paints up beautifully. Of course, it must be

painted since most people object to the dull, processed-cheese surface of bare medium-density fiberboard. The nicest thing about it is that it machines crisply. On a router, shaper or table saw, it can be raised and fielded just like solid wood, with no tearout and thus little need for sanding.

A good grade of ¾-in. or ½-in. plywood, perhaps cabinet-grade birch or lauan, makes good panel material, too. However, you'll have to glue strips of solid wood to the plywood's edges, both to hide the unsightly core and to provide a machinable surface for raising and fielding. The drawing above shows one method of doing this.

Stain-grade work requires solid-wood or veneered panels, which usually have to be glued up from smaller pieces unless the panels themselves are very narrow. Woodworkers argue endlessly over the best way to glue

Panels for wainscot can be raised on the router table, as shown in these photos, or on a table saw. Although relatively expensive, panel-raising router bits make a clean cut that requires less sanding than tablesawn panels. Use a fence with either method and feed slowly and deliberately, with hands well away from the bit or blade.

up panels. Some say it's best to orient each piece so the growth rings are in the same direction (all up or all down), reasoning that this will keep the panels from washboarding and warping the frame. Others prefer to alternate the growth rings, arguing that the frame can more easily restrain small ripples than it can large warps. I try to arrange the boards for the most attractive grain configuration, without worrying too much about the growth rings.

Regardless of the material used, panel raising is done in the same way. I've used a number of methods to raise panels, including shapers, table saws and even an antique wooden panel-raising plane. Each of these methods has merit but since I'm usually working on site, I try to stick with the fastest, simplest tools. In my experience, these are the router and the table saw.

Several companies listed in the Resource Guide (pp. 179-181) sell panel-raising router bits. Although they vary somewhat in design, all of these bits are piloted, carbide-tipped cutters with 3/8-in. or 1/2-in. shanks. They are intended to be used in a router table with a 2-hp or larger router. Never use these bits freehand. Because of their large diameter and cutting load, panel-raising bits are liable to grab the wood and jerk the router right out of your hands. Use them only on a router table, with proper hold-downs.

To raise a panel with a router, I first double-check the panel's overall size so I'm sure it will fit into the opening. The photos above and on the facing page

show a Freud panel-raising bit in use. Although the bit has a pilot bearing, it's not a good idea to use it without a fence. The fence acts as a guard, greatly reducing the chance of the bit's grabbing the work. To minimize problems with tearout, raise the cross-grain ends of the panel first so that any chipping will be cleaned up when you raise the long-grain edges.

Keep in mind that these big panel-raising bits push your router to the limit of its cutting capability. Take it slow and easy. You will get better, safer results if you make a series of shallow cuts rather than one or two deep cuts. To test the router setup, mold a scrap and try the fit in the rails and stiles. The panel should penetrate the grooves with enough play to allow for wood movement.

Tablesawn panels—If you don't have panel-raising router bits, you can do an adequate job of panel raising on the table saw. However, because of the high cutting load, even a sharp blade will tend to burn the wood a little or at least leave deep saw marks. Expect to do a lot of sanding or cleanup planing if you raise panels with the table saw. Use either a rip blade or a combination blade for this work. These blades will leave a rougher surface but they will cut faster and burn less than a crosscut blade.

One method of raising panels on the table saw is shown in the drawing on p. 160. The panel blanks are fed into a blade set at about a 15° angle, although this

can vary a little. So I can safely feed the panel into the blade, I set up the saw with a custom fence several inches higher than the stock fence. This lets me achieve a slow, steady feed so the panel doesn't wobble on its edges. The accurate feed leaves fewer burnish marks and means less cleanup later.

I can't overemphasize the need for safety when raising panels on the table saw. Always set up your cuts so the waste is on the outside of the blade, not trapped between the blade and fence, where it could bind and shoot out the back of the saw like a bullet. Make sure your panel stock is flat and straight and take slow, deliberate cuts, keeping your hands well clear of the blade. Raise the cross-grain ends first, so that the inevitable tearout will be whisked away when you raise the long-grain sides.

If you've measured accurately, the panels should fit perfectly into the frame system. Nonetheless, before gluing up, insert the panels into the frame and clamp it up. On very large panel systems, start assembly from the center and work out toward the ends. Make sure each panel fits loosely into its groove around all four edges, without bottoming out. Each panel, if tapped in the center, should rattle in the grooves slightly. This is especially true if the panels are solid wood. Panels that fit too tightly are liable to crack the frame apart when they expand during wet weather, and repairing a broken frame is very difficult. Check the shoulder of each tenon for good fit. If the panels are too long, they will bottom out in the rails, preventing the muntins from seating snugly. Where necessary, use a block plane to trim the panels. Check the frame one more time for square, and adjust as necessary.

At this point, the panel frame can be glued up. Before final assembly, however, paint-grade work should be primed on the backside, including rails, stiles and both sides of the the panels. Two coats of a good-grade primer will go a long way toward reducing moisture-induced warpage. Stain-grade work should be finished with two coats of the same finish to be used on the exposed side. Try to get finish into the panel grooves, too. This will keep glue from sticking, and you won't accidentally glue the panels to the frame during assembly. However, don't drip finish into the mortises, or the glue won't hold the joint together.

For final assembly of the wainscot, clear a flat space on the job site or shop floor and have enough clamps on hand to pull each joint together. I use aliphatic-resin glue (yellow glue) which I spread sparingly both inside the mortise and on the loose tenon. With a helper, assemble the wainscot frame from the center out, sliding each panel into place as you go. Once the assembled wainscot has been clamped up, check the frame for tight fits and for square. Then let the glue cure overnight before installing the wainscot. If I'm wainscoting an entire room, I usually assemble all of the frames first, then install them all at once.

Table-saw panel raising

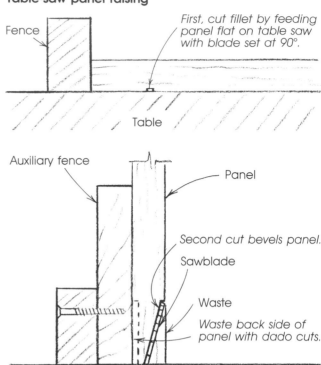

First, cut fillet by feeding panel flat on table saw with blade set at 90°.

Fence

Table

Auxiliary fence

Panel

Second cut bevels panel.

Sawblade

Waste

Waste back side of panel with dado cuts.

Hanging the wainscot

If you've used the pinch-stick or story-pole layout method, your wainscot should install easily and quickly. The chief problems will be fitting it in the corners and making sure the bottom rail conforms to an irregular floor. As with base and crown, I try to install the wainscot so corner joints are out of the direct line of sight; that way, it won't be too obvious if one opens up. If I'm paneling two or more contiguous walls and have to finish up by scribing a wainscot section between two others, I make sure the last section is the smallest one, with no windows or other features to worry about.

Assembled wainscot sections are quite heavy, so I always have at least one helper. The first section usually fits between two walls and doesn't have to be very tight since the stiles of adjacent panels will cover any gaps. Trim the stiles as necessary to get a snug fit, and align the top of the wainscoting with the chalked line. It's okay to have a gap between the bottom rail and the floor, as long as it's not wider than the shoe or base molding. I use small wedges to hold the panel section off the floor and to align it with my chalked line. If the top rail rides above the chalked line, the bottom rail may have to be scribed and trimmed, just as with baseboard.

Once the panel section is level and reasonably tight to the walls at both ends, it's ready to fasten. This can be done in any of several ways. For paint-grade work, nailing through the rails and stiles and into the back-

Panel mounting methods

End stiles scribed to fit wall

Frame screwed to backing,
holes countersunk and plugged

*An intentional gap here
can be closed by driving
a long wedge between
stile and wall.*

Wedge

Wall

Adjacent
stiles

ing is fine. The nails will be set, the holes filled and painted. For stain-grade work, blind-nailing into a sliver raised by a plane, then gluing the sliver back down, is a nice touch. Screwing and plugging, as described on pp. 165-166, is also an option. I use countersink bits and matching plug cutters made by the Fuller Co. (see the Resource Guide on pp. 179-181) to drill for the screws, and then make plugs to fill the holes. I try to pick wood that matches the color of the paneling and to align the grain of the plugs with the grain of the rails and stiles. The frame system is strong enough by itself, and a fastener every 16 in. to 24 in. vertically and horizontally will be plenty. Fasteners along the bottom rail will penetrate the bottom wall plate and be covered by the baseboard. Fasteners along the top rail will penetrate the studs or horizontal backing, and can be hidden by bed molding under the chair rail.

The next adjoining section is installed the same way but it will connect at the corner with a butt joint, a rabbet and groove or, at an outside corner, a miter. This is where making the section a little oversize pays off. As with the first section, align the top rail with your chalk mark and butt the stiles together in the corner. If the corner stile runs out into a tapered gap, scribe as necessary and trim until you get an acceptable fit. Usually, the stile at the opposite end of this section will be covered by yet another stile, so you needn't worry about a tight fit at that end. If the oppo-

site end adjoins a door casing or unpaneled wall, however, the fit will need to be tight. In these cases or on very long runs of paneling, I leave off the end stile and fit the opposite end of the panel section without it. Then I scribe the loose end stile, assemble the panel and push it snugly into place between the two walls. This loose-stile method is largely scribe, trim and try, so take very small cuts. If you make a mistake, however, it's easy to make another stile.

The final wall may have to be wedged between two previously installed stiles. This is a touchy job, and a pair of pinch sticks or an accurate tape will help you trim the panel section to near an accurate length. Then the loose-stile method described above can be used for final fitting. If the loose-stile trick isn't practical, there's one other way to fit the last section of paneling. Trim it as close as you can to final length but leave enough of a gap—about 1/16 in. to 1/8 in.—so the section can be slipped loosely into place. To close up the gap, make a long, tapered wedge and drive it into place between the wall and the back of the adjoining stile, as shown in the drawing above. The chair rail will cover any gap at the top of the paneling.

With the frames installed and nailed or screwed in place, the chair rail and/or dado cap, base and shoe can be installed as described in Chapter 7. Plugging the screw holes or filling the nails readies the paneling for varnish or paint.

Whether paint or varnish, a smooth final finish requires careful preparation, including filling nail holes, sanding and priming.

9

Finishing trim

In my experience, the last tradesman on the job is usually the most rushed and the slowest to be compensated. The concrete supplier gets paid before the driver starts a pour, but the painter seems to wait weeks for his check, usually after having rushed through a job that got hopelessly behind because the contractor couldn't stay on schedule.

Compromised quality is the usual result of this state of affairs. If the work starts behind schedule, you can be sure the painter will finish behind schedule. Hoping to make up for the lost time, the contractor or customer begins to wonder whether the trim really needs sanding or that third coat of paint. Six months later, long after the paint is dry, the answer will be all too obvious.

When you walk into a room, one of the first things you notice is the trim, and the quality of the finish makes a lasting initial impression. A neat, carefully done paint or varnish job can bring to life the best workmanship while at the same time hiding the inevitable blemishes. Unfortunately, the reverse is also true. Bad finish work—paint slopped on the floor around the baseboard or varnish dribbled on the paneling—can spoil the best trimwork.

This chapter covers the basics of painting and varnishing trim. I don't mean it to be a discourse on house painting. Other books treat the topic in far greater detail. What I'll concentrate on is explaining how to prepare the trimwork for finishing and how to select and apply the appropriate finish.

Preparation

As explained on p. 26, long before you turn to finishing the trimwork, you will have decided whether it will be stain-grade or paint-grade work. If paint-grade, you will probably be painting over pine, fir or poplar molding. Stain-grade work could be made of any of a dozen or more species of hardwood. In either case, the wood will have to be prepared to accept the finish.

The point of preparation is to create smooth, blemish-free surfaces so paint and varnish will adhere well without accenting imperfect joints, nail holes or mill marks left by a dull planer. Since trim is fastened with nails or screws, the first task is to fill all the holes left by these fasteners. Nails are easy to deal with. If they aren't already set, nails should be set at least 1/8 in. below the surface of the wood. If set much less than this, the putty used to fill the hole might not adhere and will fall out later.

The word "putty" has become a generic term, with so many kinds available. Every painter, it seems, has his or her preference. Putty used to be made up of a dough of whiting (usually a lead pigment) mixed with boiled linseed oil. Aside from being toxic, these dough-type putties were prone to shrinkage, eventually telegraphing through the paint the indentations they were supposed to hide. Shrinkage is still the culprit in the quest for a perfect putty, but modern compounds are far more reliable.

For paint-grade work, latex-based putties are the most popular. They're easy to apply, they dry fast and they sand well. Some brands are filled with tiny glass balls that minimize shrinking and improve sanding. For large areas that need filling, however, latex putties are too soft, and acrylic-based putty is probably a better choice. It sets up harder and is more resistant to dings and dents. Either type of putty is suitable for paint-grade work.

Latex and acrylic putties are best applied with the index finger. Work a small amount in the hole with a back-and-forth motion, which will keep bubbles from forming in the putty. Leave a small mound over the

The first step in finishing is to set nails at least ⅛ in. below the surface. Use a properly sized set with a cupped head. If the cup is damaged or rounded over, replace the set.

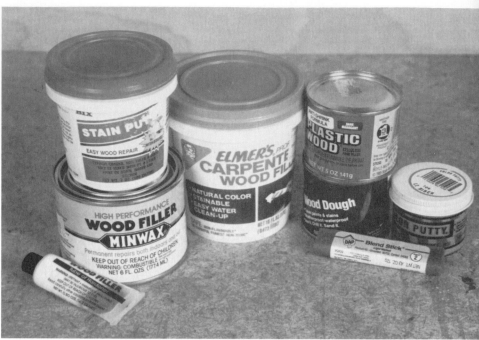

Wood fillers and putties are available in considerable variety. Minwax wood filler is a two-part filler with resin and hardener, similar to automotive body filler. Elmer's Carpenter's Wood Filler and Plastic Wood are hardening fillers. The Blend Stick, made by DAP, is a wax compound for filling nail holes after stain and finish are applied.

hole to compensate for any shrinkage, and let the putty dry overnight before sanding. Since latex putties are soft, sand them with 150-grit or 220-grit sandpaper, as described on pp. 167-169. A sanding block made of a small piece of scrap wood or a commercially made sanding "rubber" also prevents oversanding. Feel the sanded spot for any indentation and repeat filling and sanding, if needed.

Obviously, putties are no good for stain-grade work since they'd show under the varnish. Wood-dough type fillers (Plastic Wood is one brand) are one solution to filling stain-grade work. These are basically colored fillers with a binder. They're sold in various shades meant to match the wood you're using. Unfortunately, even wood of the same species changes color, often within the same board, so expecting birch wood filler to match your birch wainscot is a prayer. Buy a couple of cans of different shades and mix dollops of putty to get the shade you need.

Dough-type fillers have ingredients that inhibit shrinkage, but like the latex putties, they are not recommended for filling large holes, cracks or mars. These fillers harden to a consistency somewhere between granite and cast iron, so watch out when applying them to a softwood, like pine. When you sand, there will be a tendency to oversand the soft wood around the harder patch. I use a putty knife to force

the paste into the hole, then scrape off the excess. A rag moistened with lacquer thinner or acetone helps to keep the blade clean.

A reasonable alternative to store-bought putty is to make your own out of glue and sawdust. Carpenter's white or yellow glue works best, mixed with sawdust from the trim woods used. I use the finest sawdust I can find. One good place to look is in the drive wheels of the belt sander. Mix enough sawdust with the glue to make a thick paste. For a fast-setting putty, mix the sawdust with flexible, quick-setting epoxy glue, as shown in the top photo on the facing page. This type of fill won't take stain, so I use it on paint-grade work only. I apply home-brew fillers with a putty knife. Getting it on your fingers is much easier than getting it off, so I wear rubber gloves when working with epoxies. I keep a second putty knife handy to scrape the first one clean.

A better solution for filling nail holes in stain-grade work is colored wax sticks, which are used after the finish is applied rather than before. Wax sticks are meant for furniture repair and are sold in about 40 different colors, so you can buy several shades of the same basic color to account for variations within a species of wood. I apply wax stick with a thin, flexible putty knife and wipe it clean with a rag. No sanding is needed, and the wax won't shrink.

A site-made filler can be mixed from sawdust and fast-setting epoxy, right. The belt sander's dust bag and drive wheels are good sources for fine dust. Screw holes that are too big to be filled must be plugged or bunged. The bit shown in the photo at bottom right cuts plugs that can be freed from the board by prying with a screwdriver or by bandsawing the board through its thickness.

Plugs and bungs—Putty won't stay in a hole as large as a screw head and would look awful even if it would. Screw holes are usually filled with a matching wood plug or "bung." After being glued in, the plug is planed or chiseled flush to the surface of the molding, then sanded or scraped smooth. The plug hides any trace of the screw head.

A plug cutter—really a hollow drill bit—is used to make plugs. Although the cutter can be mounted in a portable drill, a drill press will keep the cutter from wandering and produce a more accurate plug. Cutters range in size from ¼ in. to 3 in. Some produce a plug that's slightly rounded on the bottom, which makes installation easier because the tapered end centers in the hole as it's being driven in. If the plug will be painted over, select any wood that matches the species, without regard to grain or color. Stain-grade plugs should be cut from wood that closely matches the color and grain of the wood to be plugged.

Feed the plug cutter into the wood about ⅜ in., then withdraw it. Repeat this operation until you've made as many plugs as you want. The plugs will still be attached at the bottom and can be removed by breaking them free with a screwdriver or by resawing the board in half on a bandsaw, releasing all the plugs in one operation. To set a plug, I roll it in a puddle of glue and swab glue inside the hole with a plumber's flux

To apply a fine bead of caulk between joined parts, an icing bag is ideal. Icing bags are sold by bakery-supply outlets (and by some paint stores) and can be bought with tips of various sizes.

brush. Because glue is wiped off as the plug is driven home, applying it to both surfaces ensures a good bond. Start the plug by hand and finish it with light hammer taps. If it goes in askew, don't bash it to death with the hammer: pry it out with a screwdriver and try again with a fresh plug.

When the plug is seated and driven home, it should project about ⅛ in. above the surface of the trim. Flush it off with a chisel, plane, scraper or belt sander. On flat surfaces, I chisel across the grain for the rough cut, then use a finely set block plane to flush it up, planing with the grain. On curved surfaces I chisel first and then scrape, file or sand flush. A tight, well-matched plug will be almost unnoticeable, especially if you are careful to align the grain.

Caulking—Some craftsman joke that paint-grade is really a term that slam-bam carpenters use to describe shoddy craftsmanship. Most of them know all too well that the painter's caulking gun hides all sins, or at least most of them. I don't mean to give the impression that poor joinery should be forgiven because a painter following behind with quarts of flexible caulk can fill thumb-sized cracks, but lots of minor problems in paint-grade work can be doctored with caulk. Cracks and dents and gaps between trim and the wall can be filled with flexible caulk, usually an acrylic type. This work is normally done after nail holes have been filled and a coat of sealer or primer has been applied. Even when there are no obvious cracks, caulking makes a nice, tight paint line between two parts and helps disguise the effects of wood movement.

Caulk is usually applied with a caulking gun from a tube. The gun pressurizes the tube and forces the caulk out of the nozzle. The best caulking guns aren't the common ratchet-type with a notched shaft, however. These get gunked up and are soon useless. A new style of gun has a trigger mechanism that grabs the shaft, whether it is covered with caulk or clean. Releasing the trigger also takes pressure off the tube, effectively stopping the caulk, keeping it from oozing out when not in use. Better still is a cake decorator's icing bag, shown in the photo at left. These have changeable nozzles of various sizes and can be filled with caulk from a can. Twisting the bag forces the caulk out of the nozzle at a very controllable rate.

When using a caulking tube, cut the plastic nozzle with a razor knife. Cut the hole small to start, then enlarge it if you need a bigger bead. Cut the nozzle at a sharp angle so it will fit nicely into the right angle formed by the wall and the trim. In most instances, I like to push the caulking gun rather than pull it. Pushing it puts pressure on the caulk and forces it into the crack, rather than pulling it out.

On paint-grade work, caulk is applied to any cracks between the walls and the baseboard, casings, chair rails and ceiling moldings. After the caulk is laid in the crack, immediately run a wet finger over the seam, as shown in the photos at right. A wet sponge can be used to clean excess caulk out of the complex inside corners of moldings. Caulk is also applied in the cracks where the casing meets the jamb and where the jamb meets the door and window stop.

Acrylic caulk can be smeared into molding joints to hide the hairlines that appear when the wood shrinks and the house settles. The caulk is just flexible enough to give when the wood moves but not so flexible that it will show a crack through the paint. Wipe away the excess caulk with a wet rag.

Dealing with dents—Like everybody else, I make my share of dents and hammer tracks. That's why I start trimming a room in the closet, hoping I'll use up my quota for the day where it won't be seen. Dents in paint-grade work can be filled by carefully spreading a hardening putty over the dent. Once the putty has set up, sand carefully, using a sanding block that's at least twice as large as the dent, so as to bridge the blemish and avoid making a bigger mess than the one you're trying to correct.

Dents in stain-grade work are another matter. No filler will be invisible, and sanding to remove the dent will ruin the molding or create an obvious dip. In such a case, I first try to raise the dent with steam. I heat the head of a hammer with a torch or hot-air gun. Then, with a clean, moistened rag over the dent, I work the hammer gently around the spot. This creates steam which, in turn, expands the grain. With any luck, the dent will disappear. If the dent is just too large, I consider replacing the piece or, as a last resort, fall back on the epoxy and sawdust fix. Since most fillers show up on clear work, I try to stain or paint the patch to simulate the wood grain. Obviously, it's easier to get away with this on a ceiling-level crown molding than on an eye-level casing.

Sanding

Tedious as it is, sanding is a critical part of finish work—both sanding the molding before it's applied and touchup sanding after the trimwork is installed. I'll discuss both types of sanding here, but first some notes on sandpaper.

For years, garnet paper was the carpenter's abrasive of choice. Garnet is a natural abrasive that is ground to various sizes and glued to paper. Although they're still sold in hardware stores, garnet papers seem to be giving way to man-made abrasives such as aluminum oxide and silicon carbide. These long-lasting papers leave a better-quality surface. My sandpaper of choice is open-coat wet/dry silicon-carbide paper, which I buy in four grits: 100, 150, 220 and 320. The wet/dry designation means that the paper can be used with a lubricant, which might be water or mineral spirits. Open

A standard caulking gun (top), preferably one without a notched feed plunger, is fine for caulking gaps in baseboard and casings. Cut the tube's tip at an angle and apply a fine bead, then smooth it with a moistened finger, as shown above.

Folding sandpaper

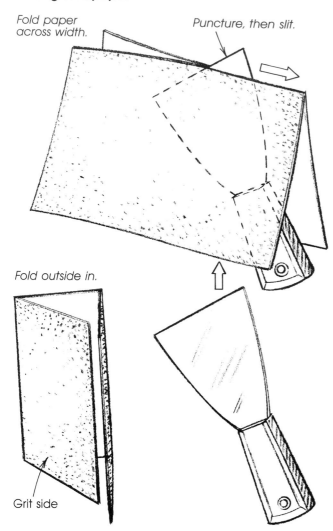

Fold paper across width.

Puncture, then slit.

Fold outside in.

Grit side

coat refers to the density of the particles glued to the paper, and it determines hows fast the paper will cut and how much it will clog. Although it cuts more slowly than closed coat, open coat clogs less so it's the most economical paper to buy, especially when purchased bulk in sleeves.

I cut full sheets of sandpaper in half with a putty knife, then fold them, outside in, into thirds so that the grit doesn't come in contact with itself. This folding arrangement, which is shown in the drawing at left, stiffens and locks the paper so it doesn't slide on itself when sanding with oil or water. Standard 9x11 sheets can be cut into smaller pieces for vibrating orbital sanders, but it is more convenient (if more expensive) to buy adhesive-backed sandpaper pads sized for sanders. These come in rolls or packs, so all you have to do is peel off the sheet and stick it to the sander. The time these pads save more than makes up for the extra cost.

I usually bring two kinds of power sanders to the job: a belt sander for coarse work and an orbital sander for finish work. Belt sanders are good for removing a lot of material from a flat surface, such as mill marks on baseboard and casing. My favorite belt sander is Porter-Cable's Model 503 with a dust bag to reduce cleanup. Placing the molding on a long, waist-height bench will alleviate backaches from sanding miles of baseboard. Also, you'll be better able to see the surface, so you'll do a better job of sanding than you would crawling along the floors.

Orbital sanders come in several sizes. One size takes a half-sheet of paper and it's good for large flat surfaces such as doors, cabinets, and flat profiles of base and casing. Palm-sized quarter-sheet sanders, like Makita's Model B04550, are good for smaller moldings and for sanding in tight quarters. Porter-Cable's Model 330 Speed-Bloc is a nice sander too, although it's larger and heavier than the Makita and other imports.

Sanding blocks or rubbers can be made of scrap wood or shaped out of large pieces of rubber, felt or leather. You can also buy them commercially from the sources listed on pp. 179-181. For profiled surfaces, I've seen nice rubbers made by carving the mirror image of the molding profile into a piece of Styrofoam, which is soft enough to conform to the profile but firm enough to support the paper.

Planer marks—Once you've worked with it for a while, your eye becomes very sensitive to the quality of a wood surface. One of the first things you notice about poorly prepared wood is mill marks, undulations that appear at regular intervals across the length of moldings. All moldings have some mill marks, but some are so small as to be undetectable. But if the molding was produced by dull knives or at improper feed rates, the marks will be painfully obvious, and no amount of stain, paint or varnish will hide them. The best solution to mill marks is to avoid them in the first place. Inspect the molding carefully before you install it, and reject badly marked pieces. If this isn't possible, you will have to sand the mill marks.

Sanding away mill marks can be done after the molding has been installed, but it's unbearably tedious. It's better to do it before the molding is installed. Because of the way light hits the moldings, normally only the flat surfaces need to be sanded, at least in paint-grade work. If profiled surfaces need work, it'll have to be done by hand. Really bad mill marks on flat surfaces can be attacked with 100-grit or 120-grit paper on a belt sander, followed by 120-grit, 150-grit and perhaps 220-grit paper on an orbital sander. Usually, 150-grit sandpaper is fine enough for paint-grade work. Sand with the grain whenever possible, to minimize cross grain scratching.

Stain-grade molding can also be sanded by machine and by hand. However, if you sand flat surfaces, you'll also have to sand the profiles. This is because light reflects differently from sanded surfaces than it does from unsanded ones. A glass-smooth surface left by a sharp molder will have a deep, silky, almost glazed, look, while a sanded surface that's just as smooth will have a cloudy, subdued look. Stain and, to a certain extent, clear finishes will amplify the difference. Surfaces to be stained should be sanded to at least 220-grit. Otherwise the stain will reveal the tiny scratches left by coarser paper.

Molding that was produced by a sticker with sharp knives will be crisp and fine, with a uniformly smooth surface. Usually material like this won't need any sanding at all, providing that it doesn't get too marked up at installation.

Sanding joints—Most joints will need touchup sanding. Badly out-of-plane joints should be recut or flushed up with a chisel, as described on p. 84. Some carpenters sand across the joint to level it, but this makes a mess for the painter, who must follow up to remove the cross-grain scratching. If they're deep enough, scratches show right through a coat of paint.

On trim that doesn't need sanding except at the joints, try to feather the sanding down the molding a foot or two so the sanded portion doesn't stand out. Using a sanding block, sand with the grain right up to the joint, but don't sand across it. Work down to the finest-grit paper you have. This will minimize scratching, and textural differences will be less obvious.

Paint-grade work

When I was learning trim carpentry during the 1960s and 1970s, wood was in. We did a fair share of painting but clear finishes, mostly oils and varnishes, were all the rage. By the mid-1980s, however, painted trim was back in style. These days, it's not uncommon to

Sanding

To avoid cross-grain scratching, sand with the grain up to the joint but stop before crossing it.

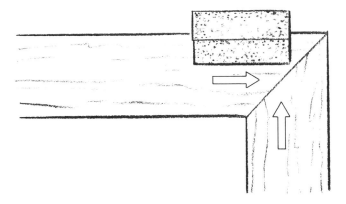

have both painted and stained trim in the same house or even in the same room.

I've always felt that painting was a misunderstood and underrated trade. Perhaps because most of us have done a little painting, we tend rank it as an also-ran skill that's more nuisance than necessity. But if you've ever carefully compared the work of a first-rate painter with an amateur's weekend efforts, you'd be surprised at the differences. Most of these have to do with careful preparation and using the right materials and tools. Of these, choosing the right paint is probably the most important.

Trim should be painted with gloss or semi-gloss enamel. Gloss is harder than flat paint, and more impervious to dirt and scuffing. Also, it's easier to clean. The paint industry has done a great job of selling latex-based paints to home owners, chiefly because they're easy to work with and they clean up quickly with water. And while it's true that gloss latex paints have improved over the years, I'm a diehard fan of oil-based enamels. I've always felt that oil-based paints brush and flow out smoother and dry to a harder, glossier surface. Because they dry more slowly, oil-based paints are more "workable" than latex, and manufacturers sometimes offer additives that alter a paint's drying charactisterics and its ability to "level" or flow out into a flat film, hiding any brush marks.

Cost seems to have very little to do with the quality of paint. At any rate, the cost of paint for the trim is such a small percentage of the total job cost that it seems silly to scrimp. I depend on *Consumer Reports* magazine (see the Resource Guide on pp. 179-181) for reliable reporting on paint quality. Given a choice, I prefer alkyd enamels made by the Pratt and Lambert Paint Co.

When you are selecting a color, don't rely entirely on the paint store's sample chip. Paints always seem to dry darker than the chip, so before committing to sev-

When possible, it's best to prime molding before it's installed. This casing has been spread out on the garage floor and sprayed front and back with primer.

eral gallons, it's a good idea to paint a sample of the trim and let it dry overnight. Stock colors can be returned to the store, as long as you don't mess up the sides of the cans. A custom color mixed by the store becomes your permanent property the instant the first squirt of pigment plops into the can. However, you can return the paint as many times as you want to have the shade adjusted.

Always make sure that the salesman keeps a record of the pigments used to make a custom color. After all, that's what the salesman is paid to do. To guard against minor color variations showing up later, some painters "box" the cans, that is, they mix together the contents of several gallons of the same color to even out shade differences.

Straight from the can, most oil enamel needs a little thinning with paint thinner. About 10% to 15% (by volume) is usually enough. Mix the paint well, either with a stick or with a paddle mixer in an electric drill. Even overnight, pigments settle to the bottom of the can. Before beginning, I always strain the paint, either through the cone-shaped filters available from the paint supplier or, in a pinch, through old pantyhose stretched over the bucket.

Primers—Raw wood should be primed before painting. A primer's function is to fill minute irregularities in the wood and provide a good surface for the paint to adhere to. A good primer dries soft enough to be easily sanded. The object of sanding is to knock down the raised grain and level the surface for the next coat of primer or paint. Primer for oil-based paints (some are intended for both latex and oil) comes thick in the can. With ordinary paint thinner, thin to the consistency of heavy cream, which usually requires 15% thinner by volume.

Sand the primer only after it's completely dry, usually the next day. For this job, 220-grit is the best. Sand lightly, and stop before you expose bare wood. Spot-prime any bare spots. Two coats of primer are better than one. Some painters mix half primer and half enamel for the second coat, then finish the entire job with just a single top coat.

Earlier in this book, I mentioned that the best time to prime the trim is before the molding is installed. It's also easier to sand at this stage. When space and the work schedule permit, I lay the molding across stickers in the garage or basement, as shown in the photo above, and prime it all at once.

After cleaning a brush, twirl it as shown to remove excess thinner. Store clean brushes in a brush box or upright, wrapped in newspaper or foil to preserve their shape.

Brush-painting trim—Brushing paint is a lost art. The skill is so difficult to perfect that painters spend hundreds of dollars per job to mask rather than teach someone to use a brush. The first rule in brushing is to use a top-quality brush. China-bristle brushes are a must, especially for good-quality oil-based paints. They cost plenty, but they will last for years if properly cared for. Don't use them with latex, however, or the brush will become "fishmouthed," losing its shape. One good way to store the brushes is hanging in a can of unboiled linseed oil or mineral spirits. Another way is to clean the brush thoroughly, then wrap it tightly in newspaper or foil to preserve the shape. Clean a brush by rinsing it thoroughly in paint thinner until the thinner runs clear. To remove the excess, twirl the brush between the palms of your hands, as shown in the photo above.

For trimwork, you need only two brushes: a 2-in. sash brush with a diagonal tip for cutting in moldings and a 2½-in. brush for large flat work. For very large flat surfaces, a 3-in. or 4-in. brush is convenient to have. One other essential painting tool is paint pots, either the tin kind that paint stores sell or the waxed paper buckets they sometimes give away to their good customers. Don't dip paint out of the can: you will make a mess and look amateurish.

Two thin coats produce a better finish than one thick coat. How thin is thin? Earlier, I said enamel should be thinned about 15% by volume. But the true test is how smoothly the paint flows off the brush. If the brush drags and grabs, the paint is too thick. You can develop an ear for proper paint consistency. In a waxed paper bucket, paint lifted into the air with the stirring paddle makes a medium-pitched plop, not high-pitched like water falling and not gooey silent like cream flowing. After a few tries you'll connect the sound to the feel of no brush drag.

For brushing, I mix about one quart at a time. The enamel is drying in the bucket as you use it, especially as you wipe off your brush and it flows down the side. The thinner evaporates and the paint becomes thicker. Thicker paint pulls the brush, causing brush marks to appear. So periodic thinning is needed to keep the paint flowing.

Every painter has a preferred strategy for trimwork. Most painters, however, roll or spray the walls first, then go back and "cut in" the trim. Some painters paint only one surface at a time (like the edges of a

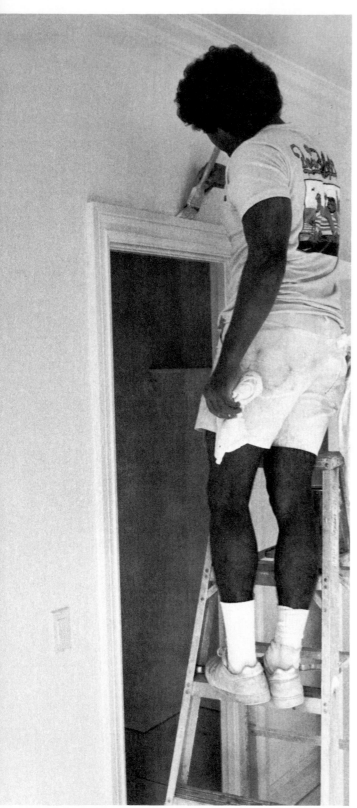

Begin cutting in casing along the edges adjacent to the walls. Then paint the flat surfaces, starting at the top and working down toward the baseboard.

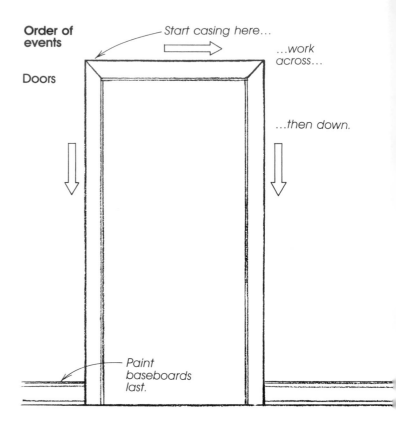

(see the drawing on the facing page)

Order of events

Doors

Start casing here...

...work across...

...then down.

Paint baseboards last.

window casing) and wait for it to dry before coming back to finish the other surfaces. The advantage of this method is that the brush doesn't mark the work as the bristles wrap around the corner. However, it's slow, and you have to make at least two trips to that window. I try to paint the entire piece at once, say, all of the baseboard or an entire window or door casing.

There's a certain order of events in painting trim. To keep from smudging the wet surfaces, work from the top down, starting with crown or ceiling molding, chair rails, doors and window casings and finally, the baseboards. I cut in the edges of the trim first, right up to the flat surface of the wall, then go back and fill in the flat surfaces on the molding. I paint small areas at a time, always working toward a wet surface, that is, brushing toward and never away from the paint that's already applied. If your cutting-in skills are sharp, paint the doors in place, taking care not to smudge paint on the hinges and lock sets. But it's better to remove the door hardware (including hinges), paint, then re-install the doors.

If an entire window must be painted, I work from the inside out, starting with the upper left-hand corner of the sash and down the left side first, then across the top of the window (see the drawing on the facing page). Next, I go down the right side and across the bottom of the sash. Muntins forming individual window lites are painted in the same pattern.

Windows

1. Lower upper sash, raise lower sash, paint upper edge first.

2. Paint across and down sides of upper sash.

3. Paint upper muntins.

4. Paint lower sash and lower muntins.

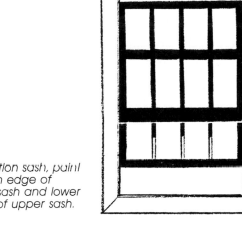

5. Reposition sash, paint bottom edge of lower sash and lower edge of upper sash.

6. Paint lower muntins.

7. Paint casing, starting in upper left corner and working across and down.

173

If trim is to be sprayed with an airless sprayer, make sure that the painter masks everything in sight. Here the countertop and cabinet interiors have been covered with taped kraft paper.

From the sash, I move to painting the casing, again starting in the upper left-hand corner and working down the edge closest to the wall. Next, I do the top and right edges of the casing, followed by the flat surfaces. There is nothing magical about this pattern—it's just a comfortable routine that keeps me from missing any spots.

If there's a real trick to painting, it's learning to cut in neatly to a straight line. Here's how an old painter taught me to do it. First, hold the brush like a pencil. Dip no more than one-third of the brush's length into the paint, then scrape one side of the brush lightly on the edge of the bucket. Apply that side to the raw wood. To cut up to an adjacent surface, start with the tip of the brush against the work, as shown in the drawing at right. Move the brush in one fluid motion toward the wet surface. Redip the brush and continue. Avoid the temptation to plant the brush in the wet film and drag it into the raw wood: this will cause streaking. Wiggling the brush up to the line causes the paint to pool, which might later result in runs or sags.

After you have painted the whole surface of a section, say a baseboard, squint across the surface obliquely and check for sags or holidays (missed spots). Going back to touch up a wet surface invites brush marks, so avoid it if possible. Brush out a sag by just tipping the brush in paint, then smooth the surface with minimal brushing. To keep the job neat and tidy, I carry a clean rag in my back pocket to wipe the handle of my brush and to clean up any drips. The best way of avoiding disastrous spills (particularly if the hardwood flooring is already finished) is to spread drop cloths in the work area. Plastic drop cloths are okay in a pinch, but heavy cloth drops cover better and last longer, and they absorb paint so you won't track it on your shoes.

Spray-painting trim—On most large jobs, and on a lot of small ones, the trim is spray painted. Because I'm not an expert on it, I won't go into the particulars here, but if you're farming out the paint work, there are a few things to consider. Spraying is faster than brushing and when done properly gives a smooth, flawless finish. Of course spraying consumes more paint and usually requires considerably more labor in masking and cleanup. Still, spraying can cost less in the long run because it can be done so quickly.

There are two major kinds of paint sprayers, the air gun and the airless spray gun. The air type uses compressed air to blow the paint onto the surface. The airless type delivers paint under hydraulic pressure. Except for clear finishes, the airless spray gun has become the choice of most painters. The airless sprayer has less overspray and covers more area in less time, although some painters say that it's harder to learn because the gun is either all on or all off, with no modulation possible.

If you intend to hire a painter to spray your trim, talk to him or her before the trim is installed. Some

Cutting in

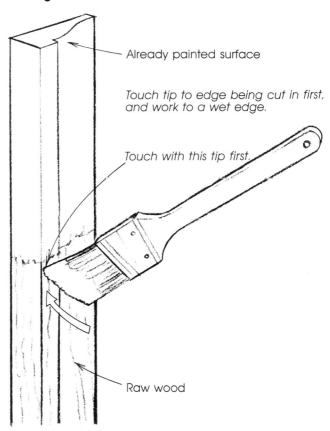

Already painted surface

Touch tip to edge being cut in first, and work to a wet edge.

Touch with this tip first.

Raw wood

painters prefer to spray the trim before it's installed and will then come back and touch it up later. This approach is certainly neater and faster than masking. If you've ever seen an airless mechanic in action, the first thing you'll notice is the protective mask and hat or head wrap. This is because even though airless spraying produces less overspray, it still makes quite a mess. Careful masking is absolutely critical. Make sure the painter masks the windows, the floors and anything else you don't want spattered with an unintentional coat of enamel.

Airless painters debate whether to mask the trim to paint the walls or conversely to mask the walls to paint the trim. I've seen both approaches work. I favor the former because I believe that a final rolled coat on the walls should be the last thing done before the owner takes the keys. I have the painter spray-prime the trim and walls in one operation, then spray-finish the trim. Finally, after the carpet is installed, the appliances are in, and all the other tradesman have had a chance to bang their tools against the walls, the painter masks the trim with one piece of 2-in. wide masking tape, covers the carpet with a drop and rolls the final coat on the walls and ceilings.

Stain-grade work

Any trim with a clear finish is considered stain grade, even though most of it never gets stained at all. As a trip to the local paint store will reveal, clear finishes are available in such incredible variety that it's hard to know where to begin. For simplicity's sake, I narrow the choices down to three basic types: oils, lacquers and varnishes.

Oil finishes are by the far the easiest to apply. Most are simply rubbed on in several coats, then buffed with a cloth or waxed, if you want extra protection from dirt and moisture. Linseed oil was once the most popular oil finish (although not necessarily for trimwork) but it has since been supplanted by a range of synthetic oils. Many of these are so-called penetrating oils that polymerize, which means that the molecules in these formulas link together to form a thin, relatively hard coating. Penetrating oils are made from natural oils like tung or linseed with additives to improve drying and hardness. Some are available in colors so that you can stain the wood at the same time you are finishing it. Some popular oils include Watco Oil and Penofin. Sources for these are listed in the Resource Guide on pp. 179-181.

Oils are favored because they protect and seal the wood without disguising its grain beneath a glossy film. However, they have some disadvantages, not the least of which is smell. Penetrating oils are generally slow to evaporate so trim treated with oil may reek for days or even weeks. Also, oils aren't as resistant to dirt and stains as other finishes, although they are easily renewed with a fresh coat. A coat of wax over the oil— Butcher's is one brand—helps keep it clean.

Oils are rubbed, brushed or sprayed, but rubbing with a rag is by far the most controllable way to apply an oil finish. Still, oiling is messy, smelly business. If possible, I recommend oiling the trim before it's installed, then touching up any rough spots. Oil both sides of the molding, but sand only the show sides. One way of preparing wood for an oil finish is as follows: belt-sand to 150-grit, then 220-grit; orbital-sand to 220-grit; and hand-sand with 220-grit to 320-grit, wiping with oil between grits or using the oil as a lubricant. Next, apply the trim and touchup-sand the joints with 220-grit, followed by 320-grit. Recoat with oil and buff to a luster, then fill the nail holes with a wax stick, as described earlier in this chapter on p. 164. Fixing scratches and spot finishing are easy to do with the oil finishes. Just sand the trim and recoat as necessary.

Two notes on safety: oil-soaked rags are susceptible to spontaneous combustion. Keep them in an approved, fireproof waste can or rinse them out thoroughly and hang them outdoors. Don't use an electric sander with oil as a lubricant. Besides gumming up the works in the sander, oil could create an electric shock and fire hazard.

Lacquer—In the furniture industry, lacquer has always been the finish of choice, and for good reason. It's among the most forgiving of finishes, easy to apply and fast to dry. Although it's not as durable as varnish, it's quickly repaired. Lacquer can be sprayed, brushed or padded on with a rag. I advise strongly against spraying indoors. The solvents in lacquer are explosively flammable, so much so that in industry, lacquers are sprayed only in very well-ventilated booths equipped with explosion-proof fans and lights. Even then, lacquer booths have been known to explode with terrific force. It's very difficult to ventilate a house adequately for spraying and almost impossible to ensure that a stray ignition source won't ignite the fumes. Leave the spraying to the professionals.

Fortunately, brushing lacquers are widely available. Although chemically similar to spraying lacquers, brushing lacquers have solvents of lower volatility, which means the film stays wet long enough for any brush marks to level out. Even at that, though, a brushing lacquer dries hard to the touch within about a half-hour. A well-stocked local paint store may have several brands of brushing lacquer, perhaps in a range of glosses. One popular national brand is Deft Clear Wood Finish (see the Resource Guide on pp. 179-181 for a source) Another brand is made by H. Behlen and sold through Garrett Wade. Gloss is a matter of personal preference. I like relatively low gloss. However, low-sheen lacquers dry to a film that's marginally softer than high-gloss blends. This may be a factor on surfaces that will get a lot of wear, such as door jambs or the area immediately around a door knob.

Prepare a finish for lacquer as described at left, sanding to at least 220-grit or 320-grit. Wipe the surface clean with a rag moistened with lacquer thinner. Before beginning finishing, make sure that the house is well ventilated and that any ignition sources such as pilot lights, gas or oil furnaces and so on have been turned off. If possible, turn the lights off and leave them off until the fumes have escaped from the room. Although an explosion is unlikely with brushing lacquer, you can't be too careful. When using lacquer, protect your lungs with a respirator designed to filter organic solvents.

Some lacquer manufacturers recommend a separate sanding sealer with their products; others, the makers of Deft, for example, say that the first coat acts as a sealer. Basically, sealers are thinned-out lacquers with additives to improve sanding. If a sealer is called for, brush it on according to the manufacturer's instructions. Use the same brushing techniques as for paint (see pp. 173-175), always working to a wet edge. Once the sealer is dry, sand it with 220-grit stearated paper, a special sandpaper available from finish suppliers that contains zinc stearate, a material that provides lubrication during sanding. Remove the sanding dust with a rag slightly moistened with lacquer thinner.

The usual lacquer finish consists of one coat of sealer and two or three top coats of lacquer, full strength from the can. Sanding between coats is optional but it will noticeably improve the final finish. Once the final coat is dry, you can rub out the lacquer film to the desired gloss with 0000 steel wool. The steel wool can be lubricated with water and a commercial steel-wool lubricant, such as Steel Wol-Wax, sold by the Star Chemical Co. (Star is listed in the Resource Guide on pp. 179-181). When rubbing out the lacquer, be careful not to smear any of the lubricant on painted walls or carpets. It's liable to leave an oily stain.

Varnishes—When better protection against dirt, moisture and abrasion is needed, varnish is the finish of choice. Retail paint stores sell three major kinds: traditional oleoresinous types made from natural oils like tung or linseed; alkyd-resin types with chemically altered natural oil; and polyurethanes, which are chemically related to plastics and so produce a very tough film. I recommend polyurethane. Because it dries hard, it offers the best protection against the abrasions most trim will be exposed to. Although they aren't totally impervious to moisture, polyurethanes do the best job of all the clear finishes in protecting the wood against moisture and liquid water.

As with lacquer, polyurethane varnishes are available in several gloss ranges, from nearly flat to semi-gloss to high gloss. The flat or semi-gloss (sometimes described by a trade name with the word "satin") is the best choice for trim. High-gloss finishes produce a thick, unappealing film that obliterates the grain, defeating the entire purpose of using stain-grade trim in the first place.

Varnishes are applied more or less like brushing lacquers. They can be sprayed, but spraying will require a lot of masking and post-finish cleanup so if you're doing the work yourself, it's probably best to brush. Sand to at least 220-grit, then clean the surface with a rag moistened with paint thinner. Some polyurethanes are sold with separate sealers, in which case you should follow the instructions on the can. Otherwise, you can make your own sealer by thinning the varnish straight from the can, then following with full-strength coats. Apply the sealer, then sand it with 220-grit stearated paper before brushing on the top coats. Once dry, the top coats can be rubbed out with 0000 steel wool with water or wax as a lubricant.

Polyurethane can be quirky stuff. If the weather is very humid, it might take a long time to dry. However, it's important to make sure it is dry before attempting to sand. Otherwise, it will gum up your paper and make an awful mess. Recoating old polyurethanes is problematic, too. Sometimes the new coats won't adhere properly and will blister or peel off. To avoid this, sand the old surface with 150-grit paper to provide "tooth" for the new varnish.

Stains and fillers—Wood is stained for two basic reasons: to change its color or to make it look like another wood. I don't use stains much unless I absolutely have to, and then only sparingly. I have always thought that if you want cherry or walnut or some other wood, it makes sense to use them in the first place, not stain some cheaper wood to look like what you want. There are times, however, when staining can come in handy. For example, it can be used to control color variations within a single species or to subdue what would otherwise be objectionable figure.

Staining to achieve uniform color works well where moldings made from different colors within the same species meet at a joint. I use commercial oil-based stains, which consist of a pigment suspended in an oil vehicle. Generically, these are known as pigmented wiping stains. As the name suggests, they are wiped on with a rag, then wiped off to achieve the desired color. Top coats are then applied over the stained wood in the usual way.

If you're planning to stain all of the trim, apply the stain and let it dry at least overnight before proceeding with finishing. Apply sealer and one or two top coats in the usual way, but make sure that the stain you're using is compatible with the top coat you plan to use. If you are attempting to even out color in the same species of wood, a very slight color change will be required. In this case, I recommend buying several shades close to the one you want, then mixing samples of them together to create the exact shade you need. Thin with mineral spirits or the thinner recommended by the stain manufacturer. Experiment on a scrap piece before staining the actual work because once you apply the stuff, there's no turning back. Usually, the only solution to an undesirable color is to apply one darker than the one you already have.

Fillers—Wood fillers are used to fill the pores in open-grain woods like oak, ash, and to a lesser extent, mahogany. Filling open-grain woods produces a smoother top coat that reflects light evenly and is less likely to show flaws, either in the wood or the joinery. A filler consists of the filler itself, a carrier and a binder. The filler can be silica, talcum or some other inert solid. The carrier, which evaporates, is usually mineral spirits, alcohol or water. The binder might be glue, varnish or shellac.

Fillers are rubbed into the wood surface and forced into the pores. The carrier evaporates, and the binder keeps the filler in the holes. Commercial paste fillers are available in colors to match the wood being filled. If you're using a neutral filler, do the filling first, followed by staining, sealing and top coats. It's very important to wipe paste fillers from the surface; otherwise, they tend to build up in places where you don't want much filler. On finished work, this will be in joints and at inside corners.

Resource guide

Builder's hardware

Hafele America Co.
301 Cheyenne Drive
P.O. Box 4000
Archdale, NC 27263
(919) 889-2322
European hinges and lock sets

Kolson Inc.
653 Middle Neck Rd.
Great Neck, NY 11023
(516) 487-1224
Lock sets and hinges

Lawrence Brothers, Inc.
2 First Ave.
Sterling, IL 61081
(800) 435-9568
(815) 625-0360 in Illinois
Residential and commercial-grade hinges

Schlage Lock Co.
2401 Bay Shore Blvd.
San Francisco, CA 94134
(415) 467-1100
Lock sets and electronic home-security systems

Stanley Hardware
Div. of The Stanley Works
195 Lake St.
New Britain, CT 06050
(203) 225-5111
Residential and commercial-grade hinges

Custom millwork

Architectural Masterworks
3502 Divine Ave.
Chattanooga, TN 37407
(615) 867-3630
Custom moldings

Brill & Walker Associates Inc.
P.O. Box 731
Sparta, NJ 07871
(201) 729-8876
English-style mantels and custom carved moldings

Classic Architectural Specialties
3223 Canton St.
Dallas, TX 75226
(214) 748-1668
Millwork

Flex-Trim Molding Co.
9077 Arrow Route
Rancho Cucamonga, CA 91730
(714) 944-6665
Flexible moldings

Focal Point
P.O. Box 93327
Atlanta, GA 30377-0327
(404) 351-0820
Foam-core reproduction moldings

House Of Moulding
15202 Oxnard St.
Van Nuys, CA 91411
(800) 327-4186
(818) 781-5300 in California
Custom moldings

Kirby Millworks
P.O. Box 898
Ignacio, CO 81137
(800) 245-3667
(303) 563-9436 in Colorado
Moldings and millwork

Maizefield Mantels
P.O. Box 336
325 Tenth St.
Port Townsend, WA 98368
(206) 385-6789
Custom mantels, turnings, staircase work

Ornamental Mouldings Ltd.
P.O. Box 336
Waterloo, Ontario N2J 4A4
Canada
(519) 884-4080
Moldings

Silverton Victorian Mill Works
P.O. Box 2987
Durango, CO 81302
(303) 259-5915
Victorian millwork specialties

Finishing supplies

Deft, Inc.
17451 Von Karman Ave.
Irvine, CA 92714
(800) 544-3338
(714) 474-0400 in California
Brushing lacquer and varnishes

The McCloskey Corp.
7600 State Rd.
Philadelphia, PA 19136
(800) 345-4530
(215) 624-4400 in Pennsylvania
Stains and varnishes

Mohawk Finishing Products, Inc.
Route 30 North
Amsterdam, NY 12010
(518) 843-1380
Oil, lacquers, varnishes and thinners

Performance Coatings Inc.
360 Lake Mendocino Dr.
Ukiah, CA 95482
(800) 468-8820
(800) 468-8817 in California
Penofin oil

Pratt and Lambert Inc.
P.O. Box 22
Buffalo, NY 14240
(716) 873-6000
Paints

Standard Abrasives
9351 Deering Ave.
Chatsworth, CA 91311
(818) 718-7070
Abrasives

Star Chemical Co.
360 Shore Drive
Hinsdale, IL 60521
(800) 323-5390
(312) 654-8650 in Illinois
Varnishes, lacquers and waxes

3M Home Products Division
Building 223-4S-01
3M Center
St. Paul, MN 55144
(612) 733-1110
Abrasives

Watco-Dennis Corp.
19610 Rancho Way
Rancho Dominguez, CA 90220
(213) 635 2778
Watco oil

Wood Finishing Supplies Co.
100 Throop St.
Palmyra, NY 14522
(315) 986-4517
All finishing supplies

Hand tools

Conover Woodcraft Specialties, Inc.
18125 Madison Rd.
Parkman, OH 44080
(216) 548-3481
Woodworking hand tools

Garrett Wade Co. Inc.
161 Avenue of the Americas
New York, NY 10013
(800) 221-2942
(212) 807-1155 in New York
Woodworking hand tools

Grizzly Imports Inc.
East of Mississippi River:
2406 Reach Rd.
Williamsport, PA 17701
(800) 523-4777;
West of Mississippi River:
P.O. Box 2069
Bellingham, WA 98227
(800) 541-5537
Miter trimmers, hand and power tools

Lee Valley Tools Ltd.
1080 Morrison Drive
Ottawa, Ontario K2H 8K7
Canada
(613) 596-0350
Woodworking hand tools

Leichtung Workshops
4944 Commerce Parkway
Cleveland, OH 44128
(216) 831-6191
Woodworking hand and power tools

Nailers
10845 Wheatlands Ave.
Suite C
Santee, CA 92071
(619) 562-2215
Carpenter's tool belts

Occidental Leather
P.O. Box 364
Valley Ford, CA 94972
(800) 541-8144
(707) 874-3650 in California
Leather tool belts

Pootatuck Corporation
P.O. Box 24
90 Main St.
Windsor, VT 05089
(802) 674-5984
Lion miter trimmers

Price Brothers Tool Co.
1053 6th St.
Novato, CA 94945
(415) 897-3153
Builder's levels

Sandvik
P.O. Box 1220
Scranton, PA 18501
(717) 587-5191
Nobex hand miter boxes and saws

Von Fange Tool Co. Inc.
Box 5
Woodville, VA 22749
(703) 829-2565
Carpenter's and cabinetmaker's hammers

Woodcraft Supply
Box 4000
41 Atlantic Ave.
Woburn, MA 01888
(800) 225-1153
(617) 935-5860 in Massachusetts
Woodworking hand tools

Woodline—The Japan Woodworker
1731 Clement Ave.
Alameda, CA 94501
(415) 521-1810
Japanese hand and power tools

The Woodworker's Store
21801 Industrial Blvd.
Rogers, MN 55374
(612) 428-2199
Woodworking hand tools, hardware

Nailers and fasteners

Duo-Fast Corp.
3702 North River Rd.
Franklin Park, IL 60131
(312) 678-0100
Air nailers and fasteners

Hilti Fastening Systems
P.O. Box 45400
Tulsa, OK 74145
(800) 727-3427
(918) 252-6350 in Oklahoma
Powder-actuated fastening systems

International Staple & Machine Company
P.O. Box 629
Butler, PA 16001
(412) 287-7711
Air nailers and fasteners

Paslode Corporation
Two Mariott Dr.
Lincolnshire, IL 60069
(800) 323-1303
(312) 634-1900 in Illinois
Air and propane-powered hoseless nailers

Senco Products, Inc.
8485 Broadwell Rd.
Cincinnati, OH 54244
(513) 388-2000
Air nailers and fasteners

Tremont Nail Co.
P.O. Box 111
Wareham, MA 02571
(508) 295-0038
Period reproduction nails

Power tools and accessories

American Design and Engineering Inc.
900 3rd St.
St. Paul Park, MN 55071
(800) 441-1388
(612) 459-7400 in Minnesota
Sawhelper chopsaw accessory tables

Black & Decker
P.O. Box 798
10 North Park Drive
Hunt Valley, MD 21030
(301) 527-7000
Chopsaws, routers, router mortising jigs, sanders and accessories

Bosch Power Tool Corp.
P.O. Box 2217
New Bern, NC 28560
(919) 636-4200
Routers, sanders and accessories

Hitachi Power Tools U.S.A. Ltd.
4487 E. Park Drive
Norcross, GA 30093
(800) 548-8259
(714) 891-5330 in Georgia
Chopsaws, routers and accessories

Milwaukee Electric Tools
13135 W. Lisbon Rd.
Brookfield, WI 53005
(414) 781-3600
Routers, sanders and accessories

Porter-Cable
P.O. Box 2468
Jackson, TN 38302
(901) 668-8600
Routers, router mortising jugs, sanders and accessories

Skil Corp.
4300 W. Peterson Ave
Chicago, IL 60646
(312) 286-7330
Chopsaws, routers, router mortising jigs, sanders and accessories

W. L. Fuller Inc.
7 Cypress St.
Warwick, RI 02888
(401) 467-2900
Combination counterbore bits and wood plug cutters

Router and panel-raising bits

Fred M. Velepec Inc.
71-72 70th St.
Glendale, NY 11385
(718) 821-6636
Custom-made carbide bits

Freud Inc.
218 Feld Ave.
High Point, NC 27264
(919) 434-3171
Panel-raising sets, cope-and-stick sets, combination bits and sawblades

Furnima Industrial Carbide
Biernackie Road
P.O. Box 308
Barry's Bay, Ontario KOJ 1BO
Canada
(613) 756-3657
Specialty router bits

MLCS, Ltd.
P.O. Box 4053
Rydal, PA 19046
(800) 533-9298
(215) 886-5986 in Pennsylvania
Panel-raising sets

Reliable Grinding
145 West Hillcrest Ave.
San Bernardino, CA 92408
(800) 424-9154
(714) 884-7258 in California
Panel-raising sets

Trade associations

Architectural Woodwork Institute
2310 S. Walter Reed Dr.
Arlington, VA 22206
(703) 671-9100

Door and Hardware Institute
7711 Old Springhouse Rd.
McLean, VA 22102
(703) 556-3990

Wood Molding & Millwork Producers Association
P.O. Box 25278
Portland, OR 97225
(503) 292-9288

Further reading

Architects Emergency Committee. *Great Georgian Houses of America.* New York: Dover Publications, 1980.

Bowyer, Jack. *History of Building.* London: Granada Publishing, 1973.

Chronicle of Early American Tools. Early American Industries Association, Publications Comittee, 60 Harvest Lane, Levittown, N.Y. 11756.

Consumer Reports magazine. Subscription department, P.O. Box 2886, Boulder, Colo. 80322.

Delta Tool Co. *Getting the Most Out of Your Shaper.* reprint. Fresno, Calif.: Linden Publishing Co., 1982.

Feirer, John L. *Cabinetmaking and Millwork.* 2nd, rev. ed. New York: Charles Scribner's Sons, 1883.

Fine Homebuilding magazine and *Fine Woodworking* magazine. The Taunton Press, Box 355, 63 S. Main St., Newtown, Conn. 06470.

Hoadley, R. Bruce. *Understanding Wood: A Craftsman's Guide to Wood Technology.* Newtown, Conn.: The Taunton Press, 1980.

Isham, Norman M. and Albert F. Brown. *Early Connecticut Houses.* New York: Da Capo, 1967.

Love, T. W. *Construction Manual: Finish Carpentry.* Solana Beach, Calif.: Craftsman Book Co., 1974.

Makinson, Randell L. *Greene and Greene: Architecture as Fine Art.* Salt Lake City: Peregrine Smith, 1977.

Radford, William A. *Old House Measured & Scaled Detail Drawings For Builders and Carpenters.* New York: Dover Publications, 1983.

Small, Turnstall and Christopher Woodbridge. *Mouldings and Turned Woodwork of the 16th, 17th and 18th Centuries.* reprint. Fresno, Calif.: Linden Publishing, 1988.

Toenjes, Len. *Building Trades Dictionary.* Chicago: American Technical Society, 1989.

The Victorian Design Book. Ottawa: Lee Valley Tools, 1984.

Whitehead, Russell F. and Frank Chouteau Brown, eds. *Architectural Treasures of Early America.* 16-vol. series. Harrisburg, Pa.: National Historic Society, 1987-1988.

Wilson, J. Douglas. *Practical House Carpentry.* 3rd ed. New York: McGraw-Hill, 1979.

Index

Senior editor: Paul Bertorelli
Designer/layout artist: Deborah Fillion
Illustrator: Lee Hov
Copy/production editor: Ruth Dobsevage
Art assistants: Iliana Koehler, Cindy Nyitray
Editorial assistant: Maria Angione
Typesetter: Lisa Carlson
Print production manager: Peggy Dutton
Indexer: Harriet Hodges

Typeface: ITC Bookman Light
Paper: Warrenflo, 70 lb., neutral pH
Printer and binder: Arcata Graphics/Hawkins, New Canton, Tennessee

Watch Craig Savage on video.

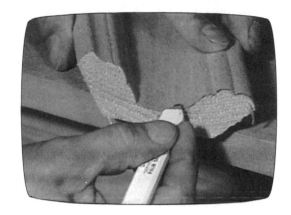

See firsthand how Savage attacks some of the same real-world problems he covers in his book. The camera looks right over his shoulder to show you how to cut butt, miter and cope joints that fit tightly. You'll learn how to install door and window casing, base molding, crown molding and more. And the video is keyed to the book, with page references right on the screen. 60 minutes

Check one: ☐ #060047 (VHS), ☐ #060048 (Beta)

Name

Address

City   State   Zip

☐ Payment Enclosed ☐ MasterCard ☐ VISA ☐ American Express

Charge Card #   Expiration Date

Signature

To order, just fill out this card and send it with your payment of $29.95, plus $2.50 postage and handling (CT residents add 8% sales tax), to the address below.

The Taunton Press
63 South Main Street
Box 355
Newtown, CT 06470
1-800-888-8286

Expert video instruction on installing doors and windows.

Using both power and hand tools, master carpenter Tom Law shows you how to square up and secure a ready-to-install opening window in minutes, fix prehung doors that arrive with warped jambs or improperly set hinges, and set and install an insulated-glass unit within a custom-built frame. Includes an illustrated booklet. 60 minutes

Check one: ☐ #060039 (VHS), ☐ #060040 (Beta)

Name

Address

City   State   Zip

☐ Payment Enclosed ☐ MasterCard ☐ VISA ☐ American Express

Charge Card #   Expiration Date

Signature

To order, just fill out this card and send it with your payment of $29.95, plus $2.50 postage and handling (CT residents add 8% sales tax), to the address below.

The Taunton Press
63 South Main Street
Box 355
Newtown, CT 06470
1-800-888-8286